WORLDCOMP'13
July 22-25, 2013
Las Vegas Nevada, USA
www.world-academy-of-science.org

PROCEEDINGS OF THE 2013 INTERNATIONAL CONFERENCE ON COMPUTER DESIGN

CDES 2013

Editors

Hamid R. Arabnia
Leonidas Deligiannidis, Ashu M. G. Solo
Fernando G. Tinetti

AF518579

FIREWALL MEDIA
(An Imprint of Laxmi Publications Pvt. Ltd.)
An ISO 9001:2008 Company
BENGALURU • CHENNAI • COCHIN • GUWAHATI • HYDERABAD
JALANDHAR • KOLKATA • LUCKNOW • MUMBAI • RANCHI • NEW DELHI
BOSTON (USA) • ACCRA (GHANA) • NAIROBI (KENYA)

This edition is for sale in India and the sub-continent.
Reprint & Revision Copyright © 2015 Laxmi Publications (P) Ltd. New Delhi, India
Original Copyright © 2013–14 by CSREA Press. All rights reserved

This volume contains papers presented at The 2013 International Conference on Computer Design (CDES'13). Their inclusion in this publication does not necessarily constitute endorsements by editors or by the publisher.

Limits of Liability/Disclaimer of Warranty: The publisher and the author make no representation or warranties with respect to the accuracy or completeness of the contents of this work and specifically disclaim all warranties. The advice, strategies, and activities contained herein may not be suitable for every situation. In performing activities adult supervision must be sought. Likewise, common sense and care are essential to the conduct of any and all activities, whether described in this book or otherwise. Neither the publisher nor the author shall be liable or assumes any responsibility for any injuries or damages arising here from. The fact that an organization or Website if referred to in this work as a citation and/or a potential source of further information does not mean that the author or the publisher endorses the information the organization or Website may provide or recommendations it may make. Further, readers must be aware that the Internet Websites listed in this work may have changed or disappeared between when this work was written and when it is read.

All trademarks, logos or any other mark such as Vibgyor, USP, Amanda, Golden Bells, Firewall Media, Mercury, Trinity, Laxmi appearing in this work are trademarks and intellectual property owned by or licensed to Laxmi Publications, its subsidiaries or affiliates. Notwithstanding this disclaimer, all other names and marks mentioned in this work are the trade names, trademarks or service marks of their respective owners.

Branches

©	Bengaluru	080-26 75 69 30	
©	Chennai	044-24 34 47 26,	24 35 95 07
©	Cochin	0484-237 70 04,	405 13 03
©	Guwahati	0361-254 36 69,	251 38 81
©	Hyderabad	040-27 55 53 83,	27 55 53 93
©	Jalandhar	0181-222 12 72	
©	Kolkata	033-22 27 43 84	
©	Lucknow	0522-220 99 16	
©	Mumbai	022-24 91 54 15,	24 92 78 69
©	Ranchi	0651-220 44 64	

Published in India by

FIREWALL MEDIA
(An Imprint of Laxmi Publications Pvt. Ltd.)

An ISO 9001:2008 Company
113, GOLDEN HOUSE, DARYAGANJ,
NEW DELHI - 110002, INDIA
Telephone : 91-11-4353 2500, 4353 2501
Fax : 91-11-2325 2572, 4353 2528
www.laxmipublications.com info@laxmipublications.com

C—
Printed at Repro Knowledgecast Limited, Thane

Foreword

It gives us great pleasure to introduce this collection of papers to be presented at the 2013 International Conference on Computer Design (CDES'13), July 22 through 25, 2013, at The New Tropicana Hotel, Las Vegas, USA.

An important mission of the World Congress in Computer Science, Computer Engineering, and Applied Computing (a federated congress to which this conference is affiliated with) includes *"Providing a unique platform for a diverse community of constituents composed of scholars, researchers, developers, educators, and practitioners. The Congress makes concerted effort to reach out to participants affiliated with diverse entities (such as: universities, institutions, corporations, government agencies, and research centers/labs) from all over the world. The congress also attempts to connect participants from institutions that have* ***teaching*** *as their main mission with those who are affiliated with institutions that have* ***research*** *as their main mission. The congress uses a quota system to achieve its institution and geography diversity objectives."* By any definition of diversity, this congress is among the most diverse scientific meeting in USA. We are proud to report that this federated congress has authors and participants from 82 different nations representing variety of personal and scientific experiences that arise from differences in culture and values. As can be seen (see below), the program committee of this conference as well as the program committee of all other tracks of the federated congress are as diverse as its authors and participants.

The program committee would like to thank all those who submitted papers for consideration. About 60% of the submissions were from outside the United States. Each submitted paper was peer-reviewed by two experts in the field for originality, significance, clarity, impact, and soundness. In cases of contradictory recommendations, a member of the conference program committee was charged to make the final decision; often, this involved seeking help from additional referees. In addition, papers whose authors included a member of the conference program committee were evaluated using the double-blinded review process. One exception to the above evaluation process was for papers that were submitted directly to chairs/organizers of pre-approved sessions/workshops; in these cases, the chairs/organizers were responsible for the evaluation of such submissions. The overall paper acceptance rate for regular papers was 31%; 7% of the remaining papers were accepted as poster papers (at the time of this writing, we had not yet received the acceptance rate for a few individual tracks.)

We are very grateful to the many colleagues who offered their services in organizing the conference. In particular, we would like to thank the members of the Program Committee of CDES'13, members of the congress Steering Committee, and members of the committees of federated congress tracks that have topics within the scope of CDES. Many individuals listed below, will be requested after the conference to provide their expertise and services for selecting papers for publication (extended versions) in journal special issues as well as for publication in a set of research books (to be prepared for publishers including: Springer, Elsevier, BMC, and others).

- *Dr. Selim Aissi (World Congress Steering Committee); formerly, Chief Strategist - Security, Intel Corp., USA; Senior Business Leader & Head of Global Enterprise Security Architecture, Visa Corporation, USA*
- *Prof. Babak Akhgar (World Congress Steering Committee); Fellow of the British Computer Society, CITP; Professor of Informatics; Co-Director of CENTRIC (Centre of Excellence in Terrorism, Resilience, Intelligence & organised Crime research), Sheffield Hallam University, Sheffield, UK*
- *Prof. Hussain Al-Asaad; Senior Member, IEEE; University of California at Davis, Davis, California, USA*
- *Prof. Nizar Al-Holou (World Congress Steering Committee); Professor and Chair, ECE Department; Vice Chair, IEEE/SEM-Computer Chapter; University of Detroit Mercy, Detroit, Michigan, USA*
- *Prof. Hamid R. Arabnia (World Congress Steering Committee); Professor, Computer Science; Editor-in-Chief, The Journal of Supercomputing (Springer); Elected Fellow, Int'l Society of Intelligent Biological Medicine (ISIBM); The University of Georgia, Department of Computer Science, USA*
- *Prof. P. Balasubramanian; Communication Engineering, Vel Tech Technical University, Chennai, India*
- *Prof. Kevin Daimi (World Congress Steering Committee); Director, Computer Science and Software Engineering Programs; Department of Mathematics, Computer Science and Software Engineering; University of Detroit Mercy, Detroit, Michigan, USA*
- *Prof. Leonidas Deligiannidis; Professor, Computer Science, Wentworth Institute of Technology, MA, USA*

- *Somdip Dey; St. Xavier's College (Autonomous), Kolkata, India*
- *Prof. Houcine Hassan; Universitat Politecnica de Valencia, Spain*
- *Dr. K. S. S. Iyer (PDPTA); Symbiosis Institute of Telecom Management, Pune, India*
- *Prof. George Jandieri (World Congress Steering Committee); Georgian Technical University, Tbilisi, Georgia; Chief Scientist, The Institute of Cybernetics, Georgian Academy of Science, Georgia; Editorial Board Member: International Journal of Microwaves and Optical Technology, Georgia*
- *Prof. Seifedine Kadry (PDPTA); School of Engineering, American University of the Middle East, Kuwait*
- *Prof. Dattatraya V. Kodavade (World Congress Steering Committee); Head of Computer Science and Engineering, D.K.T.E Society's Textile & Engineering Institute, Ichalkaranji, Maharashtra State, India*
- *Prof. B. Raja Sarath Kumar; Principal, Lenora College of Engineering, Andhra Pradesh, India*
- *Prof. Kun Chang Lee (World Congress Steering Committee); Professor of MIS and WCU Professor of Creativity Science, Business School and Department of Interaction Science, Sungkyunkwan University, Korea*
- *Muhammad Naufal Bin Mansor; Intelligent Signal Processing Group (ISP), University Malaysia Perlis, Perlis, Malaysia*
- *Prof. George Markowsky (World Congress Steering Committee); Professor and Associate Director, School of Computing & Information Science; Chair Int'l Advisory Board of IEEE IDAACS; Director 2013 Northeast Collegiate Cyber Defense Competition; Cooperating Professor Mathematics and Statistics Department UMaine and School of Policy & International Affairs UMaine; University of Maine, Orono, Maine, USA*
- *Dr. Sara Moein; Editorial Board, International Journal of Science and Technology; Faculty of Engineering, MultiMedia University, Malaysia*
- *Dr. Ali Mostafaeipour; Industrial Engineering Department, Yazd University, Iran*
- *Dr. Saurabh Mukherjee; Department of Computer Science, Banasthali University, Rajasthan, India*
- *Prof. G. N. Pandey (World Congress Steering Committee); Vice-Chancellor, Arunachal University of Studies, Arunachal Pradesh, India; Adjunct Professor, Indian Institute of Information Technology, India*
- *Prof. James J. (Jong Hyuk) Park (World Congress Steering Committee); Professor of Computer Science and Engineering, Seoul National University of Science and Technology (SeoulTech), Korea; President, KITCS; President, FTRA; Editor-in-Chiefs: HCIS, JoC and IJITCC Journals*
- *Dr. Satish Penmatsa; University of Maryland - Eastern Shore, Maryland, USA*
- *Dr. Liang Shi; Senior Researcher, McAfee, USA*
- *Ashu M. G. Solo, (Publicity Chair); Fellow of British Computer Society, Principal/R&D Engineer, Maverick Technologies America Inc., USA*
- *Prof. Fernando G. Tinetti (World Congress Steering Committee); School of Computer Science, Universidad Nacional de La Plata, La Plata, Argentina; Co-editor, Journal of CS and Technology (JCS&T)*
- *Dr. Predrag Tosic (World Congress Steering Committee); Microsoft, Washington, USA*
- *Prof. Vladimir Volkov (World Congress Steering Committee); The Bonch-Bruevich State University of Telecommunications, Saint-Petersburg, Russia*

As Sponsors-at-large, partners, and/or organizers each of the followings (separated by semicolons) provided help for at least one track of the World Congress: Aldebaran Robotics Inc., USA (http://www.aldebaran-robotics.com); Altera Corporation, USA (http://www.altera.com/); Computer Science Research, Education, and Applications Press (CSREA); Impulse Accelerated Technologies, Inc., USA (http://www.impulseaccelerated.com/); NVIDIA Corporation, USA (http://www.nvidia.com/object/about-nvidia.html); Parallella Community, Supercomputing for Everyone, USA (http://forums.parallella.org/); Pico Computing, Inc., USA (http://picocomputing.com/); SemiWiki.com, The Semiconductor Wiki Project, USA (http://www.semiwiki.com/); Solarflare Communications, Inc., USA (http://www.solarflare.com/); Stream Computing, Performance Engineers, The Netherlands (http://streamcomputing.eu/); Taylor & Francis, UK (http://www.taylorandfrancis.com/); US Chapter of World Academy of Science (http://www.world-academy-of-science.org/) ; and WEBestSOL & Webest Solutions Ltd, UK (http://webestsol.com/). In addition, a number of university faculty members and their staff (names appear on the cover of the set of proceedings), several publishers of computer science and computer engineering books and journals, chapters and/or task forces of computer science associations/organizations from 5 countries, and developers of high-performance machines and systems provided significant help in organizing the conference as well as providing some resources. We are grateful to them all.

We express our gratitude to keynote, invited, and individual conference/tracks and tutorial speakers - the list of speakers appears on the conference web site. We would also like to thank the followings: UCMSS (Universal Conference Management Systems & Support, California, USA) for managing all aspects of the conference; Dr. Tim Field of APC for managing the printing of the proceedings; and the staff of the New Tropicana Hotel in Las Vegas for the professional service they provided. Last but not least, we would like to thank the Co-Editors of CDES'13: Prof. Hamid R. Arabnia, Prof. Leonidas Deligiannidis, Ashu M. G. Solo, and Prof. Fernando G. Tinetti.

We present the proceedings of CDES'13.

Steering Committee, 2013
http://www.world-academy-of-science.org/

Contents

SESSION: PROCESSOR and INTEGRATED CIRCUIT DESIGN + LOW POWER COMPUTING + TESTING

SESSION: PERFORMANCE ISSUES + HPC AND MULTI-PROCESSOR SYSTEMS + FPGA + FILE SERVERS

SESSION

PROCESSOR and INTEGRATED CIRCUIT DESIGN + LOW POWER COMPUTING + TESTING

Chair(s)

TBA

Allocation of NBTI Aging Sensors for Circuit Failure Prediction

Samir Mahaboob Khan Kagadkar and Hussain Al-Asaad
Department of Electrical and Computer Engineering,
University of California, Davis

Abstract—*Negative bias temperature instability (NBTI) is a critical device reliability concern in nanometer-scale CMOS processes. We review the degradation effects of this phenomenon and present techniques to measure and combat NBTI aging. Such techniques involve the insertion of specialized aging sensors and their use in self-correcting dynamic reliability management systems. We propose a novel approach to optimize the allocation of such aging sensors to minimize overhead.*

Keywords: Integrated Circuit (IC) reliability, Circuit failure prediction, Negative Bias Temperature Instability (NBTI)

1. Introduction

Engineers working on the design of modern integrated circuits (ICs) fabricated in nanometer-scale technologies are in the unenviable position of having to face a plethora of issues that were benign in the past. Mounting parametric variability, radiation-induced soft errors and time-dependent device degradation make transistors increasingly unreliable components. A generation of engineers is realizing that hardware failures from these unreliable components are a distinctly realistic possibility.

Phenomena such as negative bias temperature instability, hot carrier injection, dielectric breakdown and electromigration limit circuit lifetimes. These degradation mechanisms are only increased with future technology scaling, further exacerbating an already diminished reliability. As Moore's Law packs more transistors on each chip, it is essential to design robust systems that can cope with these and other unexpected challenges.

Negative Bias Temperature Instability (NBTI) is a progressive aging phenomenon that results in reduced circuit performance. It occurs in p-channel MOS (pMOS) transistors that are stressed by negative gate voltages and elevated temperatures. NBTI has been recognized as a leading parametric failure mechanism in modern nanometer-scale ICs [1], [2].

Traditionally all parametric variations and aging effects have been tested via a go/no-go stress qualification methodology. ICs are designed to withstand a sustained combination of worst-case voltages, temperatures and parametric variation. Aging effects have been similarly factored in via their worst-case contribution to reliability degradation. As variability and degradation mechanisms worsen on modern fabrication processes, these worst-case guardbands are becoming increasingly pessimistic and resulting in lost performance and energy-efficiency.

An alternate approach is dynamic reliability management which uses specialized on-chip measurement circuitry to track variation and aging. Inputs from aging sensors and a history of past conditions predict future degradation and help optimize circuit tuning parameters such as voltage and frequency to prolong lifetimes. By minimizing pessimistic guardbands, such ICs offer optimal performances-per-joule of energy spent.

We first review the mechanisms behind and effects of NBTI degradation. We introduce sensors that track aging effects and their role in reliability management systems. In particular we explore a strategy that results in an economical allocation of aging sensors. An optimal allocation of aging sensors results in lower overhead and, hopefully, will hasten adoption of circuit failure prediction sensing in ICs.

2. Review of NBTI: Device-level and Circuit-level Effects

The phenomenon of NBTI occurs in p-channel MOSFET devices (pMOS) which are stressed with negative gate voltages at elevated temperatures. Although either negative voltages or elevated temperatures can cause NBTI, the effect is most strongly manifested when these conditions occur together. At a transistor level NBTI exhibits itself as decreases in absolute drain current I_{DSat}, transconductance g_m and absolute "off" current I_{off}, and increases in threshold voltage $|V_T|$ (V_T becomes more negative). At a digital circuit level, the increased pMOS threshold voltages and degraded drive current capabilities result in reduced performances and timing shifts. These timing shifts can eventually lead to delay faults and device failures.

Typical stress conditions are temperatures of $100 - 250°\mathrm{C}$ and oxide electric fields of a few $\mathrm{MV/cm}$. Elevated temperatures and high electric fields have become common in modern IC operation, especially when processing heavy workloads.

Various mechanisms have been described to explain the physics of NBTI. One theory that is commonly suggested is the breaking of Si-H bonds at the silicon/oxide interface resulting in the generation of dangling Si bonds. These dangling bonds act as electrically active interface traps. Under NBTI stresses, these traps are usually positively charged and result in threshold voltage increases. Details of such mechanisms can be found in [3].

Knowledge of NBTI dates as far back as the 1960s and 1970s [4], [5]. These early experiments established the buildup of positive charges at the interface Q_{it} due to NBTI, sensitivity of these charges to temperature as well as a power law dependence on aging times ($t^{0.25}$).

Commonly used surface channel MOSFET devices with SiO_2-based gate dielectric exhibit the NBTI effect. With each technology generation, more and more high-performing devices are being packed onto single dies. Such high densities and rapid switching have increased on-die temperatures ($T \approx 100°C$), especially at peak activity. The non-linear reduction of operating voltages with the technology scaling has resulted in high gate oxide electric fields. The shift to nitrided oxides on advanced CMOS devices aggravated the NBTI effects. Moreover the interface trap density introduced by NBTI has a $1/t_{\text{ox}}$ dependence on the oxide thickness t_{ox}, making the effect more pronounced on modern, ultra-thin gate oxide CMOS devices.

More recent MOS processes at the 45n and below technology nodes introduced high-k dielectrics and metal gates to combat high levels of leakage from ultra-thin SiON dielectrics. Such devices also exhibit bias temperature instability [2].

2.1 Interface States and Device-level Characteristics of NBTI Damage

The threshold voltage of a p-channel MOSFET device is given by [6]:

$$V_T = V_{\text{FB}} - 2\psi_{Bn} - \frac{|Q_s|}{C_{\text{ox}}} \quad (1)$$

The second term is the surface potential at strong inversion $\psi_s \approx -2\psi_{Bn} = -2\ln(N_D/n_i)$. $|Q_s| = \sqrt{2\epsilon_s q N_D(2|\psi_{Bn}|)}$ represents total space charge density. V_{FB} is the flatband voltage and is given by:

$$V_{\text{FB}} = \phi_{\text{ms}} - \frac{Q_f}{C_{\text{ox}}} - \frac{Q_{\text{it}}}{C_{\text{ox}}} \quad (2)$$

Here ϕ_{ms} is the work function difference between the metal and semiconductor. Q_f and Q_{it} are densities of fixed charge and interface traps respectively. N_D is substrate doping density. C_{ox} is the oxide capacitance per unit area. The other symbols have the usual meanings.

An interface trapped charge, also called an interface trap, is a dangling bond at the SiO_2/Si interface. These interface traps are electrically active defects that can act as generation/recombination sites. Since electrons and holes occupy the trap states, they contribute to threshold voltage shifts:

$$\Delta V_T = -\Delta Q_{\text{it}}/C_{\text{ox}} \quad (3)$$

Interface traps have energy states that are distributed throughout the forbidden gap, acting as acceptors in the upper half and donors in the lower half. In pMOS devices under inversion, NBTI stress leads to an activation of positively charged interface traps. This results in the threshold voltage becoming more negative (increase in $|V_T|$).

NBTI causes degradation in device characteristics and reduced performance. The MOSFET saturation drain current and transconductance are:

$$I_{\text{DSat}} = (W/2L)\mu_{\text{eff}}C_{\text{ox}}(V_G - V_T)^2 \quad (4)$$
$$g_m = (W/L)\mu_{\text{eff}}C_{\text{ox}}(V_G - V_T) \quad (5)$$

The threshold voltage changes described above result in reduced gate overdrive ($V_G - V_T$) and hence degraded drive currents and device transconductances.

2.2 Circuit-level Characteristics of NBTI Damage

Studies have shown that pMOS threshold voltages can shift by 50mV over a period of ten years. The associated drive current reduction and lower device performance translates to over 20% degradation in circuit speed [3], [7].

Negative gate bias stresses correspond to the "output high" state of the CMOS inverter operation. With speedy transition times on high performance circuits, large portions of time can be spent in the NBTI stress state. Such stresses may be coupled with high temperatures depending on device workloads and position on the die. High activity regions of the IC often reach elevated temperatures.

NBTI has been shown to be a dynamic phenomenon [1]. A large fraction of the interface traps activated under the NBTI stressing are annealed when the CMOS inverter switches to a "low" output state. This recovery phase may be explained by the diffusion of hydrogen back into the Si/SiO_2 interface thus passivating interface traps. Figure 1 illustrates threshold voltage degradation during negative bias stress and subsequent recovery under positive bias. The temperature sensitivity and the dynamic nature of NBTI degradation make the phenomenon strongly dependent on the actual computational workloads of the IC.

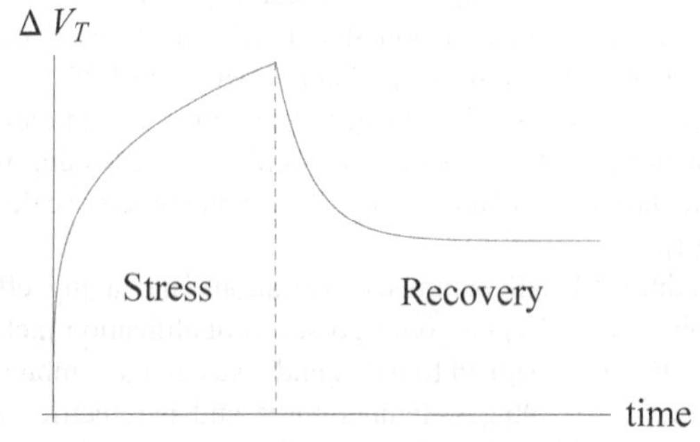

Fig. 1: pMOS NBTI vs. time illustrating both degradation and recovery when stress is removed. Note that magnitude of threshold voltage is used here.

The reduced drive characteristics and circuit speed result in delay shifts of timing paths that contain NBTI damaged gates. These delay shifts may or may not immediately manifest themselves as delay faults. For example, a timing path may possess more timing margin (slack before the onset of degradation) than the delay degradation caused by NBTI. These delay shifts can be used as indicators of NBTI, and sensors based on this principle are explored in sections ahead.

3. Combating Aging

An ideal solution to limit aging and the associated parametric degradation is to improve device fabrication process. Improved passivation of interface trap states reduces the NBTI effect. As process scaling is approaching physical and manufacturing limits, radical process improvements are non-trivial. A design engineer must recognize that aging is a realistic concern that must be dealt with proactively. Such design techniques are explored in this section.

3.1 Guardbands

This involves estimating the cumulative worst-case degradation that may occur over the lifetime of a device due to a combination of temperature, voltage, computing workload and other stresses. The clock frequency is reduced to accommodate for this worst-case degradation.

3.2 Dynamic Reliability Management

The technique of guardbands is based upon continuous stressing of a sample under pessimistic operating conditions and evaluating whether it passes or fails. In reality widely varying operation conditions and dynamic power saving methods mean most parts are not stressed to these worst-case levels. Thus by using pessimistic guardbands, we lose out on a substantial performance margin between worst-case conditions and typical conditions. This loss is illustrated in Figure 2.

An alternate approach to worst-case stress qualification is a knowledge based risk assessment and mitigation technique. A framework for application-specific knowledge-based test is defined by the JEDEC JESD-94 standard [8]. This requires a detailed knowledge of individual failure mechanisms and their models. Tests are developed to capture these failure modes under a range of operation conditions and reliability targets specific to the device's end use and application. Implementations of this knowledge-based approach are often termed as dynamic reliability management [9], [10].

The dynamic reliability management system we envisage uses real-time on-die measurements including voltage, thermal information, computing workloads and inputs from specialized on-die aging sensors. Characterization and analysis of failure mechanisms provides models that can use these inputs and past operating history to predict future degradation.

These predictions allow the adjustment of circuit control parameters as a self-correcting measure to guarantee the device is under a reasonable reliability envelope.

3.3 Self-Correction

Dynamic Voltage Frequency Scaling (DVFS) is the scaling of clock frequency and/or supply voltage dynamically and has been used to trade-off between a device's time-dependent performance and its energy consumption. At peak demand, both voltage and frequency can be scaled up to guarantee maximum performance. On the other hand these can be reduced at periods of low activity, thus ensuring low average power consumption. Since voltage scaling helps offset delay degradation on aged timing paths, this can be used to correct for NBTI degradation [11], [12].

It must be noted that higher supply voltages (V_{DD}) tend to increase the rate of NBTI degradation. Thus it is important to carefully choose supply voltages that do not unnecessarily accelerate aging effects if such voltage increases are not immediately required. Moreover higher voltages also cause increased power consumption and the associated rise in operating temperature that further exacerbates NBTI aging.

Since bias temperature instability causes increases in threshold voltage, this results in reduced subthreshold currents and a corresponding reduction in total circuit leakage power ($I_{\mathrm{sub}} \propto e^{\frac{-V_T}{mkT}}$). This presents us an opportunity of trading off this power saving for recovered performance by forward body biasing (FBB) the devices [13], [14].

A combination of the adaptive voltage scaling and adaptive body bias techniques can be used to correct for aging wearout. This correction scheme is embedded as part of a more general circuit tuning framework which dynamically matches operating voltage, frequency and body bias to application-based performance needs, power saving goals, and to combat variations in process and temperature.

4. Aging Sensors

Real-time chip- and system-level sensors measure and track the actual aging process and allow the implementation of reliability enhancement processes that can compensate for aging effects. The insertion of such sensors as part of a larger self-correcting dynamic reliability management system is one way to avoid overly pessimistic design margins.

Most modern high performance ICs already include on-chip measurement circuits such as process monitors (for example, ring oscillators) and temperature sensors. It is probably unwise to rely solely on the inputs from such conventional monitor cells [15]. Due to the time and location variability of stresses from dynamic workloads, the stresses faced by a conventional monitor might be very different from the stresses faced by various functional modules of the chip.

NBTI degradation manifests itself in a number of visible ways. Any of these signatures can be measured by specialized aging sensors and used to detect NBTI-based

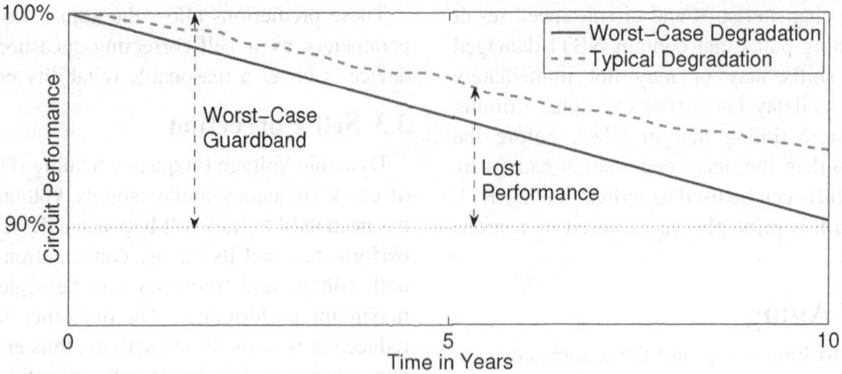

Fig. 2: Reliability degradation over time

circuit aging. Most commonly degradation in circuit speed is measured to detect NBTI. Data collected from these aging sensors is supplanted with data from conventional measurement circuits (thermal and voltage monitors) and data logs (operating history, sleep states and past measurements from on-die sensors). This information can be used to predict future reliability failures.

Some techniques for designing NBTI sensors include analog measurements. Measurement of quiescent power supply current (I_{DDQ} test) [16] or measurement of the control voltage for locking a delay-locked-loop [17] are examples of such techniques. Several other groups have suggested the use of ring oscillators to track NBTI aging [18], [19], [20]. In practice the use of analog measurements is unwieldy for measurement of in-field aging. Moreover, it is uncertain that the wearout of ring oscillator elements occurs at the same rate as data-dependent aging on paths in functional modules.

Agarwal et al. developed an NBTI measurement technique that embeds delay shift measuring circuitry within existing design flip-flops [15]. Their essential idea is to compare a delayed sample of the signal at the input of a flip-flop with the original sample. Figure 3 illustrates this idea.

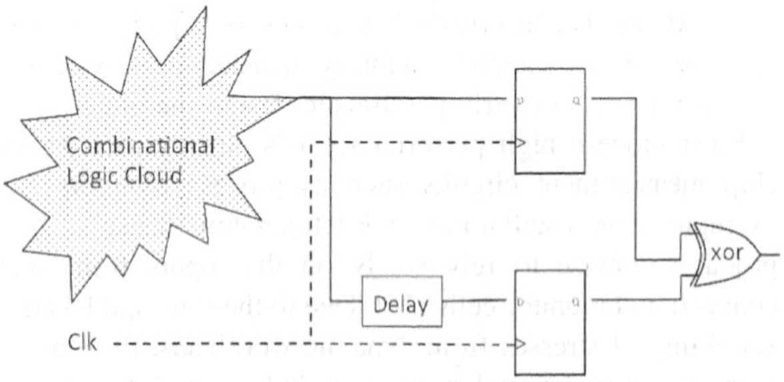

Fig. 3: Measurement circuitry that compares original and delayed samples indicating guardband violation. Adapted from [15].

They define a guardband interval as a small worst-case timing guardband that ensures circuit functionality over a short period of time, for example fifteen days. The design is closed with this safety margin and thus is ensured to work over the period of the guardband interval. Data at the output of logic cones is double sampled. A regular flip-flop takes one sample of the data and another flip-flop samples the data after a specified delay. This timing shift is implemented by a delay element with a delay equal to the guardband interval. These sampled signals are now compared via an exclusive-OR (XOR) gate. If the compared signals differ, this results in a logic-high signal at the output of the XOR gate. This indicates at least one timing path in the combinational logic cloud has sufficiently degraded due to aging thus entering the guardband and further timing degradation might cause a delay fault. If this has happened the IC enters a self-correction phase where guardbands and system parameters are adjusted to ensure future reliability [21]. Related research uses the general principle but has different circuitry of the sensor [15]. By sampling critical functional timing paths, these sensors measure in-situ aging due to real computing workloads of the device. We will consider this technique as the sensor of choice for future sections.

5. Allocation of Aging Sensors

In this section we explore a methodology to place NBTI aging sensors. A frugal insertion strategy minimizes overhead of these sensors. The insertion of aging sensors comes at the cost of area and power. For example, the sensors described earlier double sample logic outputs. The additional flip-flops add an area overhead as well as consume power when they sample data. Moreover signals from the aging sensors need to be routed to a dynamic reliability management unit for analysis which causes wiring overhead.

Since dynamic NBTI exhibits both stress and recovery (passivation) phases during circuit operation, the degradation due to NBTI is sensitive to the input patterns applied. In addition to voltage and temperature information, estimates of delay shifts should consider node switching activities from realistic computational workloads. NBTI degradation models that include activity factors indicating the fraction of time spent in stress states are presented in [22], [23]. Circuit topologies and realtime workloads cause duty cycles that vary both spatially and temporally and between gates within a logic cone.

Furthermore, dynamic on-die temperature readings are very workload dependent and temperature hotspots for one application might differ significantly from the temperature hotspots for another application. It is thus important to develop and use a well-representative mix of benchmark applications that will model realistic in-field computing workloads and temperature stresses generated therein. In addition to data-dependence, thermal profiles depend on the power-saving options in use on the device. Measures such as power gating, clock gating and other sleep states can cause large variations in temperature maps.

5.1 Optimal Placement of NBTI Aging Sensors

A naïve strategy for insertion is to place them at all flip-flops where setup timing slack is less than our guardband interval [24]. This aging estimate is based on static NBTI and is hence unnecessarily pessimistic. Agarwal et al. improve upon this strategy by performing timing analysis assuming a worst-case activity factor of 0.95 (fraction of time spent in pMOS stress state). In our opinion the overhead obtained with this empirical activity ratio is still too high for practical use on ICs. For example their analysis requires embedding aging sensors on a particularly large number of flip-flops. On two designs they report 16% and 52% of flip-flops that need embedding of aging sensors [24]. Another important consideration that is not considered explicitly in their work is the impact of thermal stress.

We propose an alternate strategy that minimizes the overhead of on-chip aging sensors by including the realistic considerations of activity ratios and temperature profiles. Timing analysis is performed on post layout netlists as a part of design closure to ensure correctness of device operation under specified performance targets. This analysis is often performed using a static timing analysis (STA) tool such as Synopsys PrimeTime. Our strategy to decide optimal locations for aging sensors is only a simple modification to an existing STA flow.

This strategy is outlined in Figure 4. Multiple vector based simulations are performed on the circuit netlist for a mix of representative real-world workloads. Such analysis is often performed on post-layout netlists to obtain dynamic power and dynamic voltage drop estimates. This simulation yields application-specific node activity information as well as temperature maps. Temperature maps could also be obtained by a separate analysis or based on previous silicon measurements. These activity and temperature maps are overlaid on the static timing analysis (STA) environment. An aging aware cell library embeds cell-level aging information specific to activity ratios at gate inputs and operating temperature. Timing slacks obtained from such application-specific timing analyses allows insertion of aging sensors optimally. Flip-flops with timing slack less than a specified guardband interval are most sensitive to NBTI aging and its associated slowdown. These are now replaced by flip-flops with aging sensors embedded within them.

Our STA flows can be sped up by eliminating non-critical end-points from our analysis. Timing paths with enough slack to tolerate pessimistic degradation can be skipped from the detailed temperature-sensitive and vector-based timing analysis. For example, end-points with more setup slacks than would be lost under worst-case static NBTI degradation at elevated temperatures are eliminated from our analysis.

Once critical end-points are identified by timing analysis, we insert aging sensors at these locations and perform incremental place-and-route to obtain final layouts. By inserting sensors on paths that are most sensitive to aging, we are able to minimize the overhead of aging sensors.

6. Conclusion

NBTI is a phenomenon that contributes significantly to reduced reliability of pMOS transistors and ICs that use these transistors as building blocks. Although we are not yet facing an insurmountable barrier due to such issues, additional complexity has been introduced on already burdened engineers. Design engineers can use measurements of in-field aging by the use of specialized on-die measurement circuits. These measurements are used to predict future circuit failures and also used in a dynamic reliability management framework to tune circuit control parameters such as voltage and body bias. We reviewed aging sensors that track NBTI degradation and explored a strategy based on application-specific data for the economical allocation of such sensors.

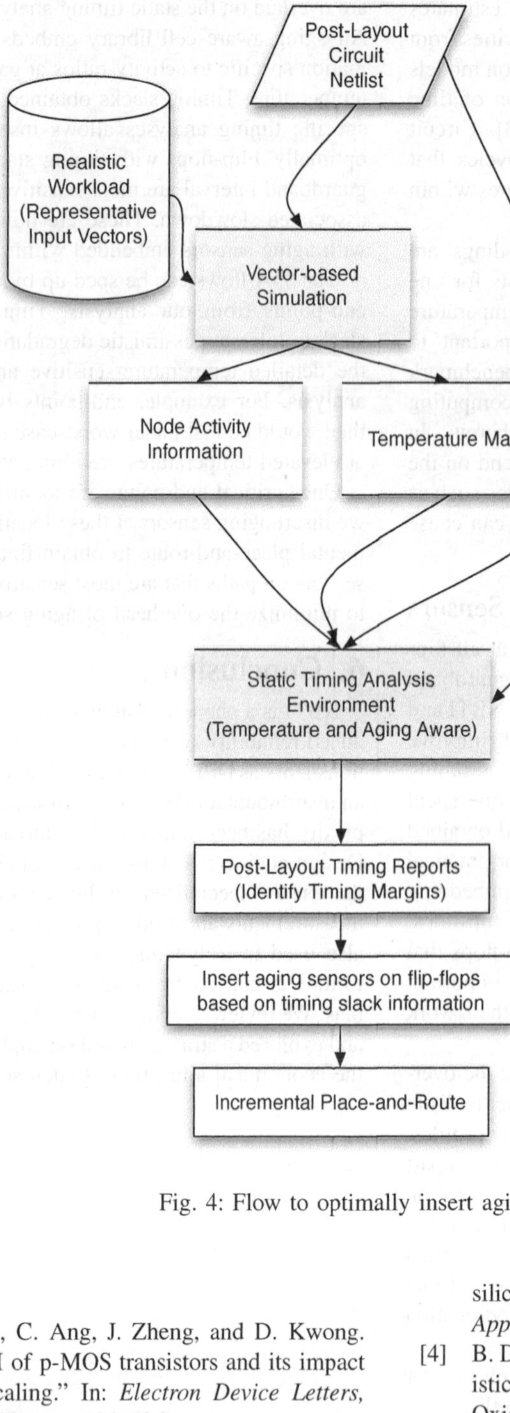

Fig. 4: Flow to optimally insert aging sensors

References

[1] G. Chen, M. Li, C. Ang, J. Zheng, and D. Kwong. "Dynamic NBTI of p-MOS transistors and its impact on MOSFET scaling." In: *Electron Device Letters, IEEE* 23.12 (2002), pp. 734–736.

[2] J. Hicks, D. Bergstrom, M. Hattendorf, J. Jopling, J. Maiz, S. Pae, C. Prasad, and J. Wiedemer. "45nm transistor reliability." In: *Intel Technology Journal* 12.2 (2008), pp. 131–144.

[3] D. Schroder and J. Babcock. "Negative bias temperature instability: Road to cross in deep submicron silicon semiconductor manufacturing." In: *Journal of Applied Physics* 94.1 (2003), pp. 1–18.

[4] B. Deal, M. Sklar, A. Grove, and E. Snow. "Characteristics of the Surface-State Charge (Qss) of Thermally Oxidized Silicon." In: *Journal of the Electrochemical Society* 114.3 (1967), pp. 266–274.

[5] A. Goetzberger, A. Lopez, and R. Strain. "On the Formation of Surface States during Stress Aging of Thermal Si-SiO2 Interfaces." In: *Journal of the Electrochemical Society* 120.1 (1973), pp. 90–96.

[6] S. Sze and K. Ng. *Physics of semiconductor devices*. Wiley-interscience, 2006.

[7] S. Borkar. "Electronics beyond nano-scale CMOS." In: *Proceedings of the 43rd annual Design Automation Conference*. ACM. 2006, pp. 807–808.

[8] J. JESD94A. "Application Specific Qualification Using Knowledge Based Test Methodology." In: *JEDEC Solid State Technology Association* (2007).

[9] E. Karl, D. Blaauw, D. Sylvester, and T. Mudge. "Multi-mechanism reliability modeling and management in dynamic systems." In: *Very Large Scale Integration (VLSI) Systems, IEEE Transactions on* 16.4 (2008), pp. 476–487.

[10] J. Srinivasan, S. Adve, P. Bose, and J. Rivers. "The case for lifetime reliability-aware microprocessors." In: *ACM SIGARCH Computer Architecture News*. Vol. 32. 2. IEEE Computer Society. 2004, p. 276.

[11] L. Zhang and R. P. Dick. "Scheduled voltage scaling for increasing lifetime in the presence of NBTI." In: *Design Automation Conference, 2009. ASP-DAC 2009. Asia and South Pacific*. IEEE. 2009, pp. 492–497.

[12] A. Tiwari and J. Torrellas. "Facelift: Hiding and slowing down aging in multicores." In: *Microarchitecture, 2008. MICRO-41. 2008 41st IEEE/ACM International Symposium on*. IEEE. 2008, pp. 129–140.

[13] J. W. Tschanz, J. T. Kao, S. G. Narendra, R. Nair, D. A. Antoniadis, A. P. Chandrakasan, and V. De. "Adaptive body bias for reducing impacts of die-to-die and within-die parameter variations on microprocessor frequency and leakage." In: *Solid-State Circuits, IEEE Journal of* 37.11 (2002), pp. 1396–1402.

[14] S. V. Kumar, C. H. Kim, and S. S. Sapatnekar. "Adaptive techniques for overcoming performance degradation due to aging in digital circuits." In: *Proceedings of the 2009 Asia and South Pacific Design Automation Conference*. IEEE Press. 2009, pp. 284–289.

[15] M. Agarwal, B. Paul, M. Zhang, and S. Mitra. "Circuit failure prediction and its application to transistor aging." In: *VLSI Test Symposium, 2007. 25th IEEE*. IEEE. 2007, pp. 277–286.

[16] K. Kang, K. Kim, A. Islam, M. Alam, and K. Roy. "Characterization and estimation of circuit reliability degradation under NBTI using on-line IDDQ measurement." In: *Design Automation Conference, 2007. DAC'07. 44th ACM / IEEE*. IEEE. 2007, pp. 358–363.

[17] J. Keane, T. Kim, and C. Kim. "An on-chip NBTI sensor for measuring PMOS threshold voltage degradation." In: *Very Large Scale Integration (VLSI) Systems, IEEE Transactions on* 18.6 (2010), pp. 947–956.

[18] V. Reddy, A. Krishnan, A. Marshall, J. Rodriguez, S. Natarajan, T. Rost, and S. Krishnan. "Impact of negative bias temperature instability on digital circuit reliability." In: *Microelectronics Reliability* 45.1 (2005), pp. 31–38.

[19] T. Kim, R. Persaud, and C. Kim. "Silicon odometer: An on-chip reliability monitor for measuring frequency degradation of digital circuits." In: *Solid-State Circuits, IEEE Journal of* 43.4 (2008), pp. 874–880.

[20] E. Karl, P. Singh, D. Blaauw, and D. Sylvester. "Compact in-situ sensors for monitoring negative-bias-temperature-instability effect and oxide degradation." In: *Solid-State Circuits Conference, 2008. ISSCC 2008. Digest of Technical Papers. IEEE International*. IEEE. 2008, pp. 410–623.

[21] Y. Li, Y. Kim, E. Mintarno, D. Gardner, and S. Mitra. "Overcoming early-life failure and aging for robust systems." In: *Design & Test of Computers, IEEE* 26.6 (2009), pp. 28–39.

[22] S. Bhardwaj, W. Wang, R. Vattikonda, Y. Cao, and S. Vrudhula. "Predictive modeling of the NBTI effect for reliable design." In: *Custom Integrated Circuits Conference, 2006. CICC'06. IEEE*. IEEE. 2006, pp. 189–192.

[23] W. Wang, S. Yang, S. Bhardwaj, R. Vattikonda, S. Vrudhula, F. Liu, and Y. Cao. "The impact of NBTI on the performance of combinational and sequential circuits." In: *Design Automation Conference, 2007. DAC'07. 44th ACM/IEEE*. IEEE. 2007, pp. 364–369.

[24] M. Agarwal, V. Balakrishnan, A. Bhuyan, K. Kim, B. C. Paul, W. Wang, B. Yang, Y. Cao, and S. Mitra. "Optimized circuit failure prediction for aging: Practicality and promise." In: *Test Conference, 2008. ITC 2008. IEEE International*. IEEE. 2008, pp. 1–10.

Implementation of a Fast Fourier Transform Processor in NULL Convention Logic

Zhen Song and Scott C. Smith
Department of Electrical Engineering, University of Arkansas, Fayetteville, AR, U.S.A.
szuark@gmail.com and smithsco@uark.edu

Abstract – *The Fast Fourier Transform (FFT) is a critical part in communication systems, because it can greatly reduce the computation requirement for signal processing. This paper presents the design of a FFT processor using NULL Convention Logic (NCL), which has been shown to have power consumption advantages over its synchronous counterpart. Performance metrics for the NCL FFT processor are obtained from Cadence simulation, and compared to an equivalent synchronous implementation.*

1. Introduction

Hardware implementations of FFT are divided into two categories, fixed-point and floating-point. Although floating-point numbers inherently have large dynamic range, hardware implementation is larger, slower, and more power consuming than the fixed-point counterpart. This is because arithmetic operations for both mantissa and exponent need to be handled in the hardware [1]. Therefore, in order to design a low-power and high-speed processor, a synchronous FFT processor is usually designed using Q15 Fixed-point format [1, 2].

2. Previous Work

1) Synchronous FFT Architecture:

The synchronous FFT processor in Figure 1 utilizes a single stage architecture. 32 butterfly units are used, one for each two points [4, 5].

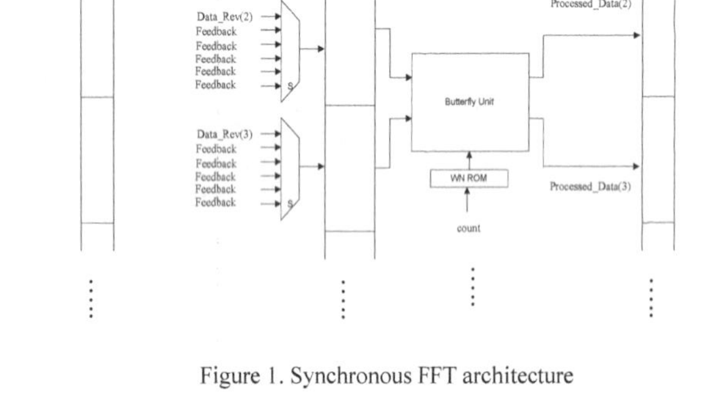

Figure 1. Synchronous FFT architecture

The feedback from each stage is hardcoded on MUX inputs. The select signal on the MUX is controlled by a counter, which counts the computation stages. A 64-point FFT requires 6 butterfly computation stages, so computing one set of input data will take 6 clock cycles. As shown in Figure 1, the 64-bit Data_in first goes through the Bit_reverse unit to get bit-reverse ordered Data_Rev. Then, for the first stage, each butterfly unit gets two points and calculates the corresponding intermediate results, called Processed_Data. These intermediate data are then fed back to the multiplexers for computations in the next stage. The MUXs take in Processed_Data from the previous stage as input for computation on the current stage. This kind of data flow continues until the final computation stage. After calculations in the final stage, a final re-order unit is used to output data in the correct order.

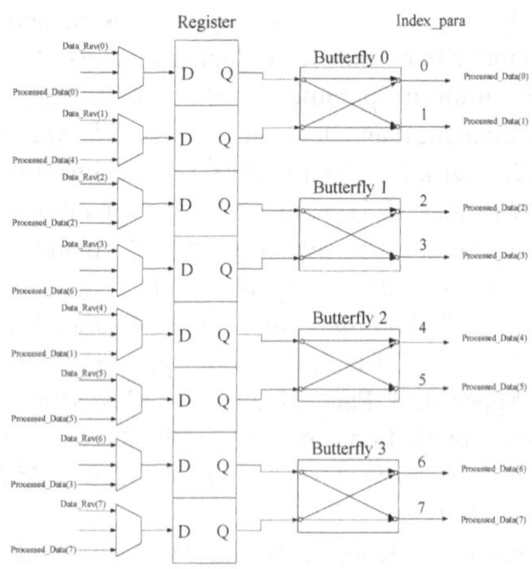

Figure 2. Hardcoded MUX inputs of 8-bit FFT

The calculation of MUX index is presented as follows [3]: in the flow graph of FFT, butterflies cross over each other in an ascending manner in each stage. The index_para for both inputs and outputs of butterfly0 are 0 and 1, 2 and 3 for butterfly1, and so on. For each node on both the right side and the left side of the butterfly groups in each stage, index_cross is used. Index_cross is the natural order we count from the first node all the way to the last node, from 1 to 64. Using excel, we can get corresponding relations to transfer index_cross to index_para on each stage and vice versa. The function to transfer index_cross to index_para on stage i is called CtoPi and the function to transfer index_para to index_cross on stage i is called PtoCi. In order to re-arrange the output of butterflies at stage i, the following equation is used:

$$CtoPi(PtoCi\text{-}1(index\_para))$$

Using the equations presented, the hardcoded MUX inputs of an 8-bit FFT are shown in Figure 2.

2) Butterfly Unit

The butterfly unit in Figure 3 computes the following equations [4, 5].:

$$X_m[p] = X_{m-1}[p] + W_N^r X_{m-1}[q]$$

$$X_m[q] = X_{m-1}[p] - W_N^r X_{m-1}[q]$$

The twiddle factor multiplier, TwiddleX, as shown in Figure 4, calculates the complex multiplication of $W_N^r X_{m-1}[q]$ inside the butterfly unit.

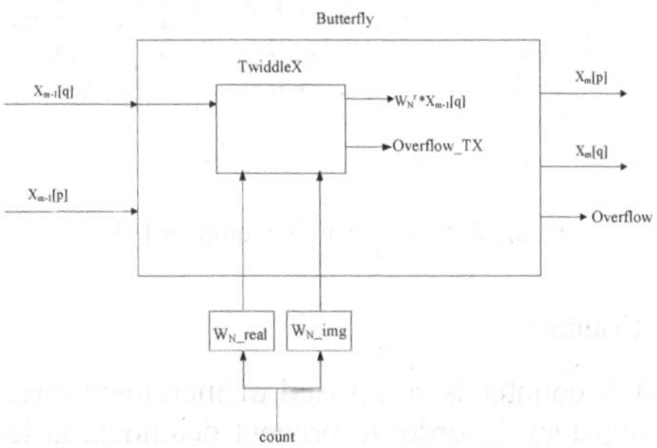

Figure 3. Butterfly unit

TwiddleX gets the value of W_N_real and W_N_img from a ROM, and calculates the following equation for complex multiplication:

$$(Xr+ j*Xi)*(W_N\_real + j* W_N\_img) = (Xr* W_N\_real - Xi* W_N\_img) + j*(Xi* W_N\_real + Xr* W_N\_img)$$

where *Xr* and *Xi* are the real and imaginary part of $X_{m-1}[q]$

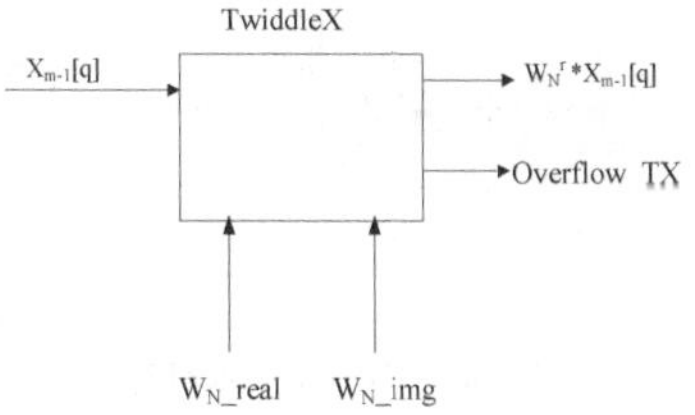

Figure 4. Twiddle factor multiplier

Each butterfly performs only 6 calculations for the entire process, so we only need to store the 6 specific W_N values in each ROM. Each addition and subtraction in the twiddle factor multiplier and the butterfly unit may cause overflow, so all overflow detection signals for these operations are combined together to get the final overflow signal at the output of the butterfly unit.

A 3-bit up-counter is used to control the FFT data path. This counter is reset to 0, and counts up whenever Enable is 1.

The corresponding algorithmic state machine diagram is shown in Figure 5.

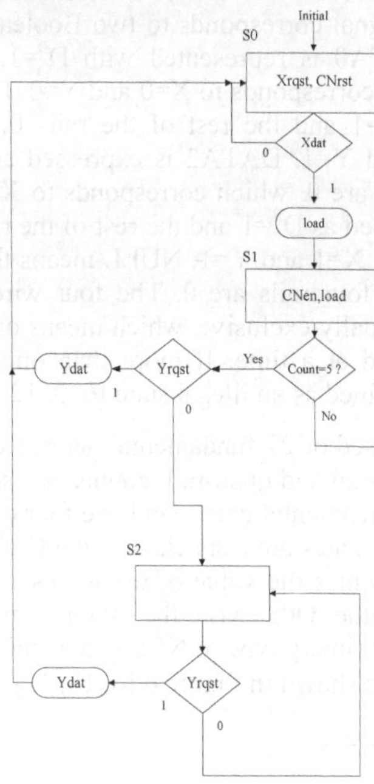

Figure 5. State machine diagram

Upon initialization, *Xrqst* is asserted to request new data, and counter is reset to 0. If *Xdat* is 1 the registers will load in the new data; otherwise they wait until *Xdat* is 1. In S1, FFT loads and calculates intermediate data until the count reaches 5. S2 is an idle state that is used to wait for *Yrqst* to be asserted before asserting *Ydat* to signify that the output is valid.

3) Introduction to NCL

Generally, asynchronous circuits fall into one of two categories: bounded-delay model or delay-insensitive model. NCL circuits belong to the delay-insensitive model, which means they can operate correctly with little timing analysis [6, 7, 8]. Symbolic completeness of expression is utilized in NCL to realize delay-insensitivity. Specifically, dual-rail and quad-rail logic are used in NCL design. Symbolically complete means that the outputs are only determined by the presence of the input signals, regardless of the timing relationship between the input signals [8].

In NCL, both dual-rail and quad-rail signals use space optimal 1-hot encoding and represent 1 bit by two wires [6, 7]. A dual-rail signal *D* consists of two wires: D^0 and D^1, whose values are from the set {DATA0, DATA1, NULL}. DATA0 corresponds to logic 0 in Boolean logic, with D^0=1 and D^1=0, while DATA1 is equivalent to logic 1 in Boolean logic, with D^0=0 and D^1=1. NULL means the dual-rail signal is not available, so D^0 =0 and D^1=0. Just as logic 0 and logic 1 are mutually exclusive in Boolean logic, DATA0 and DATA1 are also mutually exclusive; therefore, D^0 and D^1 cannot be 1 simultaneously, which is defined as an illegal state. Similarly, a quad-rail signal uses 4 wires, D^0, D^1, D^2, and D^3, which can have a value of {DATA0, DATA1, DATA2, DATA3, NULL}. A quad-rail signal corresponds to two Boolean logic signals, *X* and *Y*. DATA0 is represented with D^0=1, D^1=0, D^2=0, and D^3=0, which corresponds to X=0 and Y=0. DATA1 is represented with D^1=1 and the rest of the rails 0, which corresponds to X=0 and Y=1. DATA2 is expressed as D^2=1 and the rest of the rails are 0, which corresponds to X=1 and Y=0. DATA3 is expressed as D^3=1 and the rest of the rails are 0, which corresponds to X=1 and Y=1. NULL means the data is not available, so all four rails are 0. The four wires of a quad-rail signal are mutually exclusive, which means only one of them can be asserted at a time. If more than one rail is asserted, this state is defined as an illegal state [6, 9, 12, 13].

NCL logic is composed of 27 fundamental gates. Each rail in NCL logic, both dual-rail and quad-rail, counts as a separate variable. Each of the fundamental gates can have four or fewer variables as inputs. NCL gates are a subclass of the C-element. A C-element output assumes the value of the inputs when all inputs have the same value. Otherwise, the output remains its previous value [6]. The primary type of NCL gate is the THmn gate, where $1 \leq m \leq n$, as shown in Figure 6 [6, 10, 11].

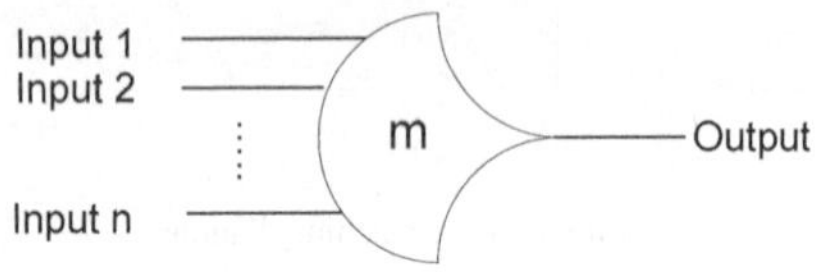

Figure 6. THmn NCL Gate [6, 10, 11]

The THmn gate has *n* inputs and threshold of *m*. The output of the gate will only be asserted when at least *m* of the *n* inputs are asserted. The inputs are connected to the arc on the left-hand side. The output is connected from the tip on the right-hand side [6].

3. NCL FFT PROCESSOR

1) NCL Components

The NCL overflow detector is designed as shown in Figure 7.

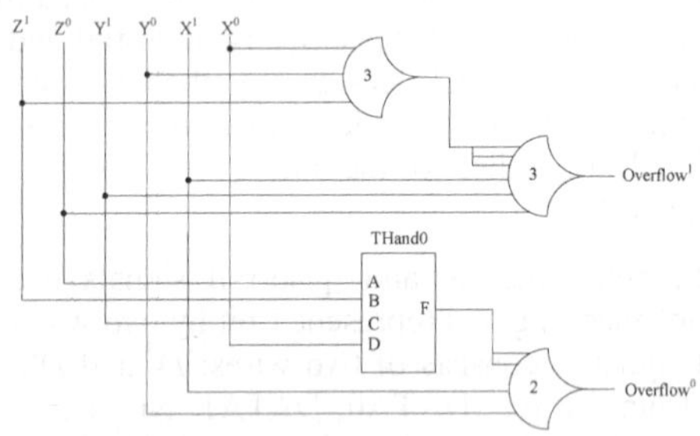

Figure 7. NCL overflow detector

a) NCL Array Multiplier

By using the Baugh and Wooley method [14], a 16-bit by 16-bit NCL array multiplier is designed, as shown in Figure 8. A partial product is generated by ANDing two bits of the input signal. Then some of the partial products are inverted according to the Baugh-Wooley scheme. In the array multiplier structure, adders only use wires to communicate to adjacent adders, thus making its layout area efficient.

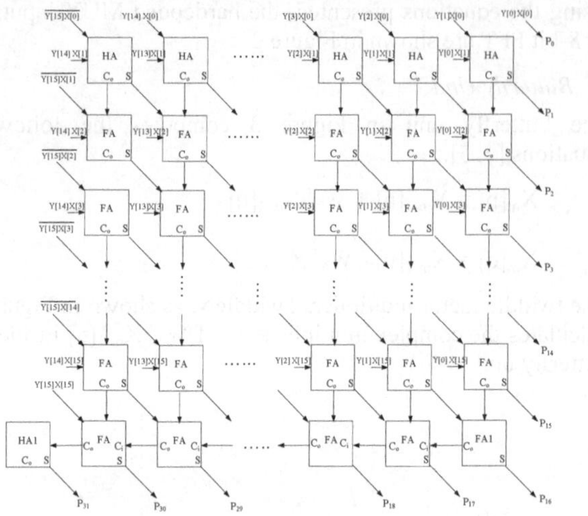

Figure 8. NCL 2-D array multiplier [14]

b) NCL Counter

The NCL counter is comprised of increment circuitry and feedback registers. In order to prevent deadlock, at least three registers are needed in a feedback loop. The internal data flow is controlled by request signal K_i and acknowledge signal K_o. Completion detection circuits are used to detect complete DATA and NULL wavefronts [7]. The up counter with three feedback registers is shown in Figure 9.

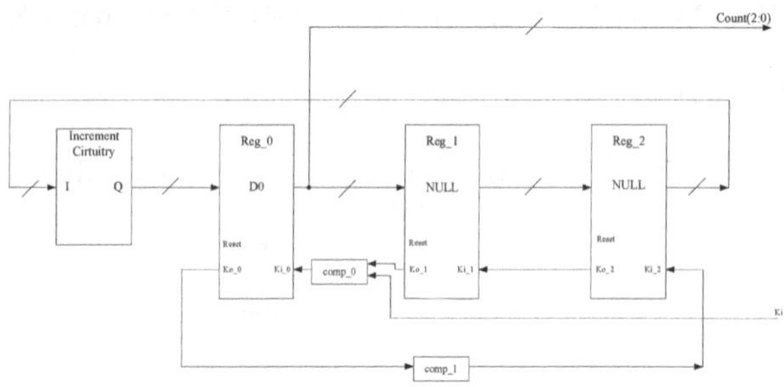

Figure 9. NCL counter [7]

Reg0 is reset to DATA0 and Reg1 and Reg2 are reset to NULL, to allow the DATA-NULL wavefront flow. This counter is initially reset to DATA0; then it counts from 0 to 5 and is rolled over. The reset signal is a standard logic signal. As a result, there is no NCL input signal for the counter. Thus, no *Ko* signal is needed. The counter increment circuitry is shown in Figure 10.

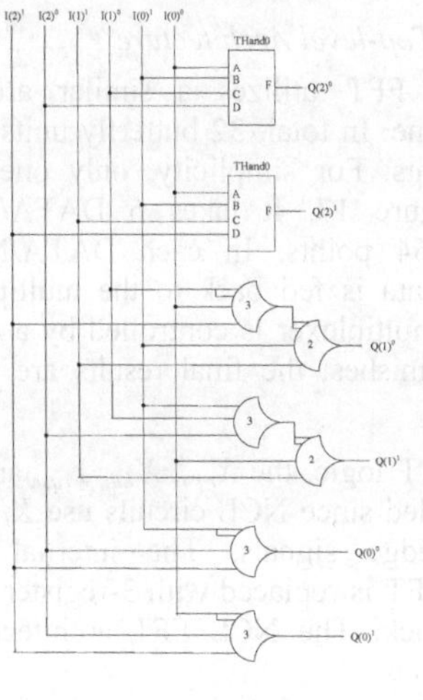

Figure 10. Counter increment circuitry

c) NCL 6 to 1 Multiplexer

In the FFT architecture, the inputs are only DATA at the beginning of the whole operation. The intermediate results then loop inside the FFT to compute the results. Therefore, the NCL multiplexer is designed to be input-incomplete with respect to the inputs, and only input-complete with respect to the select signal. Output F is DATA when select signal S is DATA and the selected input is DATA, and is NULL when S is NULL and the previously selected input is NULL. Internal control signals S_0 through S_5 are generated using TH33 gates, as shown in Figure 11.

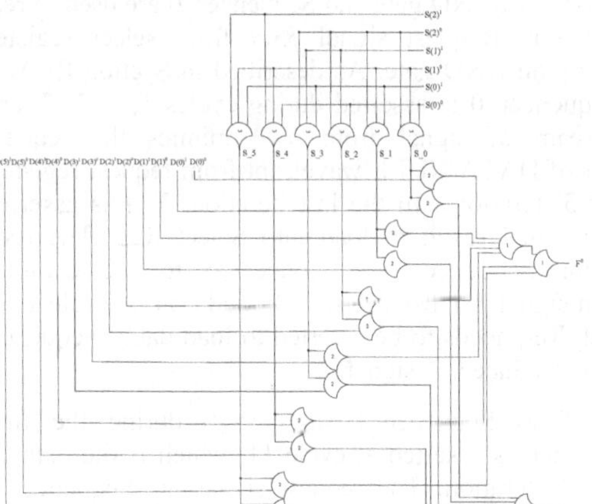

Figure 11. NCL 6 to 1 MUX

d) NCL Twiddle Factor Storage

Because the NCL circuit does not have an existing ROM, the twiddle factor values are stored using a multiplexer. The stored twiddle factor is in binary format. So, the MUX_ROM is very similar to the NCL 6 to 1 MUX, except that the twiddle factor value is directly used as D^1 and its inverse is used as D^0, as shown in Figure 12.

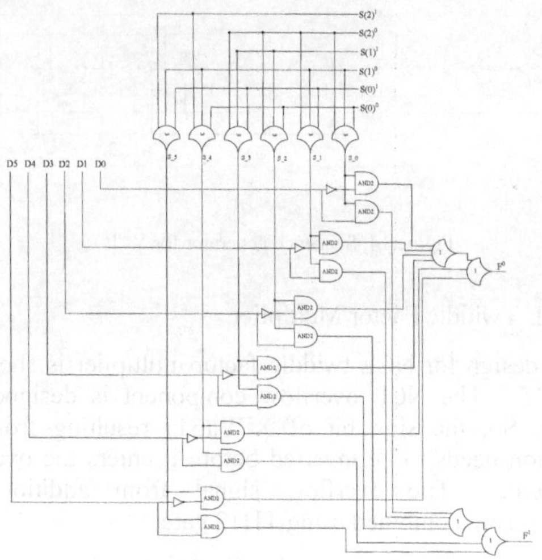

Figure 12. NCL multiplexer used as ROM

e) Sequence Generator

A sequence generator produces a specific stream of standard logic output using TH33 gates [9]. The sequence generator consists of a single-rail ring structure [15, 16].

For the NCL FFT, two sequence generators are needed that produce the following stream of bits, in order to only output the final FFT value by masking the output register's K_o during the internal iterations:

Table I. Sequence stream of Y_0 and Y_1

	Initial	1	2	3	4	5	6	7	8	9	10	11	12
Reset	1	0	0	0	0	0	0	0	0	0	0	0	0
Ki	X	1	0	1	0	1	0	1	0	1	0	1	0
Y_0	1	1	0	1	0	1	0	1	0	1	0	1	1
Y_1	0	0	0	0	0	0	0	0	0	0	0	1	0

By observing the waveforms of internal nodes, Y_0 is obtained by combining *D0*, *D2*, *D4*, *D6*, *D8*, *D10*, and *R11*, as shown in Figure 13.

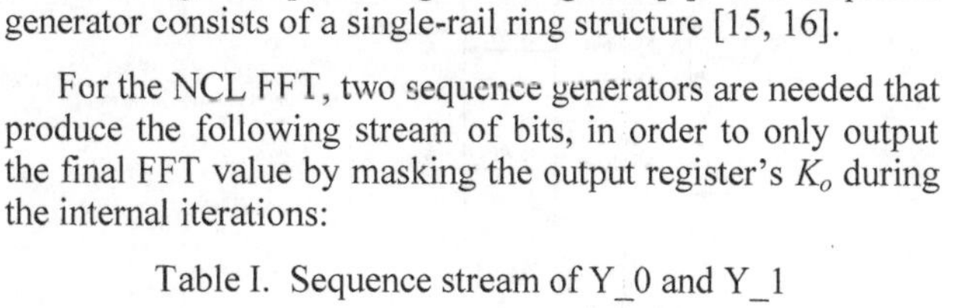

Figure 13. Sequence generator for Y_0

Y_1 is just *D0*, as shown in Figure 14.

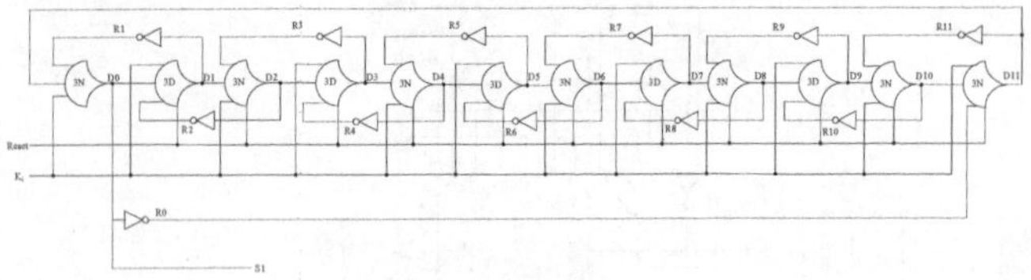

Figure 14. Sequence generator for Y_1

f) NCL Twiddle Factor Multiplier

The design for NCL twiddle factor multiplier is shown in Figure 15. The NCL overflow component is designed for addition. So, the sign bit of XiWi(31) resulting from the subtraction needs to be inverted before it enters the overflow component. The overflow signal from addition and subtraction are combined using TH12 gate.

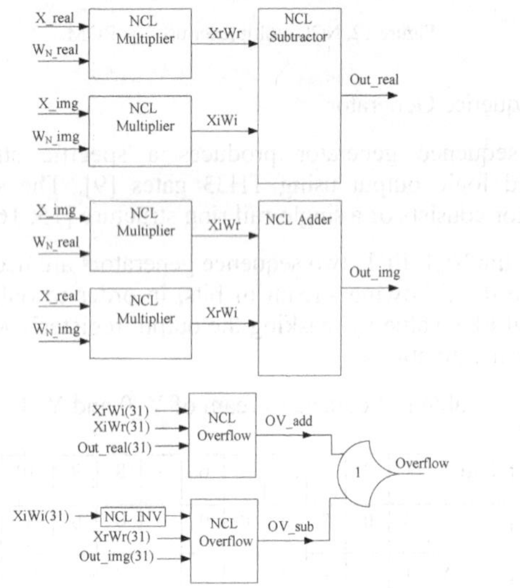

Figure 15. NCL Twiddle Factor Multiplier

g) NCL Butterfly Unit

The design for the NCL butterfly unit is shown in Figure 16. The NCL overflow signals are combined using a TH14 and TH12 gate to get the final overflow signal.

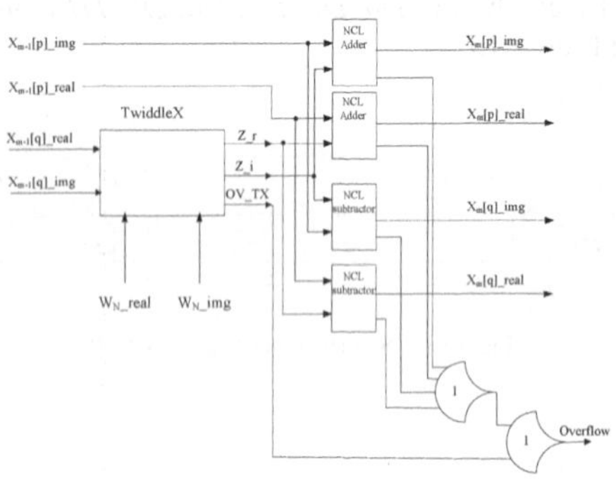

Figure 16. NCL Butterfly Unit

2) *NCL FFT Top-level Architecture*

The NCL FFT utilizes a similar architecture as the synchronous one. In total, 32 butterfly units are used; one for each two points. For simplicity, only one butterfly unit is shown in Figure 17. It takes 6 DATA/NULL cycles to compute all 64 points. In each DATA/NULL cycle, the intermediate data is fed back to the multiplexer. The select signal of the multiplexer is controlled by a counter. Once the computation finishes, the final results are re-ordered before being output.

In NCL FFT logic, the X_{rqst}, X_{dat}, Y_{rqst}, and Y_{dat} signals are no longer needed since NCL circuits use K_i and K_o as request and acknowledge signals. The internal register of the synchronous FFT is replaced with 3-register NCL feedback to prevent deadlock. The NCL FFT architecture is shown in Figure 17.

Upon reset, all NCL registers are initialized to NULL. When Data_in is ready, counter_0 outputs 0 to select bit-reversed new data to load into Reg_0. In the following 5 iterations, the intermediate results are fed back to Reg_0 through the multiplexer. In the 6th iteration, the final results are computed and loaded into Select_Reg, and new data is loaded into Reg_0 at the same time. The Final_reorder unit rearranges the sequence of results and outputs the final result. New data is loaded into NCL FFT every 6 iterations. Select_Reg is connected to the external *Ki* signal and is reset to NULL at the beginning of each new FFT computation. During these iterations, *Ko_S* from Select_Reg is always requesting DATA. In order to let the internal data feedback through, the request signal from Select_Reg needs to be masked for the first 5 iterations. An AND gate and Sequencer_0 are used to realize this function. Request signal *Ksel* from select register is masked by an AND gate. As described in Section III.A, Y_0 from sequencer_0 is asserted during cycles 1, 3, 5, 7, and 9. This stream of signal from Y_0 mimics the requesting behavior of DATA/NULL wavefront from request register for the first 5 iterations. In the last iteration, Y_1 is asserted to allow the final result to load into Select_Reg. The request signal for Sequencer_0 is connected to the completion detection signal $K_i 1$ from Reg_2. In addition, the select signal in Select_Reg needs to be asserted to load data. Sequencer_1 is used to produce this signal.

Y_1 from Sequence_1 stays at 0 during the first 5 iterations and is asserted at cycle 11, which is the data cycle for the 6th iteration. The request signal for Sequencer_1 is connected to the mask signal. As seen in Figure 17, data needs to propagate through Reg_0 and Reg_1 to arrive at the butterfly unit for computation. Two registers are used to latch the count value so that the corresponding twiddle factor value is loaded from ROM to do the computation. NCL FFT loads new data when the count is rolled over to 0, so the K_o signal is generated when count is 0. This is done by connecting $count_0^0$, $count_1^0$ and $count_2^0$ to a TH33 gate.

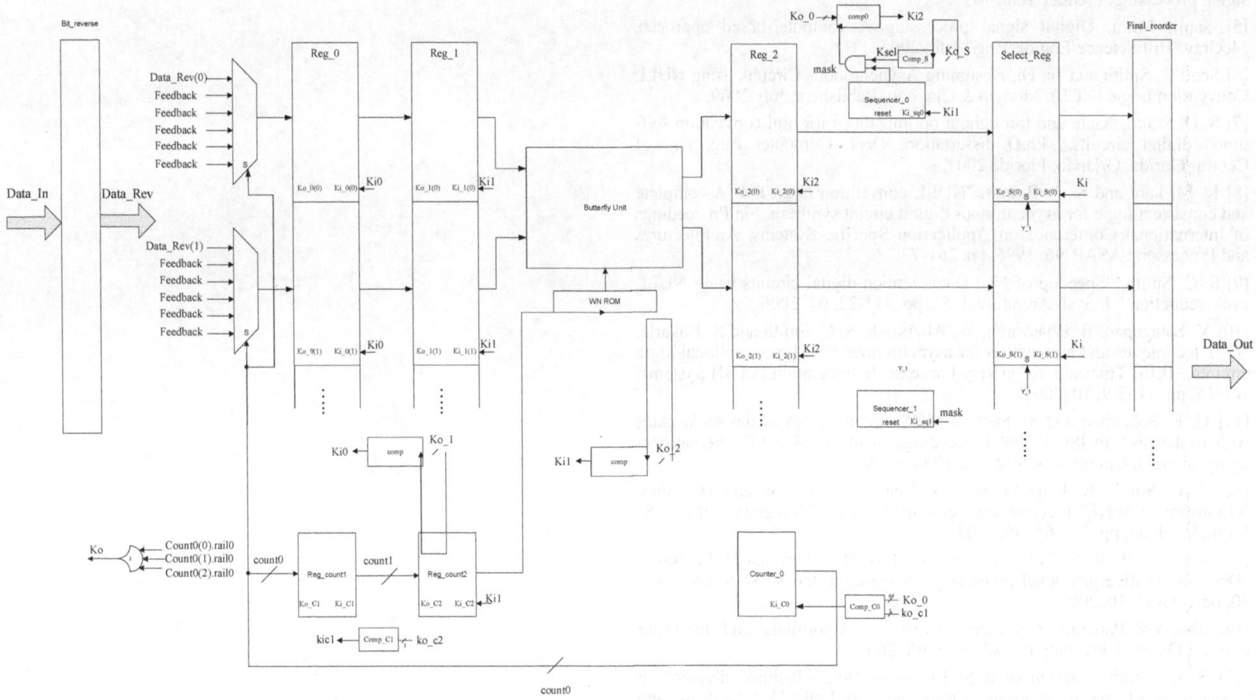

Figure 17. NCL FFT architecture

4. Simulation and Conclusion

1) Comparison of Results from NCL FFT and Matlab

The word length of Q15 format is 16 bits. Because of this finite bit-length, some least significant bits are truncated during FFT computation. This truncation error is accumulated in the feedback path. Compared with Matlab calculation results, in the worst case scenario, the last 3 bits from the NCL FFT computation are not accurate. There are 16 bits for each word, so the error rate for the NCL FFT is $2^3/2^{16} = 0.012$ %.

2) Performance of Synchronous FFT and NCL FFT

The synchronous FFT and NCL FFT are synthesized to the the IBM cmr8f 130nm process library. These synthesis results are listed in Table II, showing that the NCL FFT uses about four times as many transistors compared to the synchronous FFT.

Table II. Number of transistors used in synchronous and NCL FFT

	Number of Transistors
NCL FFT	4983104
Synchronous FFT	1335802

Power consumption and computation speed are simulated in Cadence, and shown in Table III. The average computation time for one complete NCL FFT operation is 452 ns, which means it takes 452 ns to compute the final result after getting new data. When running at this speed, the average current, *Iavg*, flowing through the NCL FFT is 0.0267 A. Running the synchronous FFT at the same speed as the NCL version requires a clock frequency of 452/6 = 75.3 ns. The average current of the synchronous FFT is 0.0354 A at this speed. Therefore, the power consumption for the synchronous FFT is 33% higher than the NCL version running at the same speed. The highest clock speed to operate the synchronous FFT without any timing violation is 9.75 ns, resulting in a calculation time of 9.75*6 = 58.5 ns to obtain the final result. At this fastest speed, the synchronous FFT requires 70% higher energy consumption than the NCL FFT and 28% more than when running it slower. Hence, although the NCL FFT is bigger and slower, it consumes less power than the synchronous FFT, even when operating at the same speed.

Table III. Comparison of NCL and synchronous FFT processor

	Computation Time (ns)	I_{avg} (A)	Energy(10^{-9} J)
NCL FFT	452	0.0267	14.49
Synchronous FFT	452 = (75.3 * 6)	0.0354	19.20
Synchronous FFT	58.5 = (9.75 *6)	0.3500	24.57

References

[1] Nasser Kehtarnavaz, Real-Time Digital Signal Processing: Based on the TMS320C6000, Newnes, 2004.

[2] Wayne T. Padgett, David V. Anderson and Jose Moura, Fixed-Point Signal Processing, Morgan and Claypool Publishers, 2009.

[3] R. Veenkant, "A serial minded FFT," Audio and Electroacoustics, IEEE Transactions on, vol. 20, pp. 180-185, 1972.

[4] Alan V. Oppenheim, Ronald W. Schafer and John R. Buck, Discrete-time signal processing, Prentice Hall, 1999.

[5] Sanjit Mitra, Digital signal processing A computer-based approach, McGraw-Hill Science/Engineering/Math, 2005.

[6] Scott C. Smith and Jia Di, Designing Asynchronous Circuits using NULL Convention Logic (NCL), Morgan & Claypool Publishers, July 2009.

[7] S. C. Smith, "Gate and throughput optimizations for null convention self-timed digital circuits," Ph.D dissertation, Dept. Computer Eng, Uinv.of Central Florida, Orlando, Florida 2001.

[8] K. M. Fant and S. A. Brandt, "NULL convention LogicTM: A complete and consistent logic for asynchronous digital circuit synthesis," in Proceedings of International Conference on Application Specific Systems, Architectures and Processors: ASAP '96, 1996, pp. 261-73.

[9] S. C. Smith, "Speedup of NULL convention digital circuits using NULL cycle reduction," J. Syst. Archit., vol. 52, pp. 411-22, 07, 2006.

[10] V. Satagopan, B. Bhaskaran, W. Al-Assadi, S. C. Smith and S. Kakarla, "DFT techniques and automation for asynchronous NULL conventional logic circuits," IEEE Transactions on very Large Scale Integration (VLSI) Systems, vol. 15, pp. 1155-9, 10, 2007.

[11] G. E. Sobelman and K. Fant, "CMOS circuit design of threshold gates with hysteresis," in ISCAS '98 Proceedings of the 1998 IEEE International Symposium on Circuits and Systems, 1998, pp. 61-4.

[12] S. C. Smith, R. F. DeMara, J. S. Yuan, D. Ferguson and D. Lamb, "Optimization of NULL convention self-timed circuits," Integration, the VLSI Journal, vol. 37, pp. 135-65, 08, 2004.

[13] S. C. Smith, R. F. DeMara, J. S. Yuan, M. Hagedorn and D. Ferguson, "Delay-insensitive gate-level pipelining," Integration, the VLSI Journal, vol. 30, pp. 103-31, 10, 2001.

[14] Behrooz Parhami, Computer arithmetic: Algorithms and hardware designs, Oxford University Press,New York, 2000.

[15] S. C. Smith, "Design of a NULL convention self-timed divider," in Proceedings of the International Conference on Embedded Systems and Applications ESA'04 - Proceedings of the International Conference on VLSI, VLSI'04, June 21, 2004 - June 24, 2004, pp. 447-453.

[16] W. Kuang, J. S. Yuan, R. F. DeMara, M. Hagedorn and K. Fant, "Performance analysis and optimisation of NCL self-timed rings," IEE Proceedings: Circuits, Devices and Systems, vol. 150, pp. 167-172, 2003.

Network-Based System for Face Recognition on Mobile Wireless Devices

Keita Imaizumi and Vasily G. Moshnyaga
Graduate School of Engineering, Faculty of Engineering
Fukuoka University
Fukuoka, 814-0180 Japan

Abstract - **This paper describes new internet-based face recognition system to be used in portable devices. In contrast to existing systems, which run computationally intensive face-recognition tasks at a mobile terminal shortening its battery lifetime, the proposed system uses mobile device only for image capturing and user-interface. All complex image processing tasks are performed by a remote high-powered network server to achieve robust and real time face recognition. The system is implemented in software and tested on Android-based Sony Tablet-S wireless terminal. According to measurements, it provides face recognition in images of 240x320 pixels in size at 10f/sec rate with very high accuracy. The paper discusses the proposed client-server architecture and the results of its experimental evaluation.**

Keywords- face recognition, face identification, network-based

I. Introduction

With emerging popularity of camera-equipped wireless multimedia devices, such as Apple's iPhone, iPad and iPod, Google's Android, and RIM's Blackberry, new applications employing face recognition can further enhance usage, intelligence and context-awareness of the devices. In this paper, we focus on real-time identification of a person from a digital image or video captured by the mobile device [1]. Providing a stand-alone mobile application can potentially benefit a user in remembering people, retrieving names of people, whom he/she has met before, and/or finding helpful information about person of interest. It could be also useful for elderly people to recall faces and names enhancing their memory and social interaction. The application can also assist law enforcement when an unknown person is being compared with images in a database in real time.

Automatic face recognition has been an active research area over the last two decades. Surveys on the methods and systems proposed can be found in [2], [3]. Although there are many systems capable of performing robust face recognition at desktops, incorporating them into mobile devices is not a trivial task. Additionally to common problems, such as face illumination, occlusion, rotation and movement of the person relatively to the camera, mobile face recognition is challenged by limited energy budget of batteries, limited computing power, limited storage, limited image resolution and size, limited network bandwidth, etc. Although it is easy for a human to detect and recognize faces, performing it on hardware requires complex algorithms and many energy dissipating computations. The high computational complexity of the task makes it unsuitable for energy and resource constrained mobile devices. While work has been done on algorithms which reduce the amount of computation for face detection and identification (e.g. a unified LDA/PCA algorithm [4], Haar-like Adabooth classifiers [5], geometric features [6], Local-Binary Pattern [7] and random incremental classifier [8], platform-driven mapping [9], etc.), there is an inherent tradeoff between computation and recognition accuracy. Unfortunately, those algorithms which recognize faces accurately are extremely computationally complex, whereas computationally simple algorithms often produce incorrect results.

Several systems for mobile face recognition have been already reported in literature. Some of them (e.g. [6, 7, 8, 11, 12, 1]) utilize fast algorithms to run the face recognition process entirely on a mobile device at the cost of accuracy and operation time. The others, such as [13-15] overcome the performance limitations of mobile platforms through effective utilization of the network resources. Rather than implementing the whole face recognition process on the energy constrained mobile device, these systems transfer the majority of computation from the device to a high-powered server on the network. For example, the Bluetooth-based system [13] implements on mobile device image preprocessing and face detection while the face recognition is done on dedicated computer (server). Similarly, [14] and [15] use the DROID phone to detect a face in an image, preprocess the face calculating the Fisherfaces weights, based on which the server performs face recognition. However, even these distributed architectures still enforce mobile devices to carry out many computations, affecting both the battery budget and the processing speed. This is due to the lack of mobile processors (e.g. ARM) for executing floating point operations and also to the fact that face detection performs exhaustive image scans at different locations and scales, yielding in hundreds of thousands of sub-windows to process, which is time consuming. By tuning out the system parameters, one can further speed-up the detector but at the cost of quality degradation.

In this work, we also employ a network-based approach to reduce computation on mobile device. Unlike related systems, we use mobile device only as input and output interface; all functions of face detection and face recognition are done by the network server. The key contribution of our work is new client-server architecture, which effectively utilizes the network as a powerful computational resource to achieve face recognition at a frame rate.

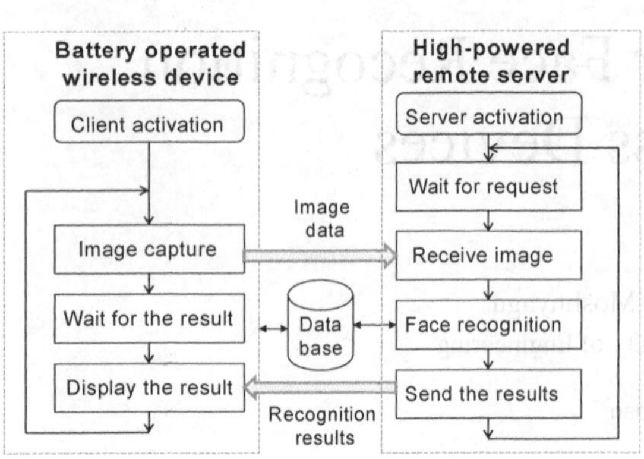

Figure 1: The face recognition flow in the proposed system

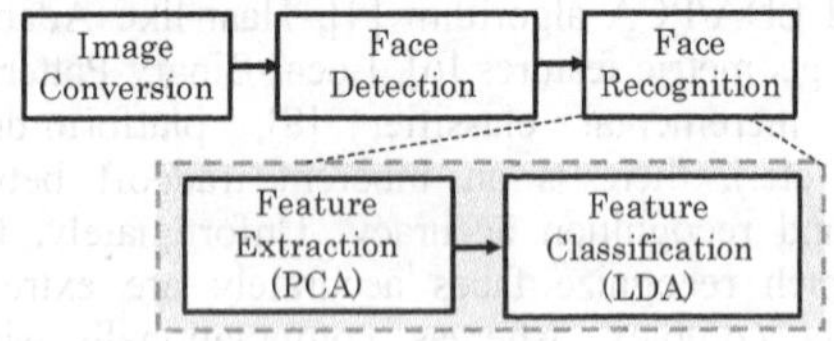

Figure 2: The face recognition tasks implemented by the server

The paper is organized as follows. Section 2 describes the proposed network-based face recognition system. Section 3 reports evaluation results. Section 4 summarizes our findings and outlines work for the future.

II. The Network-Based Face Recognition System

A. An overview

The proposed network-based face recognition system utilizes a high-powered remote server and a battery operated mobile wireless device (client), equipped with a video camera. The server has access to a face database which contains face images with corresponding information of the person. We assume that the database is shared between the client and the server through a cloud so the user has an option to upload new face images and add/delete data from database using either his/her mobile device (client) or the server (computer). Also we assume that the server is activated before the user initiates face recognition application from the wireless device. The client – server connection is set before entering the data transfer phase and released after data transmission is complete. The connection is established based on TCP/IP protocol and managed by OS through a programming interface.

The system splits the face recognition tasks between the client and the server, as shown in Fig.1. The server performs complex and accurate face recognition, while the client implements only I/O operations related to image acquisition and display of the results. The face recognition starts as the user activates the application from his/her mobile device. In this case, the client captures an image and sends it to the server with a request for processing. Upon receiving the request, the server converts image from YUV to RGB format and runs face detection and face recognition (see Fig.2) to identify the person

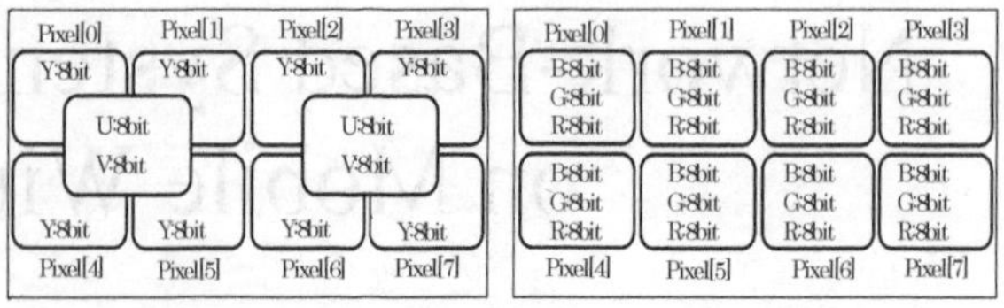

Figure 3: The image format used by the client (left) and the server (right)

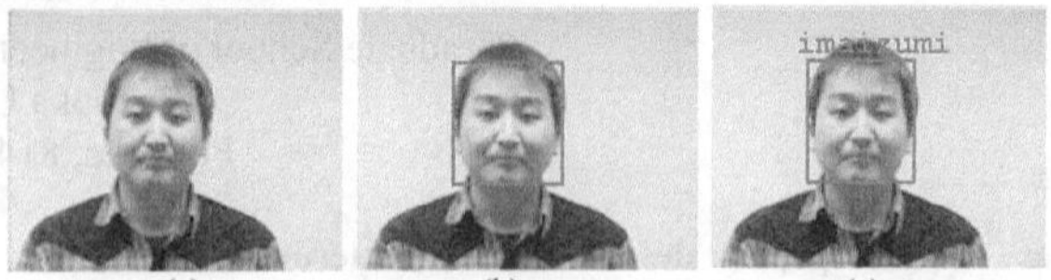

(a) (b) (c)

Figure 4: An illustration of an input image (a), the face detection result (b) and the result of face recognition (c)

of interest based on information stored in database. The results in terms of face rectangle and data identifying the person of interest are then sent back to the client, to be shown over the image displayed on the screen. In the next subsections we discuss the face recognition steps in details.

B. Image conversion

The color image captured by video camera on mobile device is represented in YUV 420 SP format, allowing reduced bandwidth for chrominance components. During transmission, the luma (Y) and the chroma (U and V) components are compressed with the sample ratio of 4:1:1 (see Fig.3); so the picture has only a quarter as much resolution in color as it does in brightness. Because the server uses RGB888 image format (Fig.3, right) for face recognition, each image is converted at the server from YUV to RGB format as follows:

$$B[i]=\{1192\times(Y-16)+2066\times(U-128) \quad (1)$$
$$G[i]=\{1192\times(Y-16)+833\times(V-128)-400\times(U-128) \quad (2)$$
$$R[i]=\{1192\times(Y-16)+1633\times(V-128) \quad (3)$$

$$B = (B[i]>> 10)\ \&\ 0xFF \quad (4)$$
$$G =\{(G[i] >> 2)\ \&\ 0xFF00\} >>8 \quad (5)$$
$$R =\{(R[i] << 6)\ \&\ 0xFF0000\} >>16 \quad (6)$$

C. Face detection

The goal of this task is to find an area corresponding to human face in the given RGB image if any. It is implemented based on Viola-Jones algorithm [5], which transforms the RGB image into the integral image representation, and then scans it with detection window to compute Haar-like face features. The features are then applied to a cascade of 25 AdaBoost classifiers to find a true face from possible candidates. The algorithm is implemented in Intel's OpenCV as cvHaarDetectObjects() using the Android's Face Detector class [16]. This class provides information regarding all the faces found in an input bitmap image. The confidence factor (a number between 0 & 1) by which the face is identified, the distance between the eyes, position of midpoint between the eyes and the face's pose (rotation around X, Y, Z axis) are the

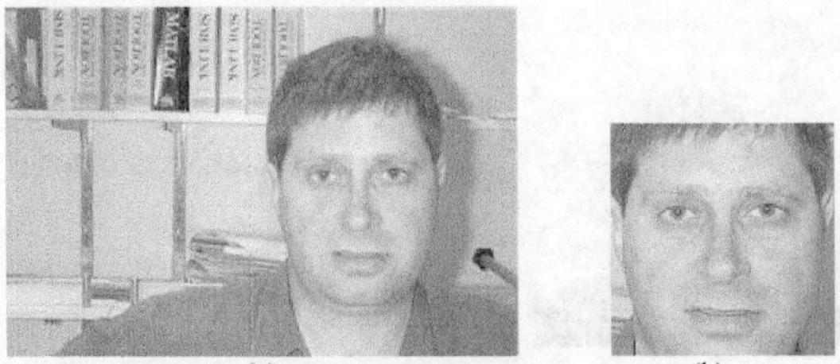

(a) (b)
Figure 5: An illustration of face sample generation

extra details the class associates with each face. A face is considered detected if the confidence ratio is above 0.3. The result of face detection is presented by a face bounding box depicted over the input image as shown in Fig. 4(b). The derived face image is preprocessed to gray scale and histogram equalization to decrease the effects of illumination, subsampled to the database sample size and applied for face recognition. If no face is detected, the server terminates the recognition process, sending a corresponding acknowledge signal to the client.

D. Face recognition

Given a set of sample images labeled with the person identity (the set is stored in database) and the unlabeled face image (x_i), (derived by face detection), the face recognition problem is to identify the name of the person in the test image. We solve the problem based on the Eigenface method [17,18] with Principle Component Analysis (PCA) for feature extraction and the Fisher's Linear Discriminant Analysis (LDA)[19] for feature reduction. Having a set of N face images, $a_1, a_2, \dots, a_N$, with each image belonging to one of C classes, $A_1, A_2, \dots, A_C$, the method calculates a mean face of each class $\Phi_j=(1/n)\times\sum_j^n a_j$, the total mean, $\Phi=(1/C)\times\sum_i^N \Phi_i$, and vectors, $D_i=a_i - \Phi_i$, which represent difference between the mean and the training face images. This covariance matrix $M=\{D_1,D_2,\dots,D_C\}$ of the face images is then subjected to LDA to find a set $V_o=\{v_1,v_2,\dots,v_k\}$ of k orthogonal vectors (i.e. eigenvectors), corresponding to the k largest eigenvalues. The LDA takes advantage of the fact that the classes are linearly separable, selecting the projection in such a way that the ratio of the between the class scatter and the within class scatter is maximized. The within-class scatter, S_W, is defined as the mean of the co-variances of samples within all classes, i.e. $S_W=1/C\,(\sum_j^C M_j\times M_j^T)$. The between-class scatter is defined as the co-variance of data sets consisting of mean vectors of each class: $S_B=\sum_j^C(\Phi_j-\Phi)(\Phi_j-\Phi)^T$. With LDA the problem is reduced to finding such a projection V_o that maximizes the total scatter $S_T = S_W+S_B$ of the data while minimizing the within scatter of the classes:

$$V_o = \arg\max_V (V\times S_T\times V^T)/(V\times S_W\times V^T)=[v_1\, v_2 \dots v_k]. \quad (7)$$

The problem is solved through transformations such as rotating and scaling the axes of tested image in different ways. Depending on the size of the data, the projection can be done onto to a lower or higher dimension. The computed eigenvector matrix V_o is then used for estimating the weights of projecting the target face x_i onto these eigenvectors. The weights are calculated as $w = V_o^T(x_i-\Phi)$. A class A_j with the minimum Euclidean distance of weights is selected. The data related to the class is sent to the client as a result. Fig.5 shows an example. If no match has been found for the given face, the system marks it as an "unknown".

E. Implementation

The proposed system has been implemented based on the Sony Tablet-S (1GHz ARM Cortex™-A9 dual core CPU, 1GB RAM, 16GB internal storage, 9.4-inch display, Android™ 4.03 OS) as a client and DELL PC (Intel® Core™ i5 2.80GHz CPU, 4GB memory, MS Windows 7 OS) as a server. The application software was created by using the Microsoft Visual Studio 2010 (Eclipse 3.6) and the Android software development kit. The client-server communication was implemented through Internet Socket API (ws2_32.lib) and TCP/IP transport protocol [20]. To support the OS-based control of the communication, a dedicated programming interface was also created. The face detection and face recognition software were programmed in C/C++ by using Intel's Open CV 2.4.2 library[21].

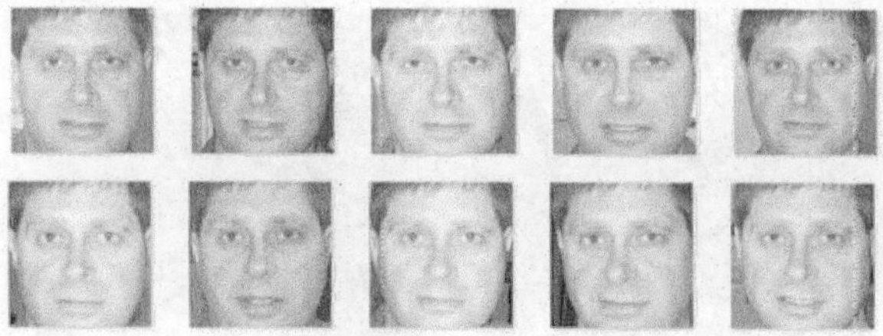

Figure 6: Example face images from the database "Faces1999"

III. Experimental Evaluation

A number of experiments were conducted to assess performance of the proposed system. The first group of experiments aimed at evaluating efficiency of face detection and face recognition software implemented on the server computer. The second group of experiment targeted performance evaluation of the entire system. Below we discuss the experiments in detail.

A. Evaluation of the face recognition software

To evaluate the ability of the developed face recognition software to detect and identify human faces correctly, we applied it to the "Faces 1999" database of 357 static frontal face images developed at Caltech [22] in total. For the sake of experiment, all the images have been manually transformed to grey-scale representation, resized and trimmed to face area only as shown in Fig.5. In such a way we prepared an experimental database of 17 different persons (9 men and 8 women), with each person represented by 10 images (170 images in total). Fig.6 exemplifies face images of the same person. All face images were 120x120 pixels in size and labeled by a unique digital tag for identification.

In the experiment, we used all 357 original pictures from Faces 1999 as an input to the developed face recognition software.

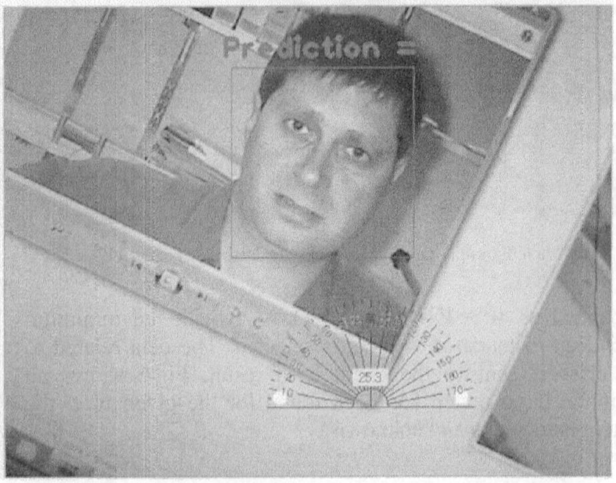

Figure 7: Example face images from the Face1999 database

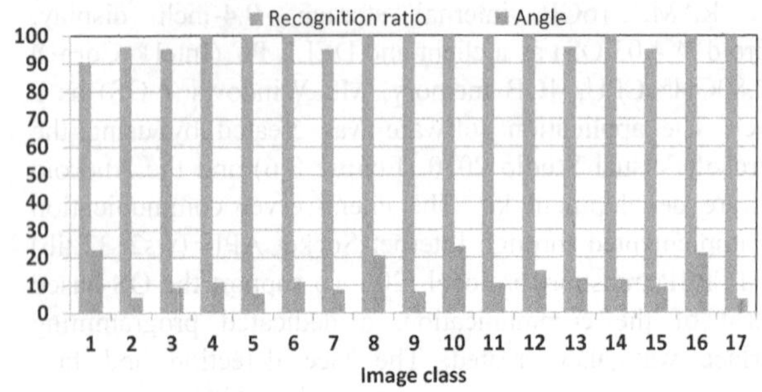

Figure 8: Recognition ratio and max.inclination angle per image

Namely, each image was captured by Logicool C600 video camera (640x480 frame size) from a display and used as an input image of a person to be identified. For each image we evaluated whether the face detection and face recognition produced correct or false results. To consider effects of face inclination, we repeated the test for each image by rotating the camera with 5° increment and determining the maximal inclination angle at which the results were correct. Fig.7 illustrates an image inclined by 25°.

Fig.8 shows the results in terms of the recognition ratio and the maximal angle at which the recognition was correct. As one can see, the recognition ratio is high, reaching 98% in average. Though face inclination affects the results, the software can correctly recognize faces inclined by as much as 24° and 12.5° on average.

The results revealed that glasses, mustaches, beard, hairstyle, gender, age, race, etc. had no bad effect on the face recognition if the corresponding features are reflected by samples stored in database. Nevertheless, there are several factors which can impede the face recognition performance. One is face brightness. Dark images might either lead to inability to detect a face (see Fig.9, top) or cause incorrect face identification (see Fig.9 bottom). Another factor which affects the results is the number of sample images in database. For example, if database

Figure 9: False results. Top pictures: the face was not detected; Bottom pictures: the face was detected but identified incorrectly

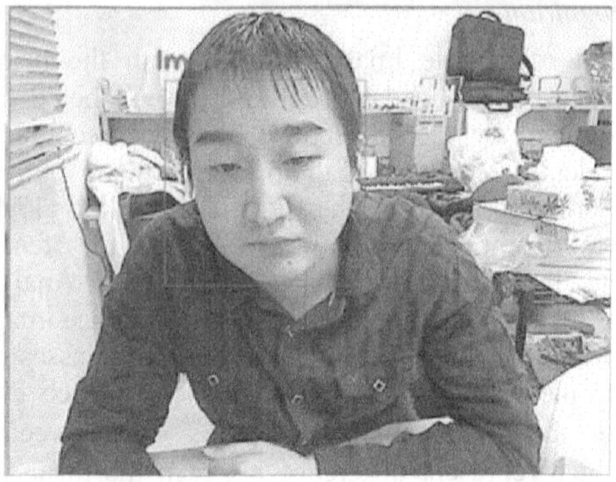

Figure 10: An example of real person recognition.

provides only a single image per person, the face recognition ratio becomes 76.5%. The recognition rate is also affected when the number of samples in each class of database is uneven. If for example, one person is represented by 10 images while the others by 2 or 3, the recognition rate does not exceed 83.3%. To increase the recognition efficiency, the number of samples in a class (i.e. for a person) has to be not only large but also the same as in the other classes.

To evaluate the software efficiency in identifying faces of real people in typical environment, we added 60 sample face image of 6 students (10 images per person, 120x120 pixels image) to the database and conducted a set of tests, in which each student appeared before the video camera at a distance ranged from 20cm to up to 2.5m. The room illumination was relatively good and the background was typical for computer lab, as shown in Fig.10. In the experiment, the students were asked to conduct five behavioral patterns: face the camera frontally with open and close eyes, turn the face up and down, turn the face to the right and to the left. Each pattern was 5 sec long and repeated twice by each user. The results (Fig.11) showed that the system was able to distinguish and track faces correctly at up to 2 m

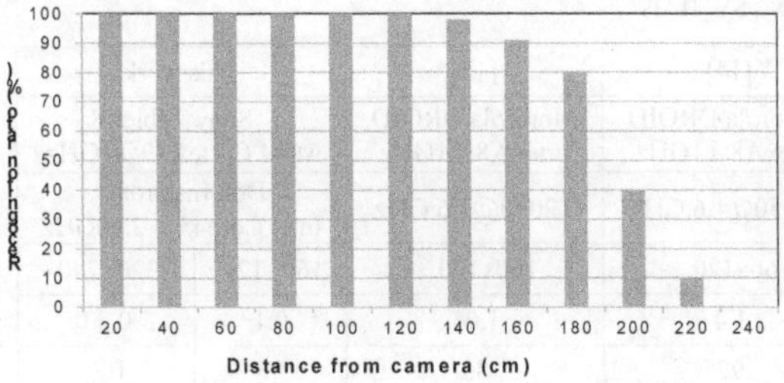

Figure 11: An example of real person recognition.

distance, recognizing them with 91% rate at up to 1.6 meter distance unless the face rotation left/right and inclination in vertical or horizontal directions is over 15°. With larger rotation, inclination and distance to the camera, the misdetection rate increases. Although our experience shows that extending the database to rotated and inclined faces improves the system performance significantly, recognizing faces at farer distances requires a more powerful camera to be incorporated into the mobile device.

TABLE I. SYSTEM PERFORMANCE (AT 1M DISTANCE)

Frame size (pixels)	160×120	320×240	848×480
Aspect ratio	1.3	1.3	1.8
Processing speed (fps)	10	3	0.43
Recognition accuracy (%)	96	100	71

B. Evaluation of the network-based system performance

The system performance was tested by running the developed face recognition system wirelessly from the Sony Tablet-S device using the 802.11n WiFi protocol and communication resources of gigabit local area network. As Tablet-S device provides three different picture formats for video capturing, we evaluated the system performance using each of them while applying the system to identification of same 6 persons. Fig. 12 shows an image observed at the screen of Sony Tablet-S device.

Table I summarizes the results in terms of the processing speed and the recognition rate versus the size and the aspect ratio of images, captured by the mobile device at the 1m distance. We observe that the system processing speed decreases as the image frame size increases. At the frame size of 160x120 pixels, it achieves speed of 10 frames per second (fps) with the recognition accuracy of 96%. As the image aspect ratio equals 1.3, i.e. the ratio of images used for sample generation, the face recognition quality is high. At the image size of 320x240 pixels, the recognition accuracy even increases reaching the maximum level due to better image quality. However, the speed of processing (320x240) images is 3 fps. The cause of this speed drop can be explained by the longer time required for transmitting and processing large images. As the frame size becomes very large (848x480 pixels) these delays become increasingly high, decreasing the speed to 0.46 frames per second.

Table II puts our system in perspective to the mobile face-recognition systems reported in the literature and online. Here

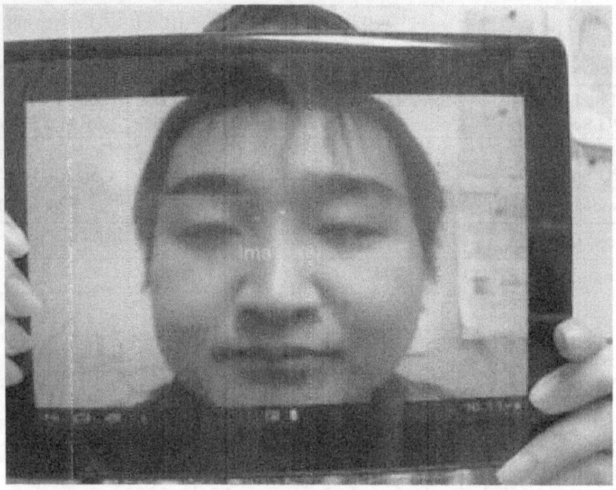

Figure 12: An illustration of face recognition result

the processing time refers to the time in seconds required to process one image frame. We observe that the proposed system outperforms the existing solutions by both the processing speed and the recognition ratio. In comparison to the related solutions, which operate on small (160x120) images at the 1 fps rate at most, our system runs 10 times faster. Moreover, it supports face recognition in larger images which is more preferable for the users. Although it looks that more powerful resources, which our system exploits in comparison to the others, is the main cause of its speed-up. However, it turns out that as long as the training is done beforehand, the bottleneck of typical face recognition system is actually the face detection, not the recognition, since the recognition images are fairly small. Detecting a face on a mobile device and transmitting it to the server is much longer than sending and processing the image at the server. Unlike the others, our system does not run the face recognition on mobile device and therefore is fast. It turns out that new client-server architecture that relieves the mobile device from any complex processing is the key the speed-up achieved by the proposed system.

IV. CONCLUSION

In this paper we presented novel client-server architecture for the network-based face recognition. Experiments showed that our system outperforms the related systems in both the processing quality and speed, allowing real-time (10fps) robust (96% accuracy) face recognition for people located up to 1.6m distance from the mobile device. In the current work we restricted ourselves to a simple case of a singular person and frontal face recognition. We are currently working on mobile recognition of multiple faces, extending the work to inclined and rotated faces, recognition of faces with partial occlusion, as well as issues related to power-aware optimizations of face recognition algorithms. Also a representative database is important to the success of the face recognition system. Therefore, in order to further improve the system, a larger mobile face database is necessary. Problems related to database development, automatic generation of sample images, etc. will be also investigated in the future.

TABLE II : COMPARISON TO EXISTING SYSTEMS

System	[11]	[12]	[13]	[14]	[15]	This work	
Mobile Device (CPU Spec.)	Motorola DROID CortexA8@1GHz	Motorola O2 XDA, Intel IR@ 520MHz	Sony-Erics.w550i ARM@300MHz	Motorola DROID CortexA8@1GHz	Motorola DROID CortexA8@1GHz	Sony Tablet-S ARM CortexA9@1GHz.	
Server PC (CPU Spec.)	Not used	Intel Core 2 Duo CPU @ 2.66 GHz	Dell Inspiron1520 Core2duo@2.1GHz	T2050@1.6 GHz	T2050@1.6 GHz	Dell Inspiron Intel Core i5@ 2.80GHz	
Frame size (pixels)	80x60	144x176	176 x 220	160x120	160x120	160×120	320×240
Processing time (s)	1.58	1.03	39	1.4	1.05	0.1	0.33
Recognition rate (%)	94	97	n/a	92	80	96	100

n/a: data is not available

REFERENCES

[1] J.Xiang, X.Chien, W.Kunz, H.Kundra, "Face as an index: knowing who is who using a PDA", ,Int. Journal of Imaging Systems and Technology, vol.13, no.1, pp.33-41, 2003

[2] R.Chepalla, C.Wilson, and S.Sirohey, "Human and machine recognition of faces: a survey", Proc. IEEE, vol.83, no.5, pp.705-740, 1995.

[3] X.Tan, S.Chen, Z.-H.Zhou, F.Zhang, "Face recognition from a single image per person: A survey," Pattern Recognition, Vol.39, pp.1725-1745, 2006

[4] J.Yang, H.Yu, and W.Katz, "An efficient LDA algorithm for face recognition", Int. Conf. on Automation, Robotics and Computer Vision, Dec.2000

[5] M. Jones, P. Viola, "Face recognition using boosted local features, Proceedings of International Conference on Computer Vision", 2003 .

[6] C.K. Ng, M. Savvides, P.K. Khosla, "Real-time face verification system on a cell-phone using advanced correlation filters, 4th IEEE Workshop on Automatic Identification Advanced Technologies, 2005, pp. 57–62.

[7] C.Schneider, N.Esau, L.Kleinjohann, B.Kleinjohann, "Feature based face localization and recognition on mobile devices", Int. Conf. Control, Automation, Robotics andVision, 2006, pp.1–6.

[8] Hadid, A.; Heikkila, J.Y.; Silven, O.; Pietikainen, M.; , "Face and Eye Detection for Person Authentication in Mobile Phones," ACM/IEEE Int. Conf. on Distributed Smart Cameras, pp.101-108, 2007

[9] Y-C.Wang, K-T.Cheng, "Energy-optimized mapping of application to smartphone platform – a case study of mobile face recognition", IEEE Workshop on Embedded Computer Vision, 2011

[10] Q.Tao,R.Veldhuis, "Biometric authentication system on mobile personal devices", IEEE Trans. Instrumentation and Measurement, vol.59, no.4, pp. 763–773, 2010.

[11] G.Dave, X.Chao, K.Sriadibhatla, "Face Recognition in Mobile Phones",Stanford Univ.

[12] J.Ren, X.Jiang, and J.Yuan. "A complete and fully automated face verification system on mobile devices." Pattern Recognition, vol.46 pp.45-56, 2013

[13] S.Kumar, P.Singh, V.Kumar, "Architecture for Mobile based Face Detection/ Recognition", IJCSE Int. J. on Computer Sc. and Engineering, Vol. 2, No. 3, 889-894, 2010

[14] A.Pabbaraju, S.Puchakayala, "Face Recognition in Mobile Devices" Electrical Engineering and Computer Science, University of Michigan, 2010.

[15] H.Yu, Face Recognition for Mobile Phone Using Eigenfaces, University of Michigan, 2010.

[16] Android Developers, FaceDetector, available online from: http://developer.android.com/reference/android/media/FaceDetector.html

[17] M. Turk and A. Pentland, "Eigenfaces for recognition", Journal of Cognitive Neuroscience 3, 72-86

[18] R.Fisher, "The use of multiple measures in taxonomic problems, Ann.Eugenics, no.7, pp.179-188, 1936

[19] K. Etemad, R. Chellappa, Discriminant Analysis for Recognition of Human Face Images, Journal of the Optical Society of America A, vol. 14, No. 8, Aug. 1997, pp. 1724-1733

[20] Internetworking with TCP/IP:Principles, Protocols, and Architecture. 1 (5th ed.). Prentice Hall

[21] Open CV (Open Source Computer Vision), available online from http://opencv.org/

[22] Faces 1999 (Front), California Institute of Technology, http://www.vision.caltech.edu/archive.html.

A Fault Injection Environment for the Evaluation of a Soft Error Detection Technique based on Time Redundancy

Luis Bustamante and Hussain Al-Asaad
Department of Electrical and Computer Engineering
University of California, Davis, CA, USA

Abstract – *This paper presents a Verilog test simulation environment designed to inject random transient faults on a 32-bit microprocessor. The purpose of the test environment is to study a hardware-assisted soft error detection technique based on time redundancy. The soft error detection method compares the states of the microprocessor of two independent executions of the same program. The simulation environment takes advantage of the redundant execution and divides the process in two phases. The first phase operates during the first execution of the program to determine the number of cycles that are required to complete the task when no faults are present. The second phase is performed during the second execution of the program to inject a soft error in the microprocessor. The hardware assistance saves the microprocessor states as the program is executing the first time and detects the soft error as they occur during the second execution.*

Keywords: On-line testing, soft errors, fault injection, time redundant double execution, error detection, built-in self-test.

1 Introduction

Design of complex digital systems requires extensive testing before fabrication to validate correct operation and to detect design or implementation errors. A typical verification environment accomplishes this by applying stimulus test vectors to the inputs of the device under test (DUT) and then monitors its response through the output ports of the device. The functionality of the design is validated when the DUT meets the design specifications. However, if after applying correct stimulus vectors, the DUT does not respond according to the design specifications, it usually means that there is a logic or implementation error present in the device. These errors are permanent as they are intrinsic to the device and can be exposed and reproduced with the appropriate stimulus. These permanent errors will remain part of the digital system until the designer takes the appropriate steps to correct them. Once the logic is corrected, the same test vectors that detected the original errors can be used again to confirm that the problem has been fixed.

The problem with the verification environment just described becomes evident when errors are caused by transient faults. These transient faults are called soft errors and they can occur randomly in any part of the semiconductor device. Soft errors are originated by high-energy subatomic particles. When these particles strike semiconductor devices, they can create electron-hole pairs with enough energy to produce charge variations large enough to change the logic state of elements in the circuit [1]. This is why soft errors are not the result of design or implementation errors, but they are caused by external disturbances that the semiconductors are exposed during operation. Because of their short duration, soft errors effects disappear and hence cannot be duplicated with traditional verification techniques. That is why a verification environment, capable of modeling the effects of soft errors, also has to have the ability to introduce random transient faults into the DUT during simulations.

The test environment we are proposing was designed to test a soft error detection technique, which is based on time redundancy with some limited support of assisting hardware. The technique simulates the effect of a soft error during the redundant execution of a task. One of the advantages of our verification environment is that it does not require special modification of the DUT's RTL. The fault injection environment is a simple and robust method that uses Verilog features combined with the specific knowledge of the DUT to create an environment that models a random soft error into any state register of a microprocessor.

Other fault injection techniques have been proposed in the literature. Some are based on VHDL [2] or dependent on making hardware modifications by inserting blocks designed to add controllability to the fault insertion [3]. The approach we propose is simple and can be used to evaluate other soft error detection methods based on time redundancy.

Before describing the proposed fault injection technique, it is important to first understand the soft error detection mechanism. For this purpose, we first describe how the time redundancy is used on a basic RISC microprocessor to detect soft errors and then we describe our soft error injection process.

2 Soft Error Detection Method

The method to detect soft errors is based on a time-redundant execution technique that requires a limited amount of hardware support to assist with this process [4]. One of the functions of the supporting hardware is to store in memory the states of the microprocessor during the first execution of a program. The time redundancy process also requires a second execution of the same program to detect any transient fault. Figure 1 shows the states of the microprocessor as they are generated during each execution of the program. The states generated by the first and second execution are then compared in order to detect any difference between them. The reasoning is that the probability that a soft error may occur in the exact same register at the same relative clock cycle of the program execution is extremely unlikely. Therefore, any difference in states between the first and second executions can be attributed to a soft error.

The soft error detection technique was applied to a microprocessor, which was modified with some limited amount of hardware to assists in the storage and comparison of the first and second execution states. One of these modifications included extending the instruction set to assist with the control of the supporting hardware.

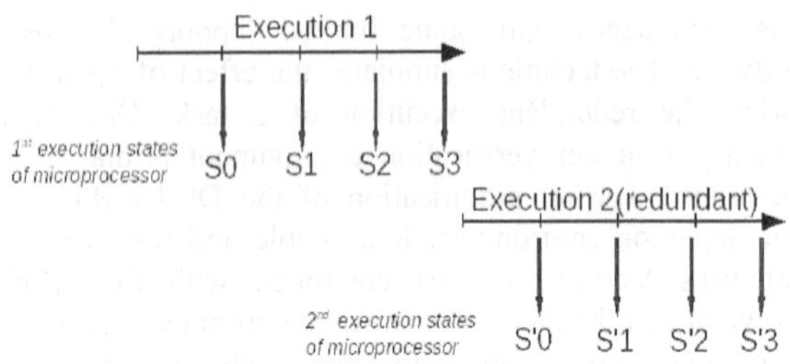

Fig. 1. State vectors S and S' generated during 1st and 2nd execution.

2.1 State Storage Module (SSM)

The state storage module interfaces with n registers of the DUT, and the current states of the registers constitute the state from the microprocessor. The DUT's state is represented by S_i where the index i represent the cycle interval at which the state is sampled. The total number of states represents the microprocessor execution states of the program and they are defined by the state vector S. Similarly, the state vector for the second execution can be represented as S'. The index k is the total number cycle intervals required to run the program.

$$S = \{S_0, S_1, \ldots, S_i, \ldots, S_{k-2}, S_{k-1}\} \quad (1)$$

The SSM accomplishes the soft error detection by storing in memory the states of the microprocessor S during the first execution of the program. After all the first execution states S have been store in memory, the SSM compares them with the second execution states S' as they are generated during simulation. If at any point of the second execution, a difference is detected by the SSM between the S and the S' execution states of the program, a soft error has been detected. The program execution is stopped and the software upper layer can be notified so that it can execute the appropriate recovery protocol procedure.

All the states generated during the first execution are stored in memory with the assistance of the SSM, as shown in Figure 2. When a particular task is targeted for soft error detection, the microprocessor signals the SSM to start storing the states of the microprocessor S_i by asserting *Execution1* and de-asserting *Execution2*. The SSM then stores the states information into memory at specific intervals until completion of the task. At this point the microprocessor is ready to start re-execution of the same task for the second time. The microprocessor accomplishes this by asserting *Execution2* and de-asserting *Execution1* to indicate to the SSM that the second execution of the task is starting. The SSM starts retrieving the first execution states S_i from memory and concurrently compares them with the

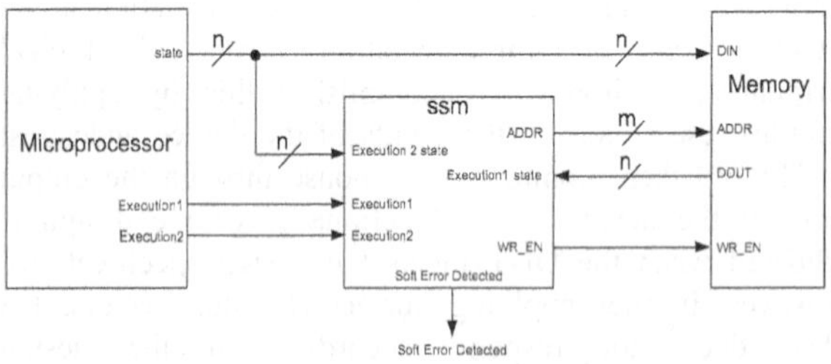

Fig. 2. SSM hardware support to store and compare first and second execution states.

states S_i' of the second execution that is in progress. If any difference is detected by the SSM logic between S_i and S'_i, then a *Soft Error Detected* signal is asserted to indicate that a soft error has been detected.

3 Device under Test (DUT)

For the purpose of testing our soft error injection environment, we designed and implemented the soft error detection assisting hardware in a basic 32-bit RISC microprocessor, also shown in Figure 2. The test environment injects a soft error randomly into any of the microprocessor state registers by inverting the *next_state* value of the register and effectively corrupting its state value when the register clock is asserted. For the purpose of controlling the SSM, the instruction set of the microprocessor was enhanced to include two additional instructions that are used to control when the execution states are saved and compared by the state storage module.

3.1 Microprocessor

The DUT is a basic 32-bit microprocessor with floating point unit. To limit the complexity of the simulation environment, the microprocessor has a reduced instruction set and the soft error detection study was limited to the control unit of the microprocessor (CU). The CU was chosen because of its critical interaction with every module in the microprocessor. This helped restrict the state space to less than 32 registers that needed to be monitored by the SSM. This is also the limit of registers that the current soft error injection environment could act on. Future research will enable a larger sample of registers from the microprocessor.

3.2 Extended Instruction Set

The microprocessor instruction set was extended to include two additional instructions that were created with the purpose of controlling the SSM. The first instruction added for this is

FES *RX*

The *FES* instruction (First Execution Start) instructs the SSM to start saving the states of the microprocessor because the first execution of the program is initiating. This instruction is executed before the first instruction of the program that is targeted for soft error detection. The *RX* operand corresponds to an address in the register file of the microprocessor that contains the return address for the program counter (PC) to start the second execution.

Similarly, the second instruction implemented to control the SSM is

SES *RX*

The *SES* (Second Execution Start) instructs the SSM to start the execution of the program by updating the PC address with the address pointing to the first line of the program. The return address was previously stored in the *RX* register by the *FES* instruction. This instruction should be run after the last line of the program that was targeted for soft error detection. Once the second execution starts, the SSM retrieves the states that were previously saved in memory and compares the states of the first and second execution.

4 Soft Error Injection

In this section, we describe our soft error injection environment and its detailed implementation.

4.1 Test Bench Specifications

To simplify the task of developing a suitable soft error injection environment to validate the soft error detection mechanism, we defined a set of minimum requirements in the specification to help us guide an efficient implementation of the test bench.

1) Soft errors can only be injected during any random cycle of the second execution of the task or program. This guarantees the environment will have knowledge of the number of cycles that the program normally requires to complete the first execution of the program.
2) Every fault injected to the hardware will always cause a flip in the state of a random register. This guarantees efficiency by minimizing the number of simulations.
3) Only one fault will be introduced during the redundant execution. This is reasonable, since multiple soft errors rarely occur in real situations.
4) The hierarchical paths of all registers are known and they can be accessed directly from the verification environment. This greatly reduces the size of the test bench and simplifies the soft error injection implementation.

4.2 Test Bench Description

The verification environment was specifically designed to meet the requirements of the soft error detection technique based on time redundancy and it consists of the following tasks and functions.

```
task count_cycles;
    output [15:0] final_count;
    integer count;

begin
    @(posedge clock);
    count <= 1;
    final_count <= 0;
    while (Execution1 == 1)
    begin
      @(posedge clock);
      count <= count + 1;
    end
        $display("count =", count);
        final_count = count;
    end
endtask
```

Fig. 3. Routine that counts the number of execution cycles.

4.2.1 Count Cycles Task

At the beginning of the first execution of the task, the Verilog task *count_cycles* is called within the test bench to count the cycles that the program requires. The task continues counting as long the signal *Execution1* is asserted. When *Execution1* is deasserted, the final cycle count is saved in the *final_count* integer variable (see Figure 3).

4.2.2 Random Integer Function

This is described by the function *rand_int* in Figure 4. This function is used to generate a random clock cycle where a soft error will be injected during the redundant execution of the program. The number of clocks cycles required to execute the task for the first execution is passed to this function to generate a cycle where the soft error will be injected.

The function *rand_int* picks a random number between 0 and *max_int*. This function is also used by the *softe_fault* Verilog task to select the random register where the fault will be injected.

```
function integer rand_int(max_int);
    integer max_int;

    parameter seed = 3;
    begin
       rand_int = {$random(seed)}%
                          (max_int-1);
    end
endfunction
```

Fig. 4. Function *rand_int* selects a number between 0 and *max_int*.

4.2.3 Register Selection

The test bench task *softe_fault* keeps a list of all the registers in the microprocessor in the form of a case statement and randomly picks one to insert the fault that will be injected during the second execution. The *softe_fault* task counts and waits for the exact clock cycle where the fault will be inserted. A simplified version of the *softe_fault* task is shown in Figure 5.

4.2.4 Main Control Initial Task

In Figure 6, we show how the tasks are called from the main initial block of the test bench. When the first execution starts, the *count_cycles* task determines the number of cycles needed, then as the second execution starts automatically, the random cycle where the soft error will be inserted has already been calculated and saved in *softe_cycle.* This value is passed to the *softe_fault* task and the soft error is randomly inserted at the exact clock cycle.

```
task softe_fault;
 input [15:0] softe_cycle;

 integer softe_location;
 parameter max_regs = 4;

 begin
  softe_location = rand_int(max_regs);
  # (10*softe_cycle);
  -> soft_error;
  case (softe_location)
  0:begin
     force tb.duv.controller0.nextstate[0]=
    ~force_tb.duv.controller0.nextstate[0];
     @(posedge clock);
    end
  1:begin
     force_tb.duv.controller0.nextstate[1]=
    ~force_tb.duv.controller0.nextstate[1];
     @(posedge clock);
    end
  2:begin
     force_tb.duv.controller0.nextstate[2]=
    ~force_tb.duv.controller0.nextstate[2];
     @(posedge clock);
    end
  3:begin
     force_tb.duv.controller0.nextstate[3]=
    ~force_tb.duv.controller0.nextstate[3];
     @(posedge clock);
    end
  endcase
 end
endtask
```

Fig. 5. The *softe_fault* task selects a random register to insert the fault.

```
initial begin
   exec_cycles = 0;
   @ (posedge Execution1);
   count_cycles(exec_cycles);
   softe_cycle = rand_int(exec_cycles);
   softe_fault(softe_cycle);
end
```

Fig. 6. The main initial block.

5 Results and Future Work

Our random fault injection and verification environment successfully inserted soft errors in the control unit of our microprocessor while it was performing calculations to generate a Fibonacci sequence. Figure 7, shows the beginning of the first execution of the Fibonacci program, which was targeted for soft error detection. Here, it can be observed that the first instruction was FES (First Execution Started) and continued with the normal program instructions. As it would be expected, current states are updated every clock cycle but only 1 in 5 states are sampled and stored in memory by the *state sample clock*. This control in the sampling clock was implemented to study the effectiveness of the soft error detection method with different clock sampling intervals. Then, the sampled states are stored by the SSM into memory and later will be compared during the states of the second execution of the Fibonacci number generator program. At the end of the first execution, the test bench counted 328 clocks and it randomly generated clock 64 of the second execution to inject the fault. The test bench also randomly selected a signal index of 2 of the *softe_fault* task to inject the soft error.

Figure 8 shows the second execution of the program. We can observe that exactly at *Execution2 count = 64* (at *t* = 3990 ns), the soft error event is injected and this event is flagged by the symbol *ϕ*. In this case, the state, in which the corruption of signal occurs, does not correspond to any sampled state by the first execution, but because the corruption propagates, when the SSM fetches a state from memory at t = 4015 ns, it detects that there is no match. It is at this point that the *Soft Error Detection* flag is asserted.

The work presented in this paper continues to evolve and as we study variations of our hardware-assisted soft error detection technique, we plan to investigate some related areas of interest. The following are research

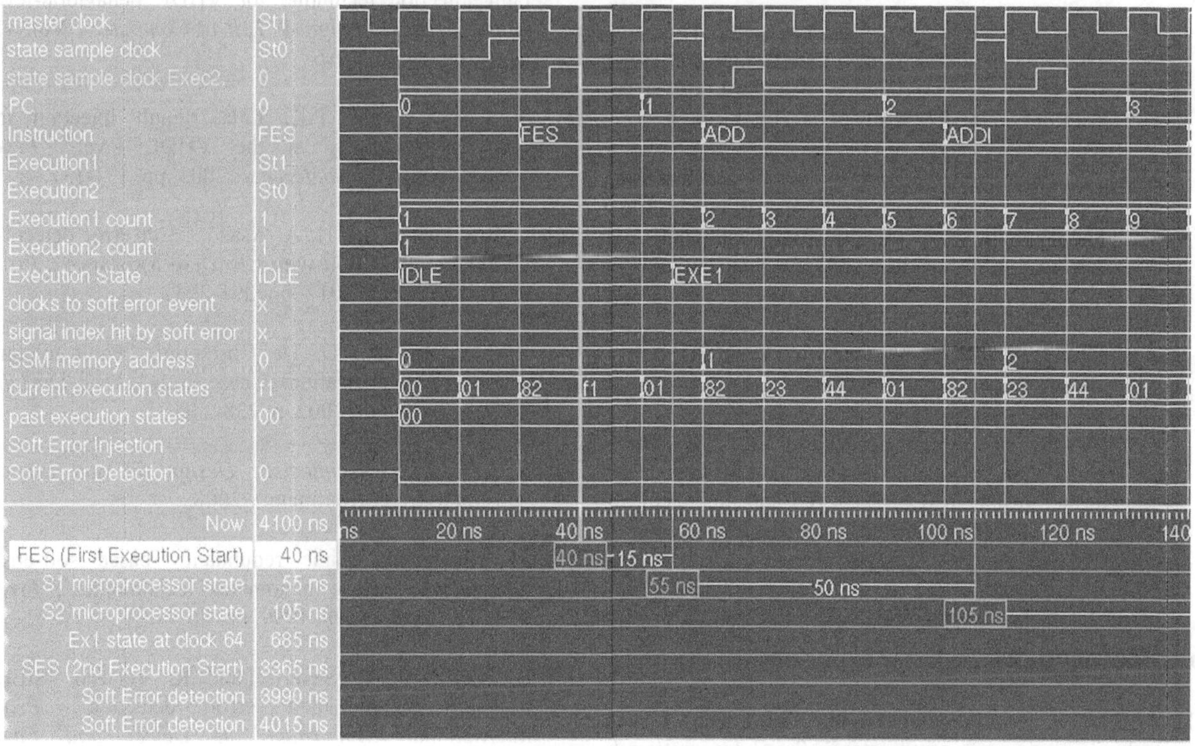

Fig 7. First Execution: Microprocessor states are sampled and stored every 5 clocks (starting after reset).

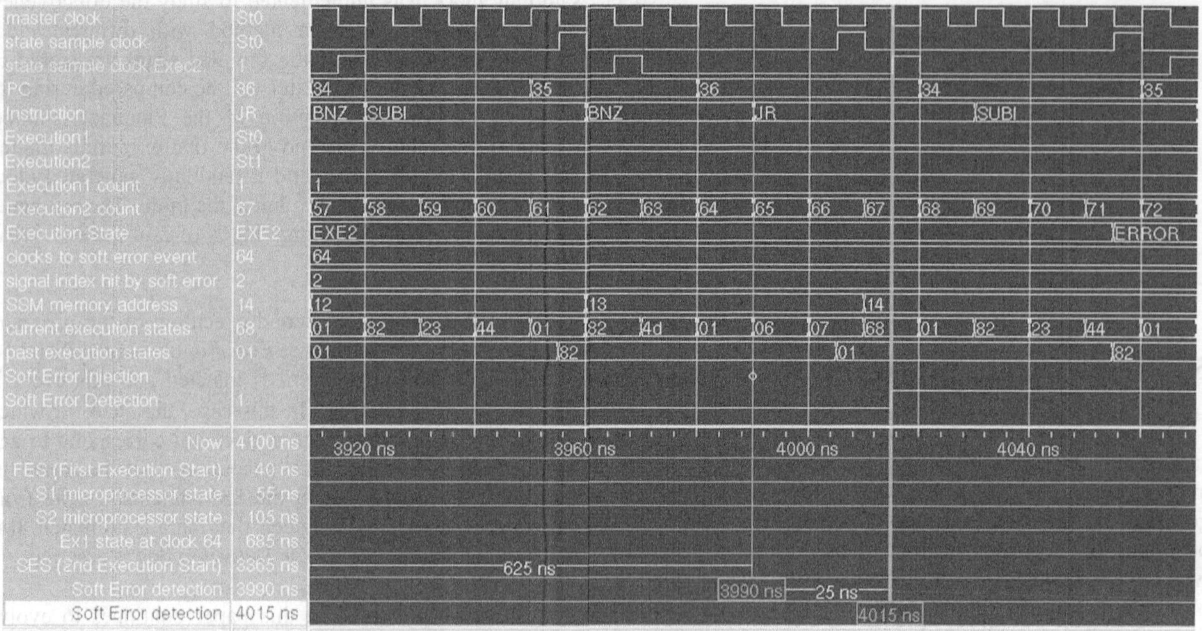

Fig. 8. Second execution: The soft error occurs at time 3990 ns and it is detected at 4015 ns.

opportunity areas we are currently considering:

1) *Fixed memory size with SSM handshake*: This will help limit memory usage for state storage. It will also allow the environment to control soft error insertion on the first cycle of execution.

2) *Additional supporting logic*: This logic is for state restoration from either a fast RAM or register file. These could lead to more efficient ways of detecting soft errors using redundant execution.

3) *Shadow registers*: The use of shadow registers could improve performance by enabling faster transitions back to a "good" known state.

4) *Insertion of soft errors during cycles where states are not sampled*: This is already in progress and further results will be analyzed and architectural benefits will be evaluated.

6 References

[1] A. Dixit, R. Heald, and A. Wood, "The impact of new technology on soft error rates," *Proc. International Reliability Physics Symposium*, 2011, pp. 5B.4.1-5B.4.7.

[2] T.A. Delong, B.W. Johnson, and J.A. Profeta III, "A fault jnjection technique for VHDL behavioral-level models", *IEEE Design & Test of Computers*, Vol. 13, No. 4, pp. 24-33, 1996.

[3] S.R. Seward and P.K. Lala, "Fault injection for verifying testability at the VHDL level," *Proc. International Test Conference*, 2003, pp. 131-137.

[4] L. Bustamante and H. Al-Asaad, "Soft error detection via double execution with hardware assistance," *Proc. AUTOTESTCON*, 2012, pp. 291-293.

[5] A. Manzone and D. De Costantini, "Fault tolerant insertion and verification: A case study", *Proc. On-Line Testing Workshop*, 2002, p. 238-242.

[6] S. Mukherjee, *Architecture Design for Soft Errors*, (Boston Morgan-Kaufmann), 2008.

[7] M. Nicolaidis, "Time redundancy based soft-error tolerance to rescue nanometer technologies", *Proc. VLSI Test Symposium*, 1999, pp. 86-94.

[8] B. Nicolescu, Y. Savaria, and R. Velazco "SIED: Software implemented error detection", *Proc. International Symposium on Defect and Fault Tolerance in VLSI Systems*, 2003, pp. 589-596.

A Comparative Analysis of Parallel Prefix Adders

Megha Talsania and Eugene John
Department of Electrical and Computer Engineering
University of Texas at San Antonio
San Antonio, TX 78249
megha.talsania@gmail.com, eugene.john@utsa.edu

***Abstract*- All modern processors, including general purpose microprocessors, digital signal processors and GPUs contain an Arithmetic Logic Unit (ALU). The computing efficiency of modern processors mainly depends of the efficiency of the ALU. An adder is the basic building block for an ALU which performs arithmetic as well as logic operations. This paper investigates the performance of six different parallel prefix adders implemented using four different TSMC technology nodes. The parallel prefix adders investigated in this paper are: *Kogge Stone Adder, Brent Kung Adder, Han Carlson Adder, Sklansky Adder, Lander Fischer Adder, and Knowles Adder.* The performance metrics considered for the analysis of the adders are: power, delay and area. Simulation studies are carried out for 16, 32 and 64 bit input data width.**

Keywords- Prefix tree adder, High speed CMOS adder, Low Power VLSI

1. Introduction

The addition of two binary numbers is one of the most fundamental and important arithmetic function in modern digital systems such as microprocessors and digital signal processors. In these systems binary adders are used in arithmetic logic units (ALU), multipliers, dividers and memory address generation. The requirements of adders are that it should be fast and efficient in terms of power and chip area. Most often, the maximum operating speed of most of the modern digital systems depend on how fast adders can process the data and hence responsible for setting the minimum clock cycle time in processors.

The major problem for binary addition is the propagation delay in the carry chain. As the width of the input operand increases, the length of the carry chain increases. To address the carry propagation problem, most of the modern adder architectures are represented as a parallel prefix adder (PPA) structure consisting of pre-processing, carry look-ahead and post processing sections. Parallel Prefix Adders have been established as the most efficient circuits for binary addition in digital systems. Their regular structure and fast performance makes them particularly attractive for VLSI implementation. The delay of a parallel prefix adder is directly proportional to the number of levels in the carry propagation stage.

This paper investigates the performance of six different parallel prefix adders implemented using four different TSMC technology nodes. The parallel prefix adders investigated in this paper are: *Kogge Stone Adder, Brent Kung Adder, Han Carlson Adder, Sklansky Adder, Lander Fischer Adder, and Knowles Adder.* The performance metrics considered for the analysis of the adders are: power, delay and area. In this paper the CMOS adders were realized using TSMC 130nm, 90nm, 65nm and 40 nm technologies. For performance comparison, the adders were realized using various prefix tree algorithms. Using simulation studies, delay, area and power performance of the various adder modules were obtained. It was observed that Kogge Stone Prefix tree adder has better circuit characteristics in terms of delay compared to adders realized using other algorithms.

The rest of the paper is organized as follows: in Section 2 a brief description of all the six different parallel prefix adders are given, in Section 3, the tools and methodology used for the research is explained. Section 4 gives results and performance analysis and finally Section 5 gives conclusions.

2. Parallel Prefix Adders

In this section the six different parallel prefix adders that are investigated in this paper are briefly described.

2.1 Kogge Stone Adder

The schematic of Kogge Stone Adder is given in Figure 1 [8]. It is widely used in high performance applications. The general concept of Kogge Stone adder is almost the same as that of the carry look ahead adder except for the second step, called parallel carry prefix chain. In the first level (L=1), generates and propagates of 2-bit are computed at the same time. In the second level (k=2), generates and propagates of 4-bit are calculated by using the result of 2-bit in level 1. Therefore, the actual carry-out value of the 4th bit would be available while the calculations in level 2 are being computed. In the third level (L=3), the carry-out of the 8th bit is computed by using the 4th bit carry result. The same method adopted in level 3 is applied to get carry-out values of the 16th bit and the 32nd bit in level 4 and level 5. All other carries of bit are also computed in parallel. In Figure 1, red boxes are propagate (P) and generate (G) generators for each bit of two inputs. Yellow boxes contain propagate block and generate block and the delay of one yellow box is equal to two gate delay (D). The blue boxes keep the original generate value transmitted from the previous level. In each level, because all carries are calculated in parallel, the delay is the running time of single yellow box.

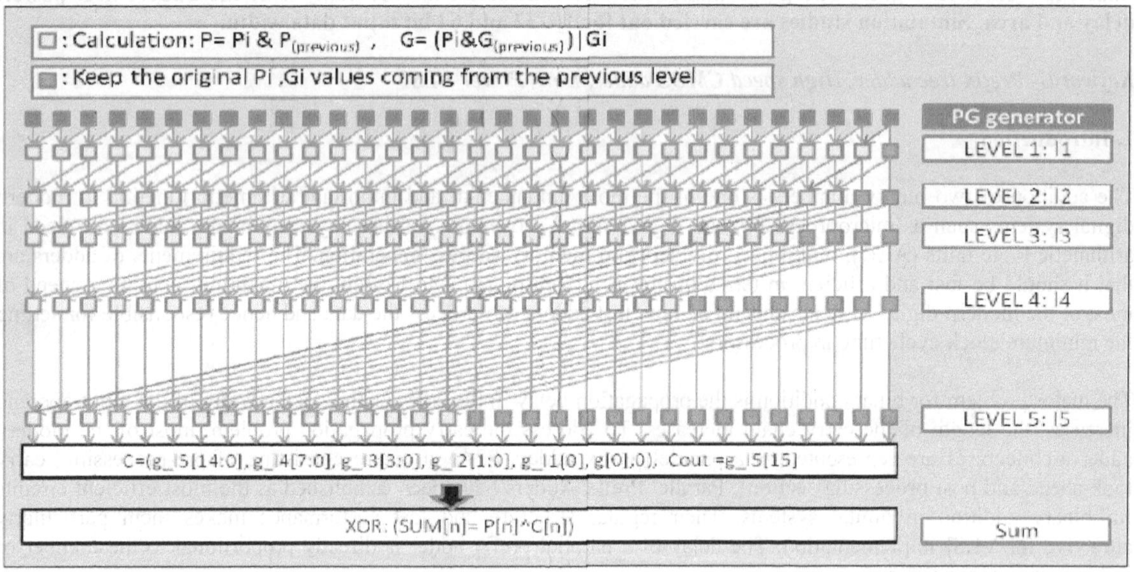

Figure 1:- Schematic of 32 bit Kogge Stone Adder

2.2 Brent Kung Adder

Figure 2 gives the schematic of the Brent Kung Adder. Brent-Kung is a parallel prefix form of the carry look ahead adder. In carry lookahead adder, as the size of the input operands is increased the delay of the result is also increased. Therefore the idea here is to have a gate level depth of O(log2(n)). It takes less area to implement than the other prefix adders such as Kogge-Stone adder and it also has less wiring congestion. Instead of using a carry chain to calculate the output, the method shown in Figure 2 is used. This will reduce the delay without compromising the power performance of the adder.

.

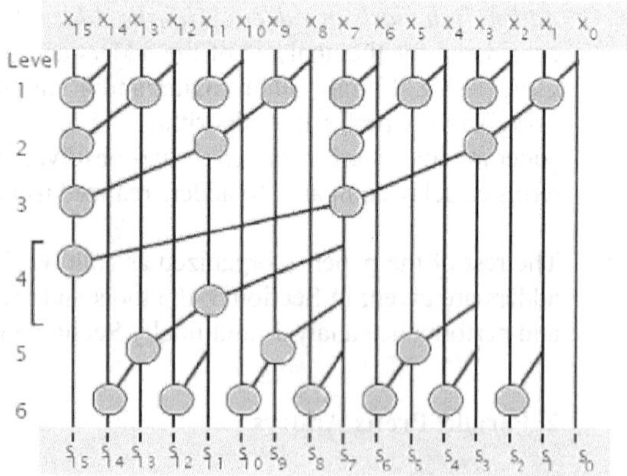

Figure 2:- Schematic of 16-bit Brent Kung Adder

2.3 Han Carlson Adder

Han Carlson adder is a parallel prefix tree. It helps to reduce complexity in Brent Kung adder [7]. It is also a hybrid design combined stages of Brent Kung and Kogge Stone adder. This scheme performs carry-merge operations on even bits only. Generate and propagate signals of odd bits are transmitted down the prefix tree. They recombine with even bits carry signals at the end to produce the true carry bits [15]. Thus, the reduced complexity is at the cost of adding an additional stage to its carry-merge path. Figure 3 represents method of 16 bit Han Carlson Adder [15].

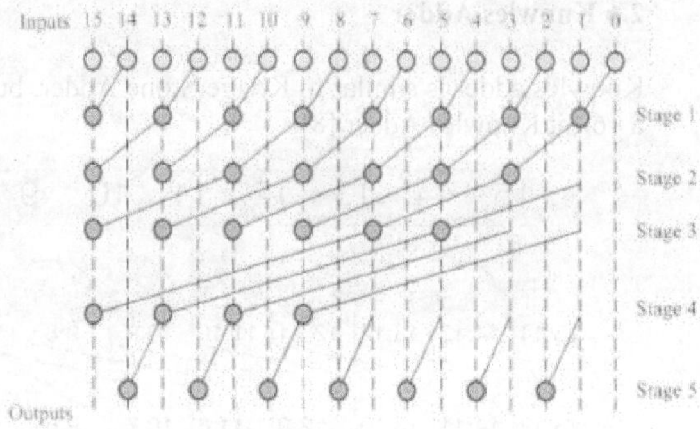

Figure 3: Schematic 16-bit Han Carlson Adder

2.4 Sklansky Adder

Sklansky Adder [7] is another form of parallel prefix adder and its schematic is shown in Figure 7. In this adder, binary tree of propagate and generate cells will first simultaneously generate all the carries, Cin. It builds recursively 2-bit adders then 4-bit adders, 8-bit adders, 16-bit adder and so on by abutting each time two smaller adders. The architecture is simple and regular, but it suffers from fan-out problems.

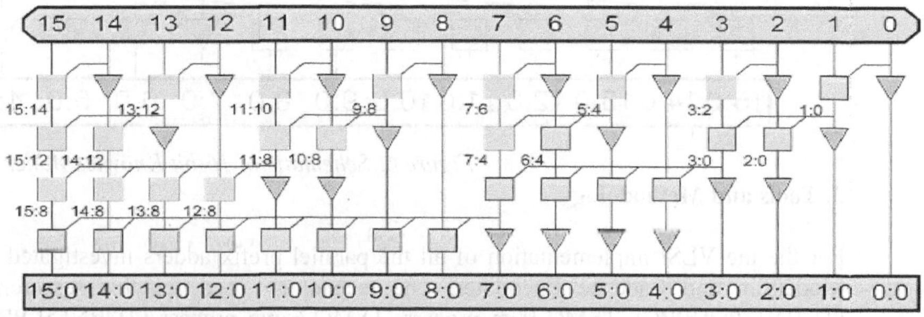

Figure 4: Schematic of 16-bit Sklansky Adder

Besides in some cases it is possible to use less propagate and generate cells with the same addition delay [7].

2.5 Lander Fisher Adder

The schematic of Lander Fischer Adder [9] is shown in Figure 5. This adder structure has minimum logic depth, but has large fan-out requirement up to n/2 [9].

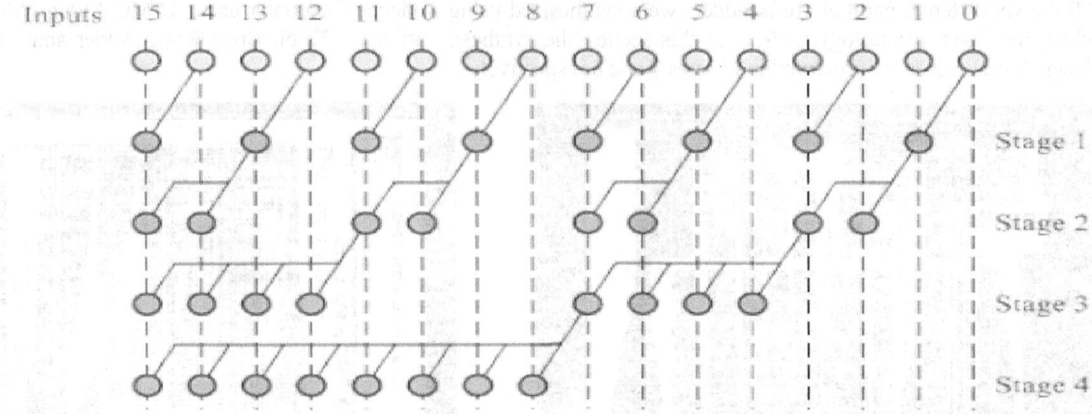

Figure 5: Schematic of 16 bit Lander Fischer Adder

2.6 Knowles Adder

Knowles adder is similar to Kogge Stone Adder, but it has different logic to calculate the output. Figure 6 illustrates a 16-bit Knowles Adder [8].

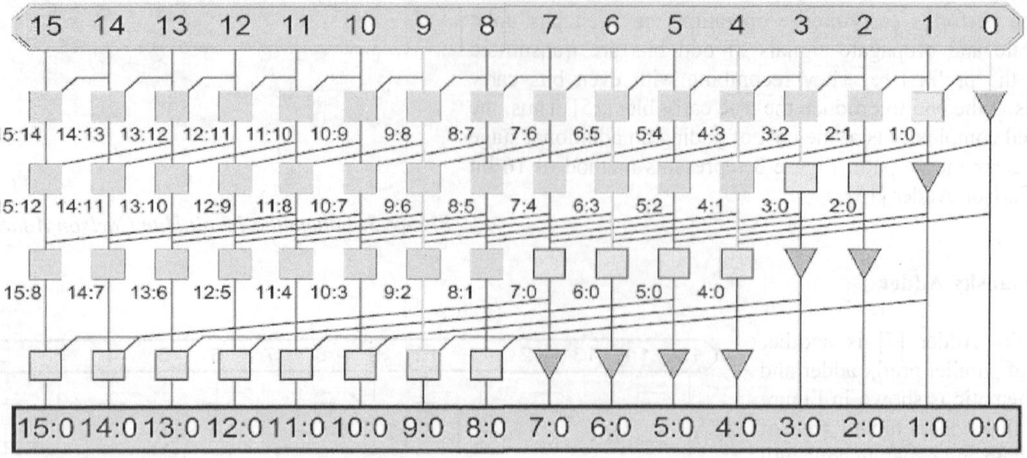

Figure 6: Schematic of 16-bit Knowles Adder

3. Tools and Methodology

For the the VLSI implementation of all the parallel prefix adders investigated in this research the tools used are ModelSim and Cadence Encounter. The technology used for this research are the TSMC 130nm process (TCBN130GHPBC), TSMC 90m process, TSMC 65nm process (TCBN65LPBWP7T) and TSMC 40nm process (TCBN40LPBWP). The simulations were carried out to obtain the power, area and the worst case delay of all the six different parallel prefix adders. The designs of each adder were generated by creating Verilog source file using ModelSim. Then each design was synthesized to simulate the functional result for functionality verification. After that each design is verified using VCS. After confirming the accuracy of each design, the source was used to create the netlist for schematic circuit diagram with Cadence Encounter. Finally, the performance evaluation for each design was calculated using TSMC 130nm, 90nm, 65nm and 40nm process libraries.

4. Results and Performance Analysis

A. Schematic and Layout Synthesis

All the six different parallel prefix adders were synthesized using Cadence Encounter using TSMC 130nm, 90nm, 65nm and 40nm technology nodes. In this section the synthesis results of 32 bit Brent Kung Adder and 64-bit Kogge Stone Adder are presented in Figures 7 and 8 respectively.

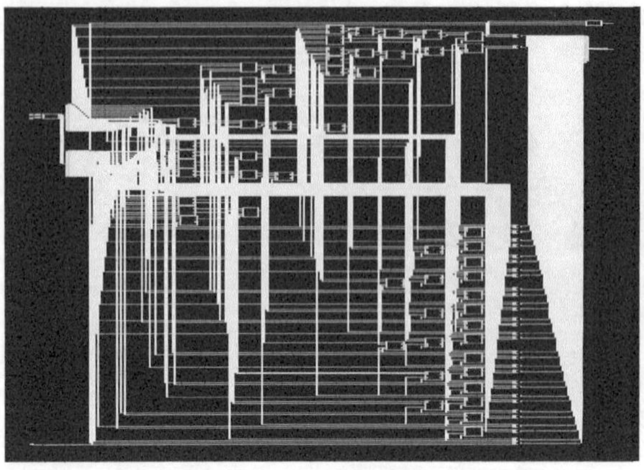

Figure 7: Schematic of 32 bit Brent Kung Adder

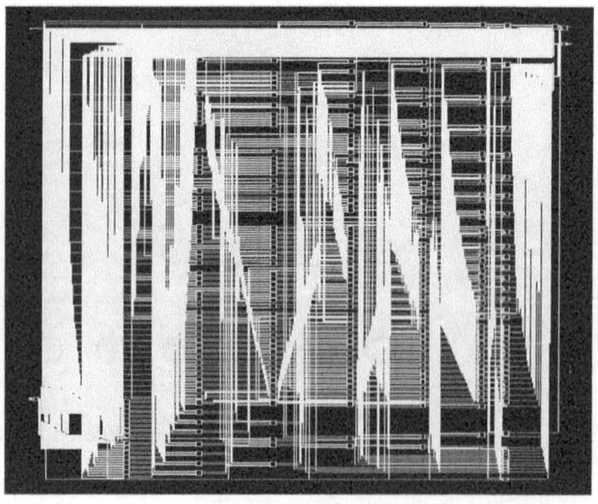

Figure 8: Schematic of 64 bit Kogge Stone Adder

Layout of low power adders were generated to analyze the area of the different parallel prefix adders using cadence encounter tool for TSMC 90nm technology node. Figure 9 illustrates the layout of 64 bit Kogge Stone Adder (KSA).

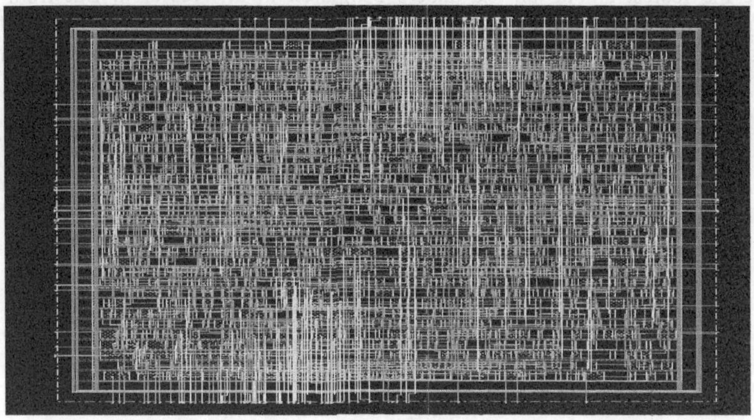

Figure 9: Layout of 64 bit KSA for TSMC 90nm technology node

B. Performance Analysis of Various Adders

The delay, power and area of all the six different prefix adders were investigated using simulations for varying input bit width for TSMC 130nm, 90nm, 65nm and 40nm technology nodes. Table 1 presents the area, power and delay results for all the six parallel prefix adders for 16 bit input width for 90nm technology node. From the results presented in Table 1 it can be inferred that 16 bit Brent Kung Adder occupies less area and power compared to any other adder investigated. But, in terms of delay it has the worst performance among all the adders compared in this study. Speed and Power are difficult characteristics to balance. As expected the 16-bit Kogge Stone Adder is the fastest adder among all the adders investigated together with Knowles Adder. This is one of the reasons why Kogge Stone Adder has been used in high speed applications.

Table 1: Comparison of area, power and delay for 16 bit input data width (90nm TSMC)

Adder	Area(µm2)	Total Power (µW)	Delay(ps)
Brent Kung	329.83	20.93	522
Han Carlson	366.05	22.48	444
Knowles	502.15	27.35	428.8
Lander Fischer	335.87	21.17	458.6
Sklansky	366.05	22.60	429.6
Kogge Stone	502.16	27.35	428.8

Table 2 presents the area, power and delay results for all the six parallel prefix adders for 64 bit input width for 90nm technology node. In this case also, Kogge Stone Adder has the best delay performance and the Brent Kung Adder has the best area and power performance.

Table 2: Comparison of area, power and delay for 64 bit input data width (90nm TSMC)

Adder	Area(µm2)	Total Power (µW)	Delay(ps)
Brent Kung	1354.99	85.08	825.9
Han Carlson	1832.34	102.51	593.9
Knowles	2345.57	127.64	565.7
Lander Fischer	1512.49	90.21	676.8
Sklansky	1681.52	99.58	831.8
Kogge Stone	2669.91	137.22	561.5

Figures 10 - 13 presents comparison of all the parallel prefix adders investigated in this research in terms of total power consumption and area using four different TSMC technologies. Figures 10 and 11 are for 32 bit adders and Figures 12 and 13 are for 64 bit adders. From the data presented in Tables 1 and 2 it can be seen that the Kogge Stone adders are the fastest among all the adders compared in this research. But from the simulation results presented in Figures 10 – 13 it can be clearly inferred that in terms of power and area performance Kogge Stone Adders are not among the best. The Brent Kung Adder exhibit the best performance in terms of area and power consumption for both the 32 and 64 bit adder categories.

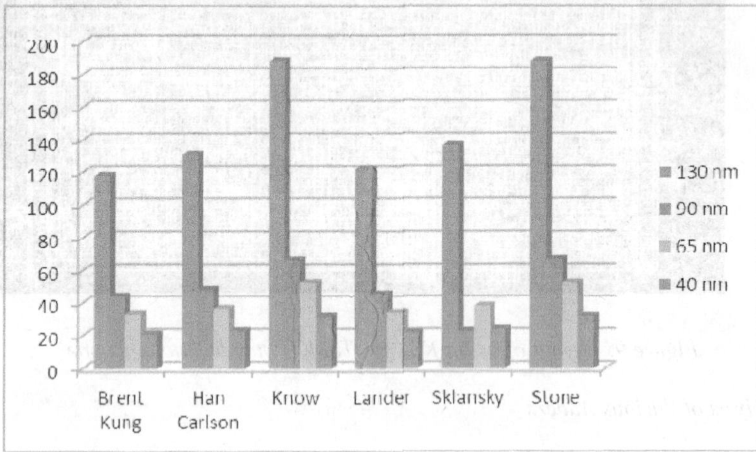

Figure 10: Total power consumption (μW) for various 32 bit adders

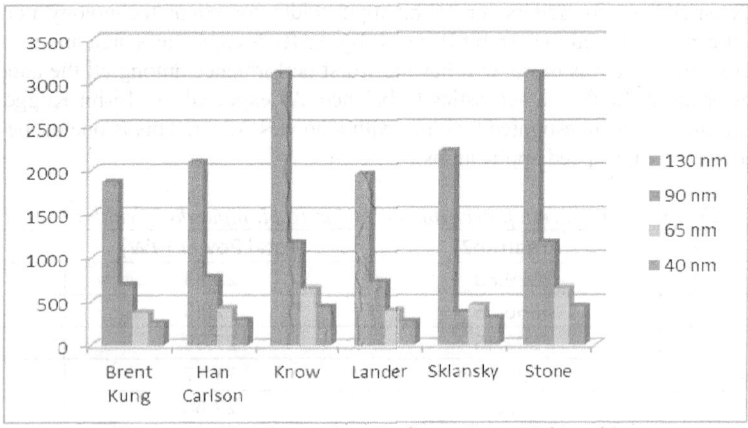

Figure 11: Total area (μm2) for various 32 bit adders

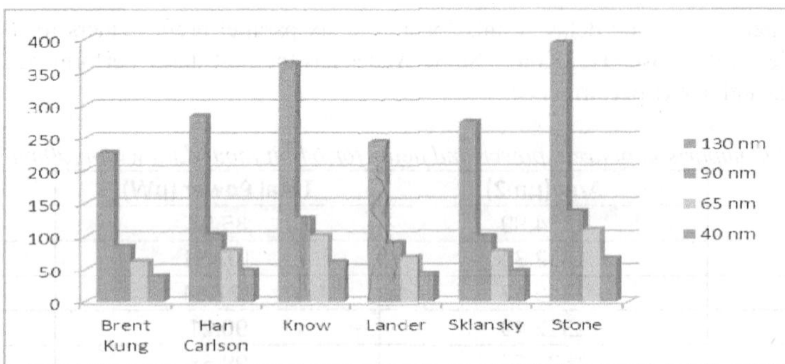

Figure 12: Total power consumption (μW) for 64 bit adders

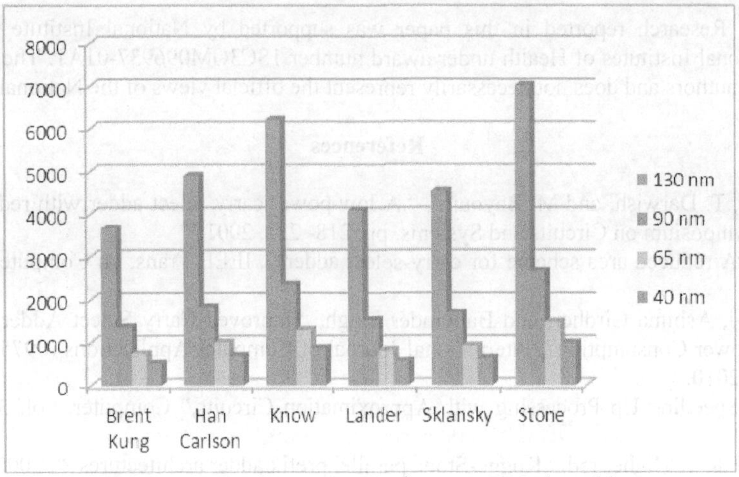

Figure 13: Total area (μm2) for various 64 bit adders

Figure 14 shows the delay comparison for all the adders for the TSMC 90 nm technology node for 16, 32 and 64 bit input data width. As expected, Kogge Stone Adder has the best performance among all the adders for all the input data width considered.

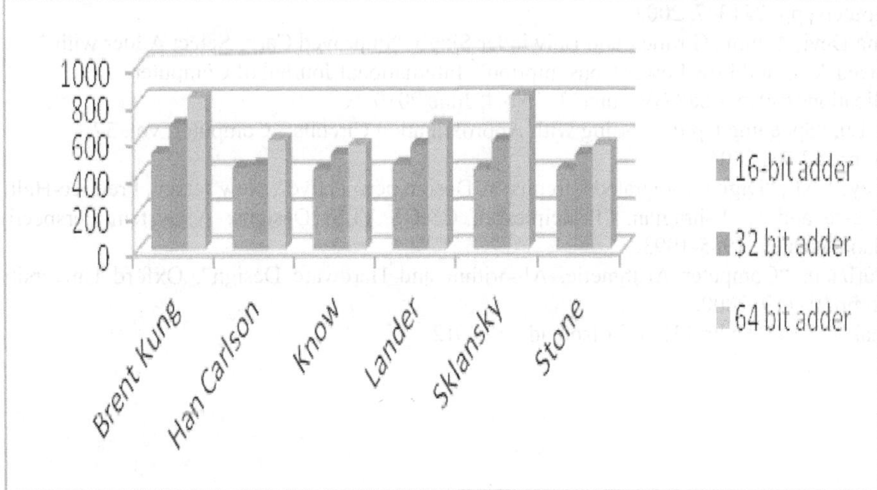

Figure 14: Delay (ps)
Comparison between all adders (90nm TSMC)

5. Conclusions

The primary objective of this research is the design, realization and performance comparison of various parallel prefix adders. In this paper several adders were analyzed to identify the optimal adder modules that can be used for the realization of high speed or low power adder structures. The addition algorithms that were studied include six different types of prefix tree adders. The performance analysis was based on the silicon area required for the implementation of the algorithm in hardware, the power dissipation during computation, and the worst case delay in performing the operation. In this research the CMOS adders were realized using TSMC 130nm, 90nm, 65nm and 40 nm technologies. Based on our simulation studies the Kogge Stone Adder has the best performance among all the adders for all the input data width considered. It is widely used in high performance applications and it has the merits of uniform structure and balanced loading in each internal node to get high speed performance. The Brent Kung Adder exhibited the best performance in terms of area and power consumption for all the input data width considered.

Acknowledgement: Research reported in this paper was supported by National Institute of General Medical Sciences of the National Institutes of Health under award number 1SC3GM096937-01A1. The content is solely the responsibility of the authors and does not necessarily represent the official views of the National Institutes of Health.

References

[1] K. Rawwat, T. Darwish, and M. Bayoumi, ".A low power carry select adder with reduces area", Proc. Of Midwest Symposium on Circuits and Systems, pp. 218- 221, 2001.

[2] A. Tyagi, "A reduced area scheme for carry-select adders", IEEE Trans. on Computer, vol. 42, pp. 1163-1170, 1993

[3] Padma Devi, Ashima Girdher, and Balwinder Singh, "Improved Carry Select Adder with Reduced Area and Low Power Consumption", International Journal of Computer Applications (0975 – 8887)Volume 3 – No.4, June 2010.

[4] S.-L. Lu, "Speeding Up Processing with Approximation Circuits," Computer, vol. 37, no. 3, pp. 67-73, 2004

[5] Gurkayna, F.K. , "Higher radix Kogge-Stone parallel prefix adder architectures ", 2000

[6] D. Harris, R. F. Sproull, I. E. Sutherland, "Logical Effort: Designing Fast CMOS Circuits" ,M. Kaufmann, 1999.

[7] P.Sunitha, "A Novel Approach For Designing A Low Power Parallel Prefix Adders", Vol. 1 Issue 8, October – 2012

[8] P. Kogge et al., IEEE Trans. Computers, vol. C-22, p. 786 (1973).

[9] D. Harris, "A Taxonomy of Parallel Prefix Networks," in Proc. 37th Asilomar Conf. Signals Systems and Computers, pp. 2213–7, 2003.

[10] Padma Devi, Ashima Girdher, and Balwinder Singh, "Improved Carry Select Adder with Reduced Area and Low Power Consumption", International Journal of Computer Applications (0975 – 8887)Volume 3 – No.4, June 2010.

[11] S.-L. Lu, "Speeding Up Processing with Approximation Circuits," Computer, vol. 37, no. 3, pp. 67-73, 2004.

[12] Rabaey, J. M., "Digital Integrated Circuits: A Design perspective", New Jersey, Prentice-Hall, 1996.

[13] N. Weste and K. Eshragian, "Principles of CMOS VLSI Designs: A System Perspective", 2nd ed., Addison-Wesley, 1985-1993.

[14] B. Parhami, "Computer Arithmetic, Algorithm and Hardware Design", Oxford University Press, New York, pp.91-119, 2000.

[15] Sudhakar, S.M.,"Hybrid Han Carlson adder",2012

A Short Survey on User-aware Power Management

Dongwon Min[1] **, Sangjun Lee**[2] **and Sung Woo Chung**[3]
[1]School of Business Administration, Dankook University, Yongin-si, Gyonggi-do, 448-701, Korea
[2] School of Computer Science and Engineering, Soongsil University, Seoul 156-743, Korea
[3]Division of Computer and Communication Engineering, Korea University, Seoul 136-713, Korea

Abstract – *This paper briefly surveys user aware power management. In the past, most power saving techniques have been focused on power and performance.. However, recently, there are some power management techniques that concentrate on user satisfaction rather than performance itself. After reading this paper, power management researchers are expected to collaborate with consumer researchers as well as HCI(Human Computer Interface) researchers.*

Keywords: User Aware Power Management, Human Computer Interface, Consumer research

1 Introduction

In the green computing where users utilize computers for a longer time with less power consumption, low power is crucial as much as performance. Especially, low power techniques are considered as much more important for mobile devices such as smartphones, pads, and notebooks. As time goes on, users need to consume more power, because they want to run more powerful (which is more power consuming) applications. In this case, however, battery usage time is reduced, which eventually makes users uncomfortable. Thus, there have been various low power techniques for mobile devices: from clock gating and power gating at the circuit level to power-aware scheduling at the operating systems level. However, most low power techniques at the operating systems level have not been applied to commercial systems, since there is a high possibility that they may hurt user satisfaction due to lowered performance.

Representative low power techniques used for off-the-shelf mobile devices are as follows: 1) DVFS (Dynamic Voltage Frequency Scaling) is adopted depending on CPU utilization, and 2) display (or even system itself) is turned off, when there is no user input for the predetermined time. Unfortunately, industries are very conservative to adopt the other previously proposed low power techniques, though they all understand that power consumption is important as same as (or even more important than) performance. The reason is that low power researchers have concentrated on power and performance, relatively ignoring user satisfaction. When users feel disturbed from mobile devices due to low power techniques, they will surely reluctant to use the mobile devices again. However, in most previous low power researches, there has not been user study to evaluate user satisfaction (disturbance). Recently, low power techniques detecting user status via HCI (Human Computer Interface) have been proposed. In addition, they are evaluated in terms of not only power consumption but user disturbance through user study widely used in consumer research. In this paper, we examine user-aware low power techniques for mobile devices.

2 User Aware Power Management

In current mobile devices, *user aware* low power techniques are very simple as follows: 1) when there is no user input for a certain time, display is turned off, and 2) when an illuminance sensor detects that it is dark enough, display backlight is lowered. This implies that mobile devices detect user status passively. On the other hand, the following subsections introduce low power techniques that actively detect user status to minimize user disturbance, still reducing power consumption.

2.1 Biometric Sensors Based DVFS (Dynamic Voltage Frequency Scaling)

Though it is apparent that ultimate goal of computer science is to satisfy the users, there is little information about the users because of the limited user input devices (e.g. the mouse and keyboard). To have more information about the users, Shye et al. added three biometric sensors: an eye tracker, a galvanic skin response (GSR) sensor, and force sensors [1]. Analyzing the information from sensors, their proposed physiological traits-based power-management system determines whether users are satisfied with the system performance. When users are considered as unsatisfied with the performance, CPU voltage and frequency are increased to boost the performance. Otherwise, they are decreased, which leads to power reduction. They also did user study to evaluate user satisfaction. However, their proposed technique requires the users to wear the eye tracker and GSR sensing device, though the force sensors are embedded in the keyboard. Note most users may be reluctant to wear the eye tracker and GSR sensing device, since they feel uncomfortable with them.

2.2 Sonar Based Display Power Management

Tarzia et al. proposed display power management technique based on sonar detecting user presence [2]. The insight here is that human bodies bounce back different sound waves compared to air and other objects. As shown in Fig. 1, the computer sends audio in the range of 15 to 20 kHz, which is inaudible to most users. It also records the audio bounced back from the user, which is different depending on user states: active (input is continued), passively engaged (looking at the computer screen), disengaged (sitting in front of the computer, not looking at the screen), distant (away from the computer, but still in the room), and absent (left the room). According to the user state, different display power mode is applied. Since most laptops have speakers and microphones, no additional hardware is required.

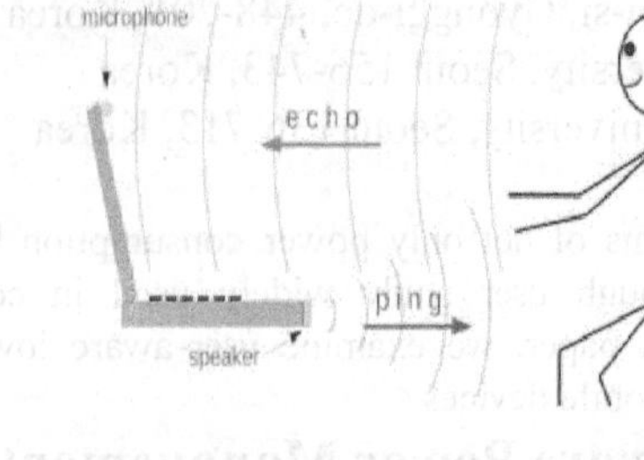

Fig. 1. User detection scheme for [2]

Their user study shows that "passively engaged" state can be discriminated from "absent" state with more than 96% accuracy. However, they did not show how their proposed technique is sensitive to external environments such as noise and room floorplan.

2.3 Camera Based Display Power Management

To detect user state more accurately, Kim et al. utilized camera for display power management [3]. Since most laptops have a camera (webcam) for interactive communication, there is no need for additional hardware. As shown in Fig. 2, there are four user states: interactive, attentive, inattentive, and away. To detect user state, they use face detection algorithm (to detect whether user face is looking at the display; not to recognize specific user face) which incurs negligible power and performance overhead. When frontal face is detected, the user state is attentive. When face is detected but it is not frontal, the user state is inattentive. When face is not detected, it is away. In case of interactive and attentive state, display power mode is normal. On the other hand, in case of inattentive state, display is in slightly low power mode (e.g. only backlight is off). In case of away mode, display is totally turned off. Note different power mode can be assigned to the user state by system vendors.

Their user study shows that power is saved by up to 14%, compared to traditional timeout based display power management. It also shows that users experienced less than one disturbance per hour, on average, which is acceptable enough.

3 Discussion

In this paper, we survey user aware operating systems level power management schemes, which are different from the traditional schemes, in a sense that information about users are utilized. Biometric sensors are used to detect user status as explained in Section 2.1. The physiological information about user status is used for DVFS (Dynamic Voltage and Frequency Scaling). The proposed technique is efficient to satisfy users but it should attach additional sensor devices to users. Sonar is used to detect user state to save display power, depicted in Section 2.2. The proposed technique does not need any additional hardware, since most laptops have speakers and microphones. However, it may be sensitive to external environments. Camera is utilized to detect user state for display power saving, explained in Section 2.3. The advantage of the proposed technique is 1) no additional hardware is required, and 2) user disturbance is quite low due to high user state detection accuracy.

We hope future researches on power management consider user satisfaction as well as performance overhead. To optimize evaluation metrics, system researchers on power management are expected to collaborate with consumer researchers for user satisfaction as well as HCI researchers for novel sensing devices.

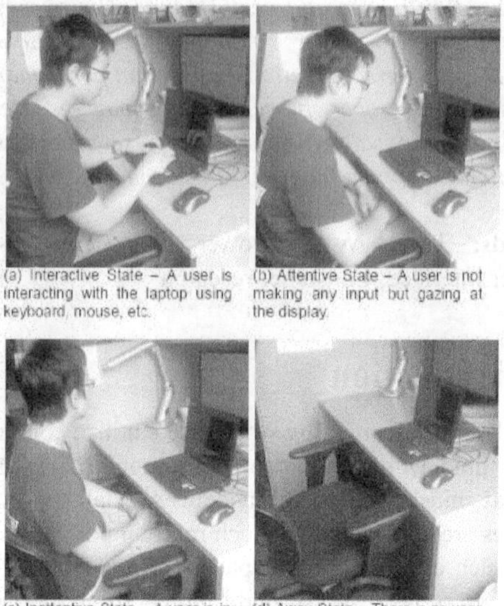

(a) Interactive State – A user is interacting with the laptop using keyboard, mouse, etc.
(b) Attentive State – A user is not making any input but gazing at the display.
(c) Inattentive State – A user is in front of the laptop but not gazing at the display.
(d) Away State – There is no user in front of the laptop.

Fig. 2. User states for display power management [3].

Acknowledgement

This research was supported by the MSIP(Ministry of Science, ICT & Future Planning), Korea, under the ITRC(Information Technology Research Center) support program (NIPA-2013-H0301-13-2006) supervised by the NIPA(National IT Industry Promotion Agency, and by the National Research Foundation of Korea (NRF) grant funded by the Korea government (MEST) (No.2012-013816).

References

[1] Shye, A., Pan, B., Scholbrock, B., Miller, J. S., Memik, G., Dinda, P., Dick, R. : Power to People: Leveraging Human Physiological Traits to Control Microprocessor Frequency. In: International Symposium on Microarchitecture, IEEE Press, Lake Como (2008).

[2] Tarzia, S. P., Dick, R. P., Dinda, P. A., Memik, G. : Sonar-Based Measurement of User Presence and Attention. In: International Conference on Ubiquitous Computing, IEEE Press, Orlando (2009)

[3] Kim, J. M., Kim, M., Kong, J, Jang, H. B., Chung, S. W. : Display Power Management That Detects User Intents. IEEE Computer Magazine, vol. 44, no. 10, pp. 60-66, IEEE press (2011)

SESSION

PERFORMANCE ISSUES + HPC AND MULTI-PROCESSOR SYSTEMS + FPGA + FILE SERVERS

Chair(s)

TBA

Performance Tradeoff Spectrum of Integer and Floating Point Applications Kernels on Various GPUs

M.G.B. Johnson, D. P. Playne and K.A. Hawick
Computer Science, Massey University, North Shore 102-904, Auckland, New Zealand
email: {m.johnson, d.p.playne, k.a.hawick}@massey.ac.nz
Tel: +64 9 414 0800 Fax: +64 9 441 8181

April 2013

ABSTRACT

Floating point precision and performance and the ratio of floating point units to integer processing elements on a graphics processing unit accelerator all continue to present complex tradeoffs for optimising core utilisation on modern devices. We investigate various hybrid CPU and GPU combinations using a range of different GPU models occupying different points in this tradeoff space. We analyse some performance data for a range of numerical simulation kernels and discuss their use as benchmark problems for characterising such devices.

KEYWORDS
MIPS vs FLOPS; computational performance; accelerator; benchmark; GPU.

1 Introduction

Graphical Processing Units [10, 11] have become almost mainstream accelerator devices in many applications areas. They remain non-trivial to program even with the advent of highly developed software libraries and tools such as NVidia's Compute Unified Device Architecture (CUDA) [12] and Open Compute Language (OpenCL) [16]. There are still some applications and parts of applications for which GPUs provide very good speedups and others for which they are less suitable. To further complicate the users decision on which platform to deploy upon there have been many different GPU models released over the last five years each of which has different design features and performance characteristics.

In this paper we use some very simple synthetic benchmarks to experiment with a range of different GPU devices and benchmark performance across them. Our particular focus of interest in integer versus floating point performance. Other factors such as memory transfer bandwidth and the exact ratio of floating point, double precision and special function evaluation units also play a part.

Our long term goal is to develop a set of GPU related benchmarks appropriate for computational fluid dynamics (CFD) [1, 2, 18] and comparing conventional CFD calculations [9] that are formulated in terms of partial differential equations that require raw floating point performance [6] with those formulated in terms of integer calculations and a lattice gas model approach [8].

There are a number of well known benchmarks for floating point performance in the context of linear algebra and matrix calculations [4, 17]. The NAS parallel benchmarks [3] also exercise some features that are specific to CFD problems as well. Other benchmarks have considered asynchronous coupling effects between the GPU and its hosting CPU [13], or have been tailored to specific applications areas such as particle dynamics [7, 15] or graph and network problems [5].

There is topical scope to consider multiple GPUs [14, 19] attached to the same CPU and driven or serviced by different cores. In this present paper however we focus on rather low-level capabilities of the various GPU accelerators we study and the main contribution is that we have been able to study quite a large collection of different vintage devices and can comment on which particular features contribute to which low level performance trend.

Our article is structured as follows: We review some of the key architectural features of graphical processing units in Section 2. We benchmark the GPUs by separating and emphasising the individual elements that make GPGPU and specifically NVidia GPUs both powerful and limiting. The areas we identified were: integer and double precision computation and global memory access. These elements represent the greatest divide between the various devices and we see in Section 3 both the strengths and weaknesses of each device relative to the other generations of NVidia hardware. We present a selection of benchmarks for low level operations in Section 4. We discuss their implications in Section 5 and offer some tentative conclusions, directions for the future and other areas for further investigation in Section 6.

2 GPU Architecture

Since the initial release of CUDA and the rise of GPGPU computing, NVIDIA has released several GPU architectures. Each of these subsequent GPU architecture releases have brought with them higher performance and additional chip capabilities that make GPGPU programs faster and easier to develop.

The GT200 released in 2008 saw the introduction of double precision processing and a reduction on the performance penalties on non-coalesced memory accesses. The GF100 Fermi architecture GPUs released in 2010 in the GeForce 400 series and saw an increase in the number of cores per multiprocessor to 32 and most significantly for the GPGPU community the introduction of an L1/L2 cache structure. The GF110 was released later in 2010 in the GeForce 500 series which brought with it performance improvements over the GeForce 400 series. The general architecture of the Fermi architecture multiprocessor can be seen in Figure 1.

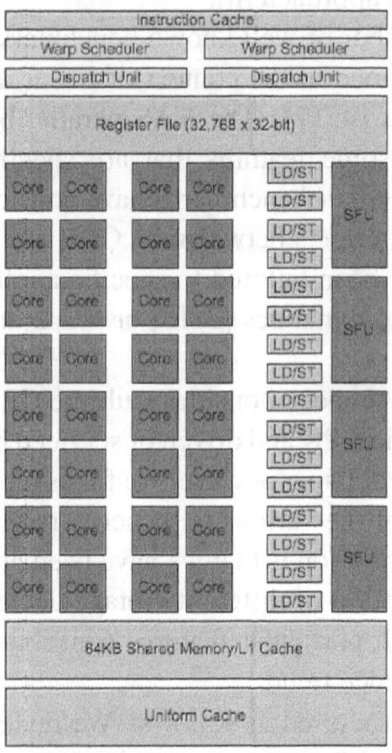

Figure 1: The architecture of a Fermi GPU multiprocessor with 32 cores, 16 Load/Store units and 4 special function units.

In 2012 NVIDIA released the new Kepler architecture GPU featuring the new generation Streaming Multiprocess architecture (SMX). These multiprocessors contain 192 cores which has allowed the maximum number of cores in a single GPU to be increased to 1,536. These GPUs provide higher performance than the previous generation Fermi devices while using significantly less power. The architecture of these GPUs is shown in Figure 2.

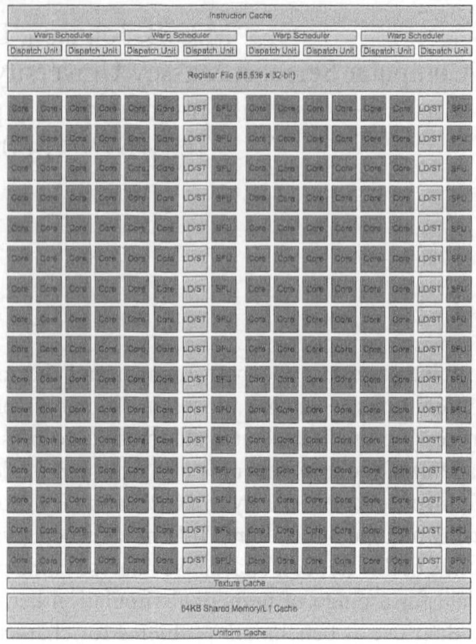

Figure 2: A Kepler architecture multiprocessor containing 192 cores, 32 Load/Store units and 32 special function units.

While these Kepler GPU have significantly higher performance than the previous generation GPUs (theoretical peak of 3090.4 GFlops for a GeForce GTX680 as compared to 1581.1 GFlops for a GeForce GTX580) the overall memory bandwidth has remained almost the same 192.2 GB/sec (GTX680) compared to 192.4 GB/sec (GTX580). This presents a problem for some GPGPU applications which maybe limited by memory speed and not computational performance. We evaluate the practical performance of these two GPU architectures and compare them in terms of computational throughput and memory access.

3 Implementation Method

We decided to reduce the benchmarks (micro benchmarks) to their simplest possible state. For computation we chose a basic Linear Congruential random number generator as shown in Listing 1. While, not the best random number generator for high quality randomness it only uses integer calculations and no memory access. Each thread has one kernel which generates one thousand random numbers. Only kernel execution time is recorded and averaged over multiple separate runs.

```
__global__ void int_compute_benchmark()
 {
    int ix = blockDim.x *blockIdx.x +threadIdx.x;
    int M = 8;
    int a = ix;
    int c = 3;
    int X = 1;
    int i;
    for(i=0; i<1000; i++)
    {
       X = (a * X + c) % M;
    }
}
```

Listing 1: Device kernel generating one thousand random numbers using a Linear Congruential generator for the integer computation benchmark.

To evaluate the double precision speed of the GPUs we use the same idea as the integer but change the algorithm to a simple quadratic equation solver as shown in Listing 2. This uses both double precision computation as well as the special function units in each of the multi processors.

```
__global__ void double_compute_benchmark()
 {
    int ix = blockDim.x *blockIdx.x +threadIdx.x;
    double linear = ix;
    double cons = blockIdx.x*blockIdx.y;
    double num1=0,num2=0;
    double power=0;
    for(int i=0; i<1000; i++){
       double quadratic = i+1;
       power=pow (linear / 2 , 2.0);
       num1= ( - linear + sqrt(power - ( 4 *
           quadratic * cons )) ) / (2 *
           quadratic);
       num2= ( - linear - sqrt(power - ( 4 *
           quadratic * cons )) ) / (2 *
           quadratic);
    }
}
```

Listing 2: Device kernel to solve one thousand different quadratic equations for the double precision computation benchmark.

We examine how memory reading and writing speed differ between the devices. Again we use the most simple example to exasperate memory transfer cost. Examining both random and coalesced reads and writes exposes the advantages and flaws for differing architecture. We expect that the random reads will perform much worse on all devices but will affect the 600 series cards the most, as the number of multi-processes have been reduced.

Listing 3 shows the algorithm we use to test the coalesced memory reads and writes. Firstly we allocate two integer arrays and populate them with random integers. The memory allocation and population is not included in the benchmark timing. Each element is then copied from array A to array B, incremented and written back to A. This allows for large coalesced reads and writes with very little other computation.

```
__global__ void
 coalesced_memory_benchmark(int *A, int *B,int *
     rStore)
  {
     unsigned int i = ((((blockIdx.y * gridDim.x)
         + blockIdx.x) * blockDim.x) +
         threadIdx.x);
         A[i] = B[i];
         B[i]++;
         B[i] = A[i];
}
```

Listing 3: Device kernel to benchmark the coalesced memory read and write speed of the devices.

```
__global__ void
 random_memory_benchmark(int *A, int *B,int *
     rStore)
  {
         unsigned int i = ((((blockIdx.y *
             gridDim.x) + blockIdx.x) *
             blockDim.x) + threadIdx.x);
         int rnd1 = rStore[i];
         int rnd2 = rStore[rnd1];
         int rnd3 = rStore[rnd2];
         int rnd4 = rStore[rnd3];
         A[rnd1] = B[rnd2];
         B[rnd3] = A[rnd4];
}
```

Listing 4: Device kernel to benchmark random memory read and writes to device global memory.

Listing 4 shows the algorithm we have used to benchmark the random memory access time for the various GPUs. Each thread must perform two random reads and two random writes to global memory. Using the same random number for multiple threads may result in some collisions. However as this is consistent across all of the benchmark it does not present any advantage to a specific device.

4 Performance Results

Figure 3 shows the plot of kernel execution time for the integer computation benchmark vs the number of thread blocks, which contain 32 threads each. We see generally predictable results. With the GTX 680 the fastest followed but the: 2090, 580, 590 and so on. The order is representative of the number of cores per GPU and for devices with

	260	480	580	590	660m	680	M2050	M2070	M2075	M2090
Compute Version	1.3	2.0	2.0	2.0	3.0	3.0	2.0	2.0	2.0	2.0
Total Global Memory(MB)	896	1536	1536	1536	512	2048	2687	5375	5375	5375
Number of Compute Cores	216	480	512	512	384	1536	448	448	448	512
Number of Multi Procs	27	15	16	16	2	8	14	14	14	16
GPU Clock Rate(MHz)	1400	1400	1590	1225	950	706	1150	1150	1150	1301
Memory Clock (MHz)	1000	1848	2004	1710	256	3004	1546	1494	1556	1848
Memory Bus(Bit)	448	384	384	384	256	256	384	384	384	384
L2 Cache(KBytes)	0	768	768	768	512	512	768	768	768	768
Const Memory Size(KB)	64	64	64	64	64	64	64	64	64	64
Shared Memory Size(KB)	16	48	48	48	48	48	48	48	48	48
Registers Per Block	16384	32768	32768	32768	65536	65536	32768	32768	32768	32768
Has ECC	No	No	No	No	No	No	Yes	Yes	Yes	Yes

Table 1: Table comparing the various NVidia GPU models that we benchmark.

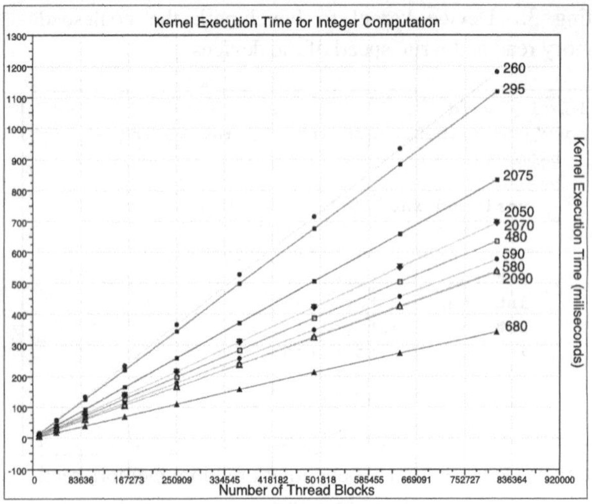

Figure 3: Integer computation test

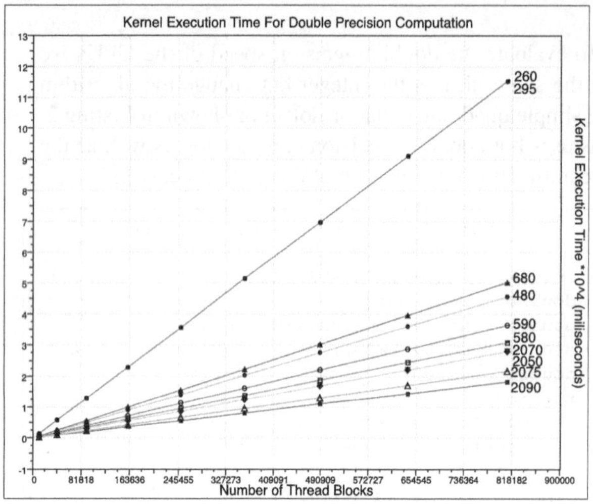

Figure 4: Double computation test

the same number of cores the clock speed separates them.

Figure 4 shows the kernel execution time for the double precision computation benchmark vs the number of thread blocks, again containing 32 threads each. Unlike the integer computation benchmark we see some unexpected results. We see that the most recent GPU tested the GTX 680 is the slowest aside from the 200 series GPUs. As expected the Tesla compute cards are the best performing cards in this test. With the 2050 and 2070 again showing nearly identical results as the main difference between them is the memory size and minute GPU clock rate difference. The 2075 shows an improvement over the 2070 and 2050 which is then followed by the 580 and 480.

We see in Figure 5 the results of the random access memory benchmark. Again the results of this test are unusual as the most recently released GPU the GTX 680 is not the fastest as it is beaten by the 480, 580 and 590. We believe this is due to the smaller number of multiprocessors in the 680 with eight compared with sixteen in the 580 and 590 and 14 in the 480. Because the multiprocessors handle the memory operations for the cores within each one, randomly accessing the memory will significantly affect the devices with lower numbers of multiprocessors.

Figure 6 shows us the results of the coalesced memory access bench mark. We see that unlike the random access benchmark the 680 performs very well. The 580 also performs well and comes in a close second. The GPUs seem to be grouped into three distinct groups with the 260 and the 295 performing surprisingly well compared to the Tesla GPUs.

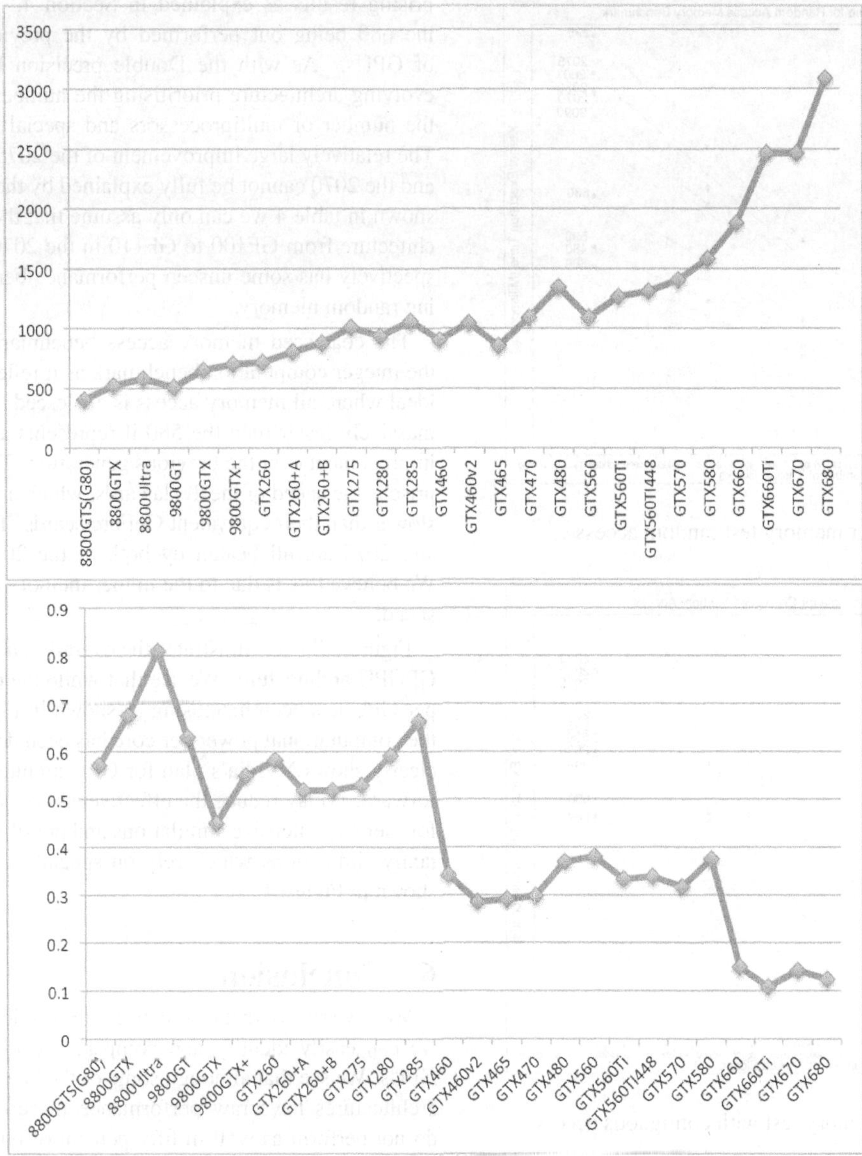

Figure 7: GFlops (above) and GFlops per core (below)

5 Discussion

GPUs are primarily designed to render computer graphics and only recently have begun to be used for general purpose computing (GPGPU). Producing graphics requires primarily integer calculations and we see the result of this in Figure 3 where each generation of NVidia GPU performs better than the previous. The main factor in the integer computation performance seems to be the number of cores followed by the clock speed. We see evidence of the impact clock speed makes in the difference between the 580 and 590 which have almost identical specifications aside from a lower GPU clock speed and lower memory clock speed. The 2075 is also significantly slower than the 2070 and the 2050 as with the memory benchmark this cannot be explained by the specifications.

Double precision has historically been a weak point for GPGPU and specifically the NVidia GeForce consumer GPUs. In the Tesla series they have concentrated on bridg-

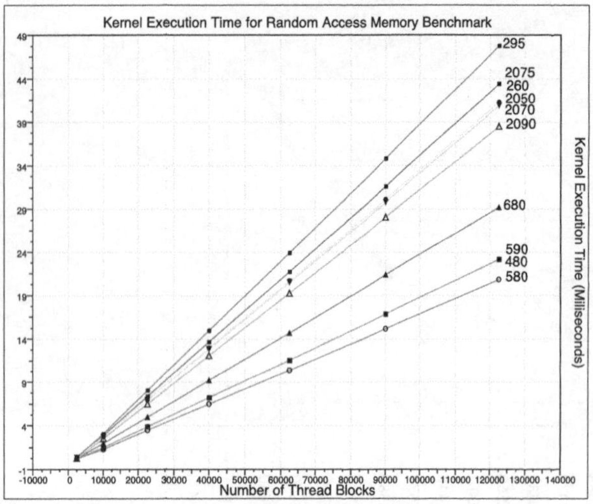

Figure 5: Integer memory test random access

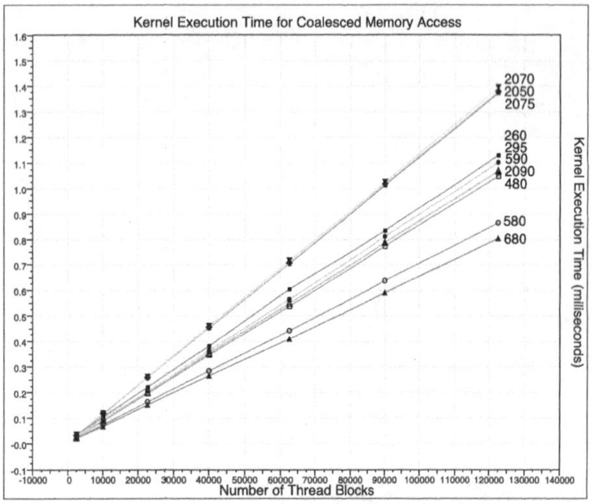

Figure 6: Integer memory test with contiguous access

ing this divide and we see the results of this in Figure 4. The Tesla cards: 2050, 2070, 2075 and the 2090 all perform much better than their GeForce counterparts. More surprisingly the best of these cards was the oldest Fermi architecture card, the 480. The 680 being the slowest card despite being one of the new generation Kepler is reflective of the growing divide between the consumer graphics cards and the professional level GPGPU devices such as the 2090 and consumer graphics focused GeForce cards such as the 680. Although the 680 has many more cores that all of the other GPUs, the ratio of special function units to compute cores is much lower.

The random access memory benchmark shows some surprising results as explained in Section 4. Again we see the 680 being out performed by the previous generation of GPUs. As with the Double precision benchmark the evolving architecture prioritising the number of cores over the number of multiprocessors and special function units. The relatively large improvement of the 2075 over the 2050 and the 2070 cannot be fully explained by the specifications shown in table 4 we can only assume that the change in architecture from GF100 to GF110 in the 2070 and 2075 respectively has some unseen performance benefit in accessing random memory.

The coalesced memory access benchmark is similar to the integer computation benchmark as it reflects the NVidia ideal where all memory access is coalesced. The 680 is not massively faster than the 580 it represents an evolutionary improvement over the previous generation. The biggest surprise is the speed of the Tesla cards, which are mostly much slower than their equivalent GeForce cards. The 2050, 2070 and 2075 are all beaten by both of the 200 series cards. We believe this is due to the higher memory clock and core speed.

Figure 7 (lower) illustrates the overall trend of the NVidia GPGPU architecture. We see that while the overall GFlops per GPU has been increasing as shown in Figure 7(above), the computational power per core has been decreasing. This clearly shows NVidia's plan for GPU architectures moving forward. It may reduce the effectiveness of NVidia GPGPU for memory intensive simulations and possibly more importantly simulations which rely on special function units as shown in Figure 4

6 Conclusion

We have shown that by creating simple micro benchmarks we can easily identify and compare specific functions of GPUs. We see that although some of the latest NVidia GPU architectures have raw performance in certain areas they do not perform as well in fifty percent of our benchmarks. While we do not propose buying older generation GPUs, it may give insight into why simulations are not performing as well on some GPUs and not others. We also show that there is a growing divide between the GeForce consumer cards and the professional GPGPU Tesla GPUs. The next generation of GPUs that have been announced are the K20x and its GeForce cousin the Titan show the continuing trend towards the many core less multiprocessors architecture.

References

[1] Abbott, M., Basco, D.: Computational Fluid Dynamics: an introduction for engineers. Longman (1989)

[2] Acheson, D.: Elementary Fluid Dynamics. Oxford Applied Mathematics and Computing Science Series, Clarendon Press (1990)

[3] Bailey, D., Barscz, E., Barton, J., Browning, D., Carter, R., Dagum, L., Fatoohi, R., Fineberg, S., Frederickson, P., Lasinski, T., Schreiber, R., Simon, H., Venkatakrishnan, V., Weeratunga, S.: The nas parallel benchmarks. Tech. Rep. RNR-94-007, NASA Ames Research Center, Moffett Field, CA, USA. (1994)

[4] Dongarra, J.J., Luszczek, P., Petitet, A.: The LINPACK Benchmark: past, present and future. Concurrency and Computation: Practice and Experience 15(9), 803–820 (2003)

[5] Graph500.org: The Graph 500 List. `http://www.graph500.org/`, last accessed November 2010

[6] Griebel, M., Dornseifer, T.: Numerical Simulation in Fluid Dynamics A Practical Introduction. No. ISBN 0-89871-398-6, SIAM (1998)

[7] Hawick, K.A., Playne, D.P., Johnson, M.G.B.: Numerical precision and benchmarking very-high-order integration of particle dynamics on gpu accelerators. In: Proc. International Conference on Computer Design (CDES'11). pp. 83–89. No. CDE4469, CSREA, Las Vegas, USA (18-21 July 2011)

[8] Johnson, M.G.B., Playne, D.P., Hawick, K.A.: Data-parallelism and gpus for lattice gas fluid simulations. In: Proc. International Conference on Parallel and Distributed Processing Techniques and Applications (PDPTA'10). pp. 210–216. CSREA, Las Vegas, USA (12-15 July 2010), pDP4521

[9] K.Srinivas, C.A.J.Fletcher: Computational Techniques for Fluid Dynamics. Springer Series in Computational Physics, Springer-Verlag (1992), a Solutions Manual

[10] Leist, A., Playne, D.P., Hawick, K.A.: Exploiting Graphical Processing Units for Data-Parallel Scientific Applications. Concurrency and Computation: Practice and Experience 21(18), 2400–2437 (25 December 2009), CSTN-065

[11] Luebke, D., Humphreys, G.: How gpus work. Computer pp. 96–100 (February 2007)

[12] NVIDIA® Corporation: NVIDIA CUDA C Programming Guide Version 4.1 (2011), `http://www.nvidia.com/` (last accessed April 2012)

[13] Playne, D.P., Hawick, K.A.: Comparison of GPU Architectures for Asynchronous Communication with Finite-Differencing Applications. Concurrency and Computation: Practice and Experience (CCPE) Online, 1–11 (7 April 2011), `http://onlinelibrary.wiley.com/doi/10.1002/cpe.1726/abstract`

[14] Playne, D.P., Hawick, K.A.: Classical mechanical hard-core particles simulated in a rigid enclosure using multi-gpu systems. In: Proc. Int. Conf. on Parallel and Distributed Processing Techniques and Applications (PDPTA'12). pp. 76–82. CSREA, Las Vegas, USA (16-19 July 2012)

[15] Playne, D.P., Johnson, M.G.B., Hawick, K.A.: Benchmarking GPU Devices with N-Body Simulations. In: Proc. 2009 International Conference on Computer Design (CDES 09) July, Las Vegas, USA. pp. 150–156. WorldComp, Las Vegas, USA (13-16 July 2009)

[16] Stone, J.E., Gohara, D., Guochun, S.: Opencl: A parallel programming standard for heterogeneous computing systems. Computing in Science & Engineering 12(3), 66–73 (May-June 2010)

[17] TOP500.org: TOP 500 Supercomputer Sites. `http://www.top500.org/`, last accessed November 2010

[18] Tritton, D.: Physical Fluid Dynamics. Clarendon Press, 2 edn. (1988)

[19] Zaspel, P., Griebel, M.: Solving incompressible two-phase flows on multi-gpu clusters. Computers & Fluids In press, 1–9 (2012)

Performance Measures of an Implementation of a Parallel Compiler

Deepa. Komathukattil[1], **Roger. Eggen**[1], **Sanjay. P. Ahuja**[1] **and Behrooz. Seyed. Abbassi**[1]
[1]Computing and Information Sciences, University of North Florida, Jacksonville, FL, USA

Abstract - *Parallel programming is prevalent in every field mainly to speed up computation. Advancements in multiprocessor technology fuel this trend toward parallel programming. However, modern compilers are still largely single threaded and do not take advantage of the machine resources available to them. A good deal of research has been reported on compilers that add parallel constructs to the programs they are compiling, enabling programs to exploit parallelism at run time. Auto parallelization of loops by a compiler is one such example. Parallelizing the compilation process itself has received less attention.*

Parallelization brings along with it issues like synchronization and communication overhead. In the semantic analysis phase of a compiler, these issues are of particular relevance during the construction of the symbol table. This paper presents an approach to parallelizing program compilation during the semantic analysis phase. The parallel compiler developed here augments the work done formerly on a concurrent compiler developed at the University of Toronto. The performance speedup obtained using the parallel compiler is evaluated using a shared memory multiprocessor and a distributed Beowulf cluster.

Keywords: Parallel processing, Compilers, Parsing, Shared memory, Distributed processing.

1 Introduction

A compiler translates a program written in one language into an equivalent program written in its target language [1]. The target language can be machine code or intermediate code. Research continues to this day towards generating efficient machine code. Figure 1 illustrates the different phases of a compiler. Every phase in the compiler plays a distinct role. The scanner also called a lexical analyzer breaks the source code into atomic units of the language called tokens. The parser performs syntax analysis on the tokens provided by the scanner. It verifies that the source code conforms to the syntactic structure defined by the grammar of the language. The semantic analysis phase verifies that the source code has meaning. In this phase, the compiler typically enters information about the data types, scopes and other attributes associated with identifiers into the symbol table. This information guides the semantic analysis phase. In the optimizer phase, the compiler may include code improvements or optimizations to the source code.

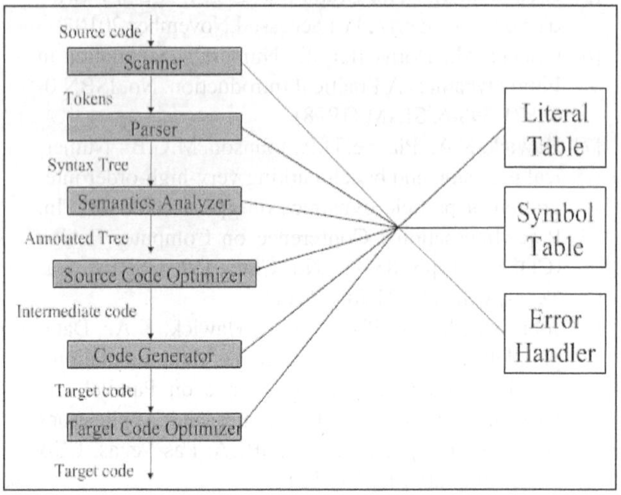

Figure 1: Phases of a Compiler [1]

Compilation of large programs could take a substantial amount of time. With the availability of multi core processors, parallel computing is emerging as a prevalent computing paradigm. Modern compilers are now capable of applying optimizations that produce highly efficient code targeted for multiprocessors. The industry focus is largely on producing optimizing compilers that add parallel constructs to the programs, therefore allowing the developers of the code to be oblivious of the underlying machine architecture. However, the compilation process itself is far from optimized. Adding parallel constructs to the program can affect the overall time needed for compilation. Parallelizing the different phases in the compiler will allow the compiler to employ more time consuming optimizations. Although compilation in parallel sounds promising, achieving overall speedup, efficiency and ease of implementation has been an elusive research goal to date.

Seshadri and Wortman [7] propose various techniques for parallelizing the semantic analysis phase. The techniques used in [7] are discussed in further detail in section 2.1. The present study enhances the work done in [7] and proposes a new technique for parallelizing the semantic analysis phase. Lexical analysis and code generation appear to be easily parallelizable as compared to semantic analysis [3, 5]. The parsing technique used in the proposed parallel compiler is top down recursive descent parsing. The compiler performance is evaluated on two different computer hardware architectures: a shared memory multiprocessor architecture and a Beowulf cluster.

Section 2 summarizes related previous work on parallel parsing and compiling. Section 3 discusses some of the implementation issues faced when designing a parallel compiler. The technique used for concurrent semantic analysis is discussed in section 4. The host environments used to evaluate the performance of the parallel compiler are discussed in section 5. Section 6 evaluates the performance metrics obtained for the parallel compiler and the speedup attained with the parallel version as compared to the sequential version of the compiler. Speedup is measured as a ratio of execution time of the sequential algorithm to the execution time of the parallel algorithm.

2 Related Work

The work of Seshadri and Wortman [7] discussed in section 2.1 is chosen as the primary reference in view of the fact that it is also trying to solve the same problem; achieving parallelism in the semantic analysis phase. In addition, the authors present a well-structured analysis of the problem at hand.

2.1 Parallelizing the Semantic Analysis Phase

The concurrent compiler developed at the University of Toronto [6, 9] takes the approach of applying parallelism in the semantic analysis phase of compilation. The compiler is built for source languages that require identifiers to be declared before they are referenced. The lexical analysis stage is sequential and is enhanced to recognize structural boundaries and split the source code into blocks for further processing. Scope boundaries determine parallel blocks. Some of the major challenges encountered in this approach were the construction of the symbol table and error reporting. The symbol table would have to be protected by mutual exclusion mechanisms to prevent simultaneous writes to the table. This could result in a lot of time spent by a process just waiting to get a lock on the symbol table and consequently slow down processing. Moreover, the symbol table lookup operations for identifiers had to take into account that the tables could be incomplete. Because of concurrent processing, the declaration of an identifier might not be processed before the identifier is used. It is not possible to know at this point if the declaration does exist and will be processed subsequently. The authors term this scenario as the "doesn't know yet" (DKY) problem. The authors [7] propose the following three strategies for dealing with the DKY problem.

2.1.1 DKY Avoidance

In this approach, parent scopes are processed before any child scopes resulting in simplified symbol table management. If an identifier declaration is not found while performing a symbol table lookup then it is safe for the compiler to flag it as an error. However, this strategy can affect parallel processing. The amount of parallelism achieved would heavily depend on the structure of the program being compiled.

2.1.2 DKY Handling

In this approach, DKYs are allowed to occur; the process encountering the DKY is suspended until another process resolves the DKY. This complicates and slows down symbol table operations.

2.1.3 Hybrid Approach

Semantic analysis is split into two phases. In the first phase, all the declarations in the program are processed and the symbol table is constructed from this information. In the second phase, statements of the program are processed. This eliminates any synchronization issues in the second phase and simplifies the compiler algorithm used for parallelism. However, this approach requires an extra parse of the program.

Experimental results show that performance of all three approaches was alike. The performance difference between DKY handling and DKY avoidance was small due to significant identifier cross usage between scopes. Though expected, the hybrid approach did not outperform the other two approaches. The compiler was built for Modula-2+. Declaration processing in Modula-2+ took more time than statement processing and hence the hybrid approach did not achieve a significant speedup over the other approaches. The average speedup factor for the above three approaches was approximately 2.5.

2.2 Parallelizing the Lexical Analysis Phase

G. Srikanth [8] and Kumar *et al.* [3] parallelize the lexical analyzer's scanning and tokenizing phases. Aho-Corasick is used for pattern matching because of its high-speed string search capabilities. In order to split the input, a static block size is first determined based on the input file size. Based on this static block size, the input file is then split into dynamic blocks using the newline character as a delimiter. These blocks are processed in parallel. A 50% reduction in execution time was observed as compared to the sequential version.

2.3 Parallelizing the Code Generator

Gross *et al.* explored parallelism in the optimization and code generation phases of compilation [2]. The structure of the programming language used as an input to the compiler consists of a high-level module. This module can contain one or more sections. Sections in turn can contain one or more functions that constitute a unit of work. Parallelism is achieved by spinning off processes for each section in the program. Processes communicate via messages, as there is no global shared memory involved in the host architecture. Experiments show a speedup factor ranging from three to six over that of the sequential version of their compiler.

3 Implementation Issues

The challenge with parallelizing the semantic analysis phase is symbol table creation and management. The semantic analysis phase accesses the symbol table frequently to perform additions, deletions and read operations. It is critical for these operations to be efficient and performed in near constant time. As with any kind of parallelism that involves a shared data structure, concurrency and synchronization problems could negate any performance benefit attained.

The traditional compiler algorithms for sequential compilers ensure that the outer scopes are built and that declarations are added to the symbol table before the processing of the inner scopes begin and before these declarations get used. This makes error reporting straightforward because the compiler can flag an error when encountering an identifier not found in the symbol table. A parallel compiler will have to take into account that the outer scope processing might not have completed while the inner scope is processed. The compiler will have to defer error reporting until all related scopes are processed.

4 Parallel Compiler Design

The source program is divided into multiple parallel units such that each unit can be processed and compiled in parallel. The approach for data partitioning used in the present study is the same as the one used in [7]. Scope or function boundaries are used to partition data. This approach to partitioning reduces the dependency between processes and can save some expensive communication between processes.

The parallel compiler is implemented using the Master-Worker design pattern. A Master-Worker design pattern allows identical computations to be performed in parallel. Figure 2 demonstrates the master worker pattern.

4.1 Master

The main process invoked when processing begins is the master. The master is responsible for lexical, syntax and semantic analysis as well as intermediate code generation for all global variables and function declarations. The master does not analyze the function body itself. The master first invokes lexical analysis on the input file specified. During the lexical analysis phase, the master looks for any tokens that indicate the start of a function. If the master finds a function declaration, it invokes a worker and passes the file pointer handle that holds the start of the function to the worker. The master then skips to the end of the function and continues with lexical analysis on the rest of the file, invoking workers when needed. A thread pool dictates how many workers can be active at a time.

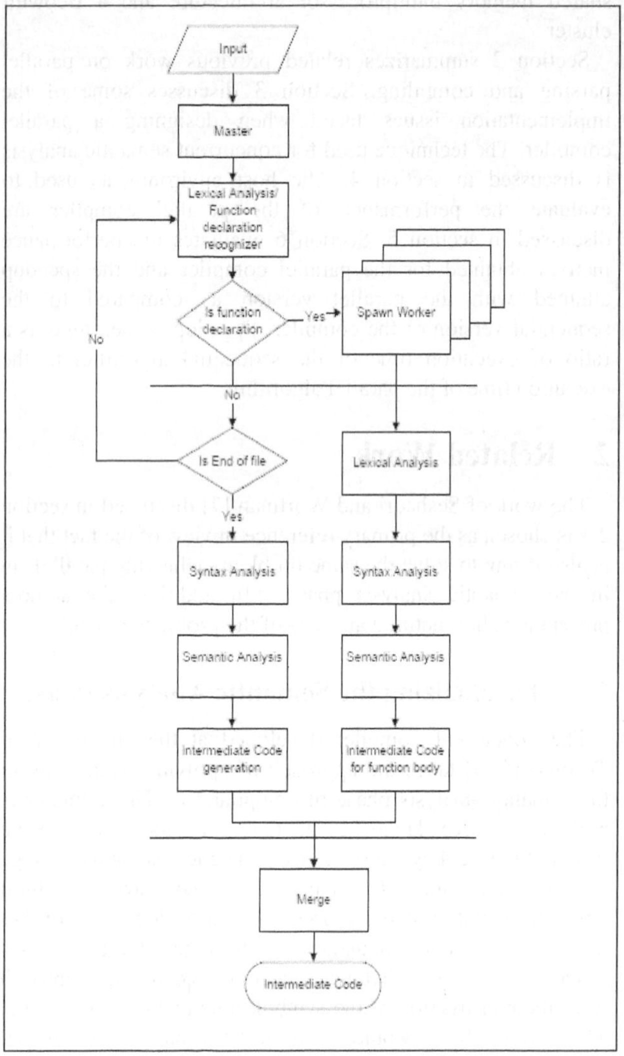

Figure 2: Parallel Compiler Structure

Once the master is done with the lexical analysis stage, it continues with syntax analysis, semantic analysis and intermediate code generation. In the semantic analysis phase, the master builds the symbol table referred to as the master symbol table. The master symbol table contains all global declarations. The master waits for all workers to complete their processing. It then validates and combines the outputs from all workers.

4.2 Worker

The worker is responsible for lexical, syntax and semantic analysis as well as intermediate code generation for the function body. The worker first invokes lexical analysis on the function body. It stops its lexical analysis when it finds the end of function. When the worker has enough information about the attributes of the function that it is processing, it sends an update message to the master with this information. Attributes of a function include its return type, number of arguments and the data type of those arguments. The master updates its symbol table with this information so that the function declaration is available for use by other workers. This is the only scenario in which the worker sends an identifier over to the master so that the function declaration can be added to the master symbol table.

In the semantic analysis phase, the worker keeps track of any DKY's. When the worker encounters an identifier with a DKY, the worker marks that identifier as a dummy and adds it to a dummy symbol table. As processing continues, the worker starts guessing the attributes related to the dummy identifier. The logic behind the guesswork is to assign values to the identifier that will avoid a compile error at that point in time. For example, consider that the worker comes across a statement as below:

SUM = ADD(2,3);

Supposing the worker did not find the declaration of the identifier SUM in the master symbol table. It first adds SUM to the dummy symbol table. In order for the above statement to not throw a compile error, the type of SUM needs to be the same as the return type of the function ADD. Two scenarios are possible here: ADD is found in the master symbol table, or ADD also had a DKY. If ADD is found in the master symbol table, the worker assigns the return type of function ADD to the data type of SUM. It stores this information in the dummy symbol table. If ADD had a DKY, the worker cannot deduce any information about the data type of SUM. In this case, it stores the fact that SUM and ADD are related by type. The parser can deduce this information from the order of parsing inherent in a recursive descent parser. Information about identifiers related by type is stored in a related identifiers list.

For future lookups of the same identifier by the same worker, first the master symbol table will be searched and then the dummy symbol table. If the master did process the identifier by this point in time, the entry from the master symbol table is retrieved. The entry from the dummy symbol table will be retrieved only if the master has not processed the identifier yet. The dummy symbol table is local to the worker; the master symbol table is never updated with the information from the dummy symbol table. When the worker has finished processing its block, it hands the intermediate code it generated along with the dummy symbol table back to the master. If a related identifiers list was created during processing, that list is also sent back to the master.

When all workers have finished processing their respective functions, the master has all the information necessary in its master symbol table to validate the results from the workers. Validation includes verifying that any identifiers with DKY's are in fact present in the master symbol table. In addition, any information that was guessed by the workers is validated against the entry in the master symbol table. If there is a disparity between the guessed attributes and the attributes found in the master symbol table, the identifier is flagged as an error. Consider the previous statement:

SUM = ADD (2, 3);

Let us assume that SUM is of type integer and return type of ADD is a float. If SUM had a DKY and ADD did not have a DKY, the worker would have added SUM to the dummy symbol table and assigned float as its type. When the master is validating the results from the workers, it finds a conflict between the declaration for SUM in the dummy symbol table and the master symbol table and reports the conflict as an error. If SUM and ADD both had a DKY, they would be added to the related identifiers list. When examining this related identifiers list, the master would catch the fact that SUM and ADD have different types.

Creating dummy identifiers and guessing their attributes reduces the overhead involved with inter-process communication. This approach of having a separate master symbol table and individual worker symbol tables drastically minimizes the amount of concurrent writes to the symbol table.

5 Host Environment

The parallel compiler was run on two different host systems to evaluate which computer architecture would suit the program better. Following are the specifications for the two systems.

5.1 Uranus

Uranus is a thirteen-node Beowulf cluster with Gigabit Ethernet network. All nodes are made up of 2.83GHz Intel Xeon processor. On this distributed Uranus cluster, communication between the master and the workers was achieved using Java's remote method invocation (RMI) interface. In order to run the tests the workers are first started on the remote nodes. The parallel compiler is then invoked which in turn invokes the master.

5.2 Atlas

Atlas is a shared memory multiprocessor machine. It has a Quad Quad-Core Intel Xeon processor with a total of 64 threads running at 2.00 GHz along with 128 GB RAM. In order to take advantage of the shared memory system in Atlas two versions of the program were created. The first version does not use any RMI. The master, at runtime, first creates and starts workers and then invokes them with tasks. This program is referred to as the Atlas program. Since the master and workers run on the same Java Virtual Machine (JVM), they can easily take advantage of the shared memory system provided by Atlas. In the second version, the workers are first started and initialized before the compiler is invoked. The master does not create or initialize the workers. This is similar to the program developed for Uranus in 5.1. It uses RMI for communicating between the master and the workers. This program is referred to as the Atlas RMI program.

Theoretically, both the versions above have their advantages and disadvantages. In the Atlas version, the workers have the advantage that their copy of the master symbol table is always current since the master symbol table is a shared data structure. This should lead to fewer DKY's. The disadvantage though is that the workers have to go through initialization every single time the program runs. This is because the master creates and initializes the workers. This initialization time adds to the overall response time of the compiler. On the contrary, the response time for the Atlas RMI program will not be dependent on the time it takes to initialize workers. However, since the workers and the master do not run on the same JVM, they communicate with each other using RMI. In this case, the master symbol table becomes distributed.

6 Results

Compiling a program, whose size is measured in KLOC (Thousand Lines of Code), can take a significant amount of time on a traditional sequential compiler. Relatively smaller programs might not benefit from parallel compilation. Ideally, the speedup in compilation time should be n where n is the number of processors involved in compilation. Linear speedup would be the ideal goal, but probably overly optimistic. The overhead associated with communication between multiple processes can prevent linear speedup. The implementation overhead can also contribute to this reduction in performance. In addition, the programming style used in the input program can negatively affect the execution times.

6.1 Performance Results

The test bed comprises of input programs with different sizes and different programming styles. This includes programs that have a lot of identifier cross usage between scopes resulting in DKY's. The sequential response time in the following graphs is represented by the value shown in the graphs when the number of parallel threads is equal to one. Figure 3 shows the response time of the parallel compiler for a relatively large program with ten thousand lines of code. The parallel response times are significantly smaller than the sequential response times.

The speedup obtained largely depends on the number of functions in the input and on the size of these functions. For an input program that has many small functions in it, the overhead of delegating each of these functions to the workers proves to be costly. This overhead can decrease the speedup obtained.

Scheduling of tasks and processor assignment are good candidates for improvement. Currently, a simple first come first serve strategy is used to schedule tasks on different processors. As discussed previously, if the size of the function is small, parallel execution could take more time as compared to its sequential counterpart. A better approach would be to group together all the small functions and process them together using one processor.

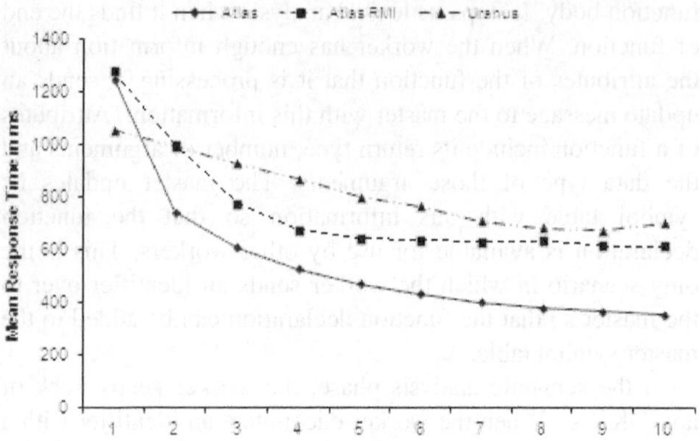

Figure 3: Response times for 10000 LOC

6.2 Performance Comparison

For smaller programs, namely programs in the range of 500 lines of code, the Atlas RMI program performs better than the Atlas program. Figure 4 shows a consolidated view of performance of all three programs on an input with 500 lines of code.

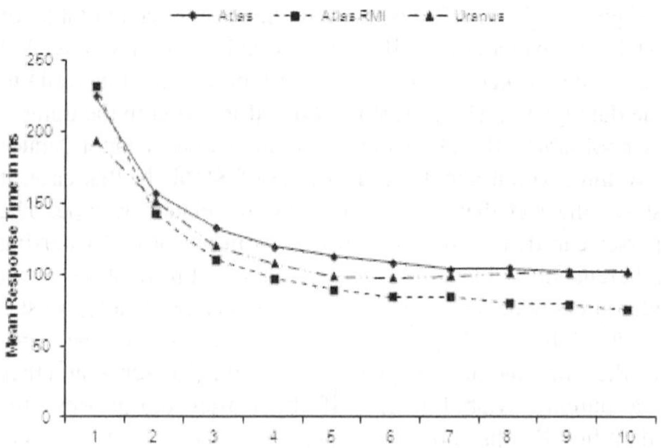

Figure 4: Comparison of response times for 500 LOC

As discussed in section 5.2, the Atlas program does not initialize workers in advance. The time taken to initialize workers in the Atlas program contributes towards the total response time of the program. For smaller programs, this initialization time results in a significant addition to the overall response time and hence the Atlas RMI program performs better than the Atlas program.

In comparison, as the size of the program increases the initialization time of workers is negligible compared to the time spent on remote method invocations. Hence, for larger programs the Atlas program performs better than the Atlas RMI program. Figure 5 shows the performance of all three programs on an input with 5000 lines of code.

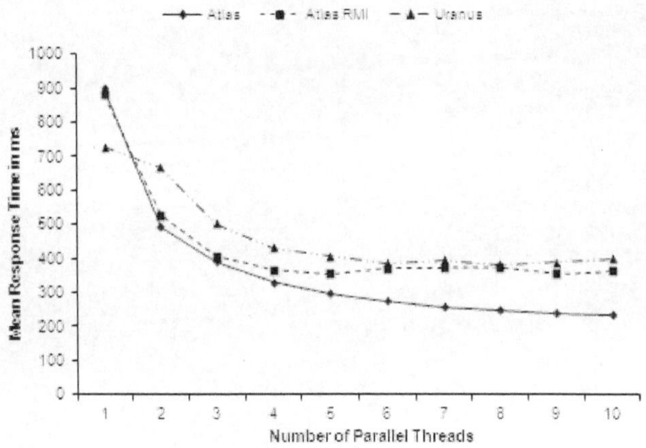

Figure 5: Comparison of response times for 5000 LOC

The sequential response time for an input of any given size on Uranus is better than the sequential response time for the Atlas programs. The same cannot be said for the parallel response times. The programs for Uranus and Atlas RMI are the same. Both initialize workers in advance and the master and workers communicate using RMI. However, the speedup obtained using Atlas RMI is marginally better than that obtained using Uranus. This is true for inputs of any given size.

6.3 DKY versus No DKY

During execution of the parallel compiler, if any of the parallel threads encounter a DKY situation they guess the attributes of the identifier and move on. Workers add these attributes along with their guess information to a list. Depending on the style of programming, there could be a sizeable amount of DKY attributes in this list. The master has to compare this list with the master symbol table to uncover any errors. In order to evaluate the overhead introduced by this validation, a comparison was made between the response times obtained by an input with no DKY versus response times obtained from the same input program written such that there would be many DKY identifiers.

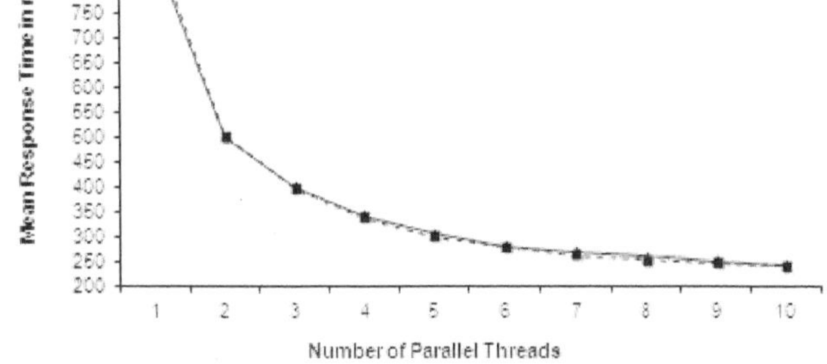

Figure 6: DKY versus No DKY for Atlas

Figure 6 demonstrates the results obtained from this comparison using an input with 5000 lines of code for Atlas. The results show that the overhead introduced by this validation is negligible.

7 Conclusion

Improving the speed of the first four phases of compilation allows the compiler to apply more time-consuming optimizations. Substantial improvements in compilation time can be achieved using concurrency. On the parallel compiler using 10 parallel processors, the speedup achieved was 3 for smaller programs and 3.5 for larger programs. As expected, the implementation overhead prevented linear speedup.

The most significant contribution made here is the strategy of making use of the parsing technique itself to deal with symbol table management. The natural order of parsing in a recursive descent parser guides this strategy. This guides the semantic analysis phase eliminating the need for blocking or suspending threads. It also eliminates the need for an extra parse of the program. This addresses the limitations of the approaches used in [7]. Significant identifier cross usage in the program does not affect the speedup obtained as shown in section 6.3. The technique used for splitting the program and parallel processing of individual functions neither introduced nor masked any syntax or semantic errors.

This research also compares the implementation of the parallel compiler on two different host environments namely a thirteen-node distributed Beowulf cluster and a shared memory multiprocessor machine. The parallel compiler performs best on the shared memory multiprocessor machine.

8 References

[1] Kenneth. C. Louden. Compiler Construction Principles and Practice, Publication Date: January 24, 1997, Edition 1.

[2] T. Gross, A. Sobel, and M. Zolg. "Parallel compilation for a parallel machine," In Proceedings of the ACM SIGPLAN 1989 Conference on Programming language design and implementation (PLDI '89), ACM, 91-100.

[3] P.J.Satish Kumar , M. Rajesh Khanna, H. Shine and S. Arun. "Implementing High Performance Lexical Analyzer using CELL Broadband Engine Processor," International Journal of Engineering Science and Technology, vol. 3, pp. 6907-6913, 2011.

[4] J. Cohen and S. Kolodner. "Estimating the Speedup in Parallel Parsing,", IEEE Transactions on Software Engineering, vol. SE-11, pp. 114-124, 1985.

[5] D. Sarkar and N. Deo. "Estimating the Speedup in Parallel Parsing," IEEE Transactions on Software Engineering, vol. 16, no. 7, pp. 677-683, July 1990.

[6] V. Seshadri, S. Weber, D. B. Wortman, C. P. Yu, and I. Small. "Semantic analysis in a concurrent compiler," In Proceedings of the ACM SIGPLAN 1988 conference on Programming Language design and Implementation (PLDI '88), ACM, New York, NY, USA, 233-240.

[7] V. Seshadri and D. B. Wortman. "An investigation into concurrent semantic analysis," Softw. Pract. Exper. 21, 12 (December 1991), 1323-1348.

[8] G. U. Srikanth. "Parallel lexical analyzer on the cell processor," in Secure Software Integration and Reliability Improvement Companion (SSIRI-C), 2010 Fourth International Conference on, 2010, pp. 28-29.

[9] David B. Wortman and Michael D. Junkin. "A concurrent compiler for Modula-2+," In Proceedings of the ACM SIGPLAN 1992 conference on Programming language design and implementation (PLDI '92), ACM, New York, NY, USA, 68-81.

SDD: Selective De-Duplication with Index by File Size for Primary File Servers

Hitoshi Kamei[1], Tomonori Esaka[1], Satoru Kishimoto[1], Takayuki Fukatani[2], Takaki Nakamura[3] ,and Norihisa Komoda[4]
[1]Hitachi, Ltd., Yokohama, Kanagawa, Japan
[2]Hitachi Europe Ltd., Bracknell, Berkshire, United Kingdom
[3]Tohoku University, Sendai, Miyagi, Japan
[4]Osaka University, Suita, Osaka, Japan

Abstract – *We propose a method, called SDD, for improving performance of file level de-duplication for primary file servers. The processing time of the de-duplication is increasing because more and more files are being stored in the servers, therefore the de-duplication process cannot finish during assigned time. According to previous studies, large files stored in the servers are dominant in terms of the storage space, while rather small files are dominant in terms of file count. SDD sets a file size threshold to narrow down target files. We develop and evaluate a prototype system using SDD, which increases the throughput of the de-duplication processes.*

Keywords: De-duplication, File Server, File System, Indexing

1 Introduction

In order to share information in nowadays digital communications world, an increasing number of files are being stored in primary file servers. This game change concerns mostly server administrators, who are responsible for managing infra-structures and cost. One of the common solutions for this problem is the use of de-duplication [1]. De-duplication finds redundant data from file system volumes and eliminates them, thus reducing storage foot-print. Examples of products that use de-duplication are EMC Data Domain [1] [2] and NetApp's A-SIS [3].

We can classify de-duplication in terms of its abstraction level, i.e., block level de-duplication [2] or file level de-duplication [4]. Block level de-duplication detects duplicate datasets in the entire file system volume by using fixed or variable block sizes, while file level de-duplication detects duplicate files. Typically, block level de-duplication leads to a more effective redundancy elimination, but imposes a larger management overhead to the system. Therefore, file level de-duplication is usually considered to be more suitable for primary file servers, where latency and throughput are highly prioritized when compared to storage space availability.

De-duplication is commonly executed during low-usage periods, such as on weekends or in the night. However, the amount of files stored in servers is rapidly growing, and problems arise when de-duplication processes are unable to finish during assigned periods. This scenario has pointed out the need for better file level de-duplication techniques.

In this paper we present the selective de-duplication method (SDD) for improving file level de-duplication performance on primary file servers. In a nutshell, the proposed method sets a threshold that represents the minimum file size considered for de-duplication.

This paper is organized as follows. Section II presents the state-of-art method on file level de-duplication and current challenges. Section III describes the SDD method. Section IV presents our prototype system. Section V reviews related work, and Section VI summarizes our work and draws conclusions.

2 File level de-duplication and challenges

This section summarizes file level de-duplication and the challenges of using them on primary file servers.

2.1 Summary of file level de-duplication

File level de-duplication consist of a detection process and a deletion process.

1) Detection process

The detection process finds files with identical "bodies", which are referred to later as 'duplicated files'. Generally, duplicated files can be found by referring to their hash values. Conventional methods calculate the files' hash values by hash functions, such as SHA-1 or SHA-256, when they are stored on the server. Moreover, hash values are recalculated and updated if the files are modified. To detect duplicated files, the detection process searches for identical hash value on a registry or database.

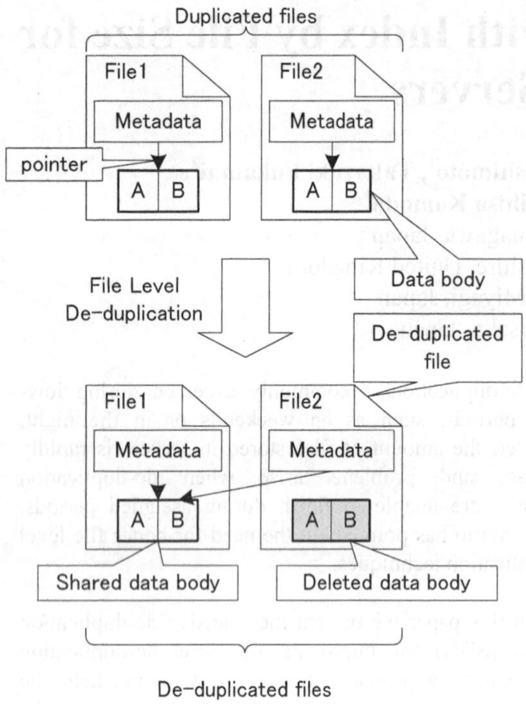

Fig. 1. Example of deletion process. The deletion process deletes all duplicated data bodies except one and sets a pointer to it in the de-duplicated files

This is an effective method for detecting files that have the same data. However, there is a very low probability that distinct file bodies present the same hash values. Therefore, for the sake of certainty, some file servers compare files that have the same hash value byte-by-byte.

2) Deletion process

The deletion process selects one of the duplicated file, possibly randomly, and deletes the bodies of the other ones.

Figure 1 shows an example of the deletion process. There are two duplicated files, File1 and File2, selected by the detection process described above. These files comprise a metadata header and a data body, and the metadata header points to the data body. The deletion process deletes the data body of File2 and updates File2's pointer to point to File1's data body, achieving a de-duplication ratio of 50%.

2.2 Challenges of file level de-duplication for primary file servers

Figure 2 illustrates the conventional de-duplication process and its common issues.

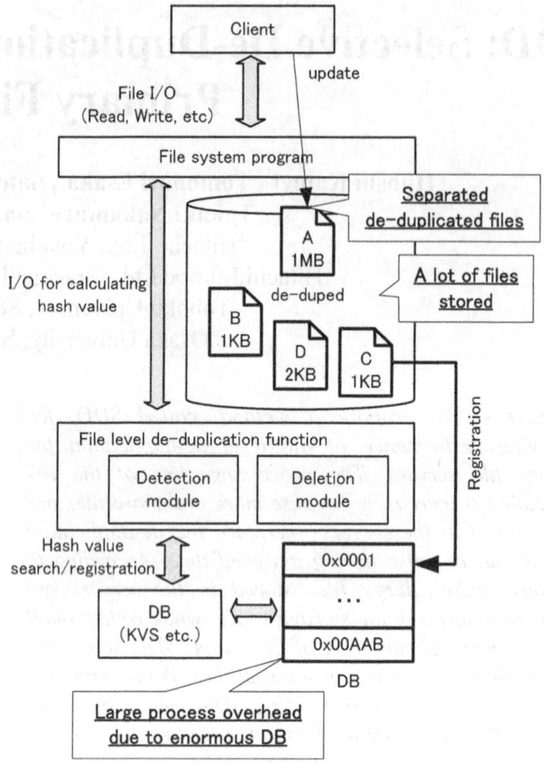

Fig. 2. Processes of conventional de-duplication and problems: Hashing all the files and updating de-duplicated files makes challenges.

One of the issues with de-duplication is that, even though file-level de-duplication tends to optimize management overhead costs when compared to block-level de-duplication, calculating hash values for every file and managing them might impose an important burden on primary file systems, where potentially millions of files may be stored [6]. Furthermore, file servers accessed by multiple users present higher operation throughput (file creation, update, deletion etc.).

Additionally and more importantly, when a de-duplicated file is modified, it has to be separated from its "set", which might involve extensive data copying, even for small modifications.

3 Proposed method for reducing file level de-duplication cost

Here we present the selective de-duplication method, or SDD, for reducing the management cost of file level de-duplication on primary file servers.

3.1 Policies for reducing costs

The SDD method sets two policies, as described below.

1) SDD Policy 1: file size

Matsumoto et al. [5] concluded that files of about 1KB dominate file systems in terms of the number of files; however, the file system volumes also likely to have a significant number of large files that are over 1MB. Meanwhile, Mayer et al. [6] described that a few large files might use a large amount of a file system volume. Therefore we can process most of the data in file system volumes by handling large files. Accordingly, we set a threshold on the minimum file size that is to be processed in order to narrow down target files.

Meanwhile, if files to be processed are different in size, it means they cannot be de-duplicated. So by checking only the same sized files, we can avoid detection overheads on files that absolutely cannot be de-duplicated.

2) SDD Policy 2: file age

Mayer et al. [6] concluded that most files are updated shortly after being created. Hence, if these files are selected for de-duplication, they may soon be separated again. Hence, one can prevent such files from being de-duplicated by referring to their last modification time.

3.2 Methodology

The SDD method can be described by three key points.

1) Using search engine to find large files

The proposed method employs a search engine to find such files, using the policies described above. The search engine crawls through the file system, and when it finds files that matches the policy, it adds it to a list. After crawling, it executes the de-duplication process over the selected files.

2) Sharing of data body between de-duplicated files

As opposed to conventional implementations of de-duplication processes [7], the SDD method proposes the separation of the data body from the de-duplicated files altogether. The separated body, referred to as a shared file, or SF, is a special-purpose hidden file of the file system and works as a base reference where the de-duplicated files metadata point to.

As a consequence, when a de-duplicated file is updated, it keeps the reference to the SF plus the differential data that has been modified, as in a "diff" process. Figure 3 illustrates this scenario.

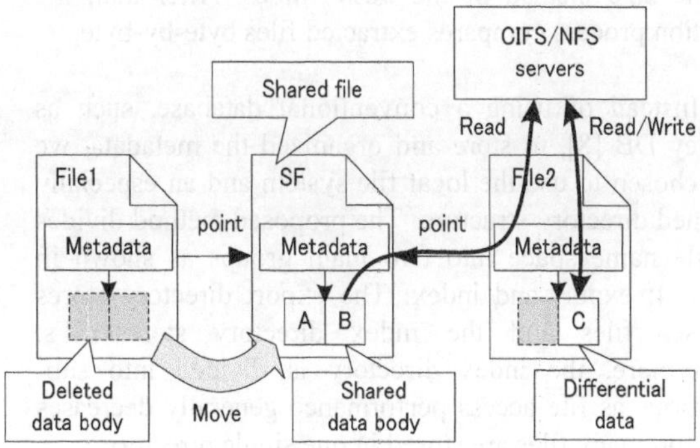

Fig. 3. Sharing data body between two de-duplicated files. De-duplicated files point to a shared data file. The de-duplicated files store differential data in their data body

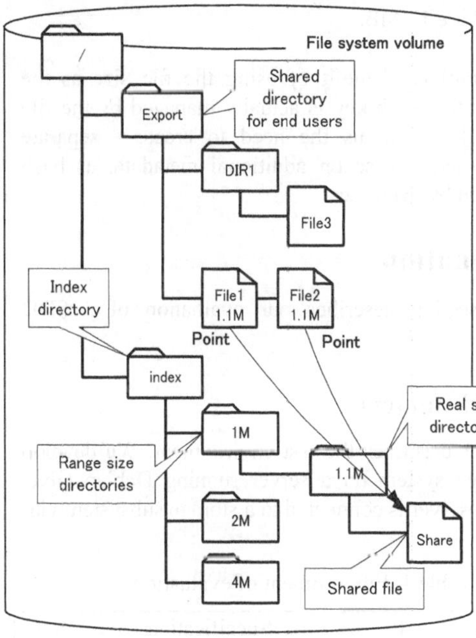

Fig. 4. The name space in the file system volume is divided into two parts. The "export" directory has files stored by end users and the "index" directory stores SFs. De-duplicated files in the export directory point to the shared file in the index directory

3) Using file size as a database key

The proposed method registers the file size as a database key instead of its hash value. Therefore, it can narrow down the files to be de-duplicated by referring to the file size instead of the hash values. After that, the detection process compares extracted files byte-by-byte.

Instead of using a conventional database, such as Berkley DB [8], to store and organized the metadata, we have chosen to use the local file system and an especially designed directory structure. The proposed method divides the file name space into two main groups as shown in Figure 4: export and index. The export directory stores end-user files and the index directory stores SFs. Furthermore, the index directory is divided into sub-directories as file access performance generally decreases when too many files are stored in one single directory.

We also employ a hierarchical sub-directory division in which SFs are distributed to directories reserved to its specific file size. For example, the 1MB sub-directory has sub-directories ranging from 1MB to (2MB - 1B), as depicted in Figure 4. Moreover, the 1.1MB sub-directory has SFs that are 1.1MB.

An additional benefit of using the file size as the basic key is that such key is actually managed by the file system itself, saving us the need to create a separate indexing structure base on additional metadata, as hash tags managed by databases.

4 Evaluation

This section describes our evaluation of a SDD prototype.

4.1 Environment

Table 1 describes the test environment. We develop the prototype system on a server running Debian GNU /Linux. The server is connected to a storage subsystem via Fibre Channel. The dataset is stored in the storage subsystem. The dataset is about 490GB and have about 1.14 million files.

Table 1 Environment of evaluation

Item	Specification
CPU	Intel® Xeon(TM) CPU 3.60GHz
Memory	8GB
Internal HDD (for OS)	SEAGATE ST373207LC, 73.4 GB
Operating System	Debian GNU/Linux, Linux 2.6.30.1 w/ file level de-duplication function
File System	XFS w/ file level de-duplication function
Storage Subsystem (volume)	HDD: 75GB, RAID Level: 1+0, Connection: Fibre Channel, One LV is created by LVM. The size of LV is 590GB.
Dataset characteristics	Office data
Size of dataset	490GB

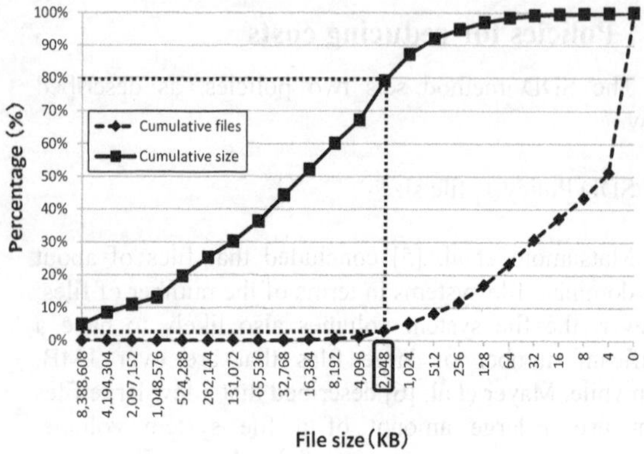

Fig. 5. Characteristics of our dataset. The over 2MB files occupy our dataset about 80% in terms of the capacity; however; the files are less than 5% in terms of the number of files

Figure 5 shows the main characteristics of our dataset. The x-axis represents the maximum file size in a decreasing log scale. The solid line graph is the percentage of cumulative total size. The dashed line graph shows the percentage of the cumulative number of files. For example, focusing on 2MB, these graphs show the cumulative values that sum up 2MB files in terms of the total size and the number of files. These graphs show that files that are over 2MB account for 3% in terms of the number of stored files but 80% in terms of occupied capacity. Therefore, when the prototype system processes the files that are over 2MB, it includes 80% of the dataset while keeping the size of index directory small.

4.2 Results

Figure 6 shows the de-duplication performance of our prototype system. The x-axis is the threshold described in Section III in a decreasing log scale. The y-axis stands for throughput in a log scale. In this evaluation, we vary thresholds from 0B to 1GB and observe the performance. Note that when threshold is 0B, all files are processed. Figure 7 shows the storage reduction rates, also according to the threshold.

4.3 Analysis

1) De-duplication performance

When the threshold is set to 0B, the dataset can be reduced by 24.3% and throughput is 18.7 MB/s. On the other hand, when we set threshold of 128KB, the dataset can be reduced by 23.2% and throughput is 114.9 MB/s. Hence, the reduction rate reaches 98.9% in comparison to

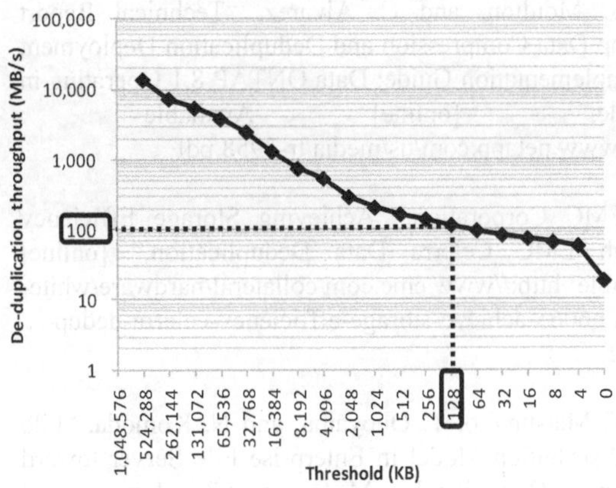

Fig. 6. De-duplication throughput of prototype system. When the threshold is set 128KB, the throughput is over 100MB/s.

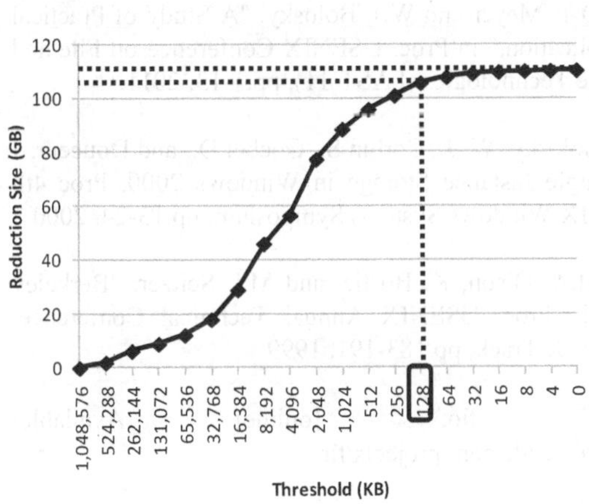

Fig. 7. Reduction size of dataset. When the threshold is set 128KB, the reduction rate reaches 98.9% of the total reduced size in our dataset.

when all the files are processed. Therefore, for our dataset, throughput of the de-duplication increases 6.1 times while keeping roughly the same reduction efficiency. Note that these results are for our dataset, which means that distinct datasets might present distinct results. The dataset we used was generated from a file server in an office environment with about 100 users.

These results show that by setting an appropriate threshold, we can achieve good throughputs and reduction rates.

2) I/O performance of de-duplication files

Figure 8 shows read I/O performance and figure 9 shows write I/O performance. We evaluate random and sequential I/O performance of partial block I/O and full block I/O by using fio[9]. Partial block I/O means accesses to file data that are less than 4KB, and full block I/O

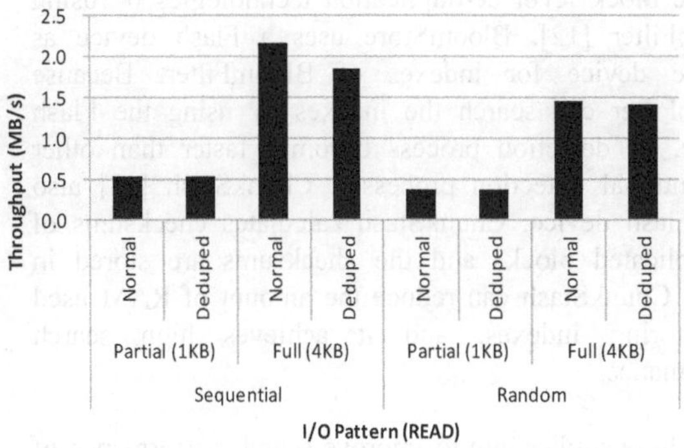

Fig. 8. Read I/O performance. The proposed method affects performance of sequential full read. The performance declines 15%. However, other read I/O patterns aren't affected.

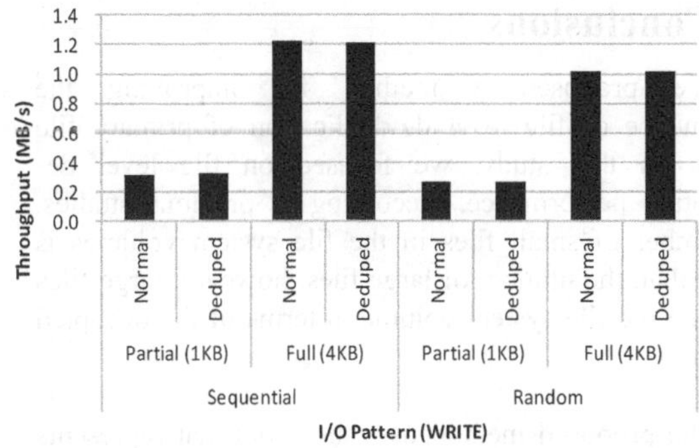

Fig. 9. Write I/O performance. In terms of write throughput, there are little overhead by the proposed method.

means access to file data that equals to 4KB. To avoid cache interferences, we delete all the cached data before every evaluation by using Drop_Caches [10] of Linux function. The file size used in this evaluation is 318KB based on the study of Mayer et al. [6].

These results show that read performance is not affected except for that of sequential file read. Performance of sequential full read, however, declines at about 15%. The reason is that read-ahead techniques don't perform well in this scenario: if there are differential data on a de-duplicated file, the read operation issues read I/O to the de-duplicated file and the corresponding SF. Meanwhile, write performance is not affected by proposed method.

5 Related work

Some other studies have aimed to reduce processing time of the de-duplication technologies. BloomStore [11] intends to improve the search performance of KVS that stores the hash values of blocks of the file system volumes for the block level de-duplication technologies by using BloomFilter [12]. BloomStore uses a Flash device as storage device for indexes of BloomFilter. Because BloomFilter can search the indexes by using the Flash device, its detection process becomes faster than other conventional detection processes. ChunkStash [13] also uses Flash device. ChunkStash calculates checksums of de-duplicated blocks and the checksums are stored in RAM. ChunkStash can reduce the amount of RAM used for storing indexes, and it achieves high search performance.

These studies aim to improve search performance of KVS to achieve high throughput of block level de-duplication technologies. That is, they don't focus on using file metadata to improve the performance of the file level de-duplication technologies.

6 Conclusions

We proposed a method for improving the performance of file level de-duplication of primary file servers. In this study, we focused on file level de-duplication performance. According to previous studies, the number of small files in the file system volumes is greater than the number of large files, however; large files dominate the file system volume in terms of the occupied amount.

The proposed method uses threshold that represents the minimum processing size and date, which allows us to discard small and recent files on which file level de-duplication would probably be inefficient. Moreover, the proposed method doesn't use a dedicated database, proposing the file name space as the storage medium. Furthermore, in order to share data, the proposed method creates files to share data and de-duplicated files point to the shared file. If the de-duplicated files are modified, SDD doesn't need to update the management information.

We implemented and evaluated a prototype system on the Debian/GNU Linux. We confirmed that SDD improved the performance of file level de-duplication. In particular, when we set 128KB as the threshold, SDD was about six times faster than it was when it processes all the stored files.

7 References

[1] B. Zhu, K. Li, and R.H. Patterson, "Avoiding the Disk Bottleneck in the Data Domain Deduplication File System," in Proc of the 6th USENIX Conference on File and Storage Technologies (FAST'08), pp.269-282., 2008

[2] "EMC Data Domain DD800 Series," [online] Available: http://www.datadomain.com.

[3] S. Moulton, and C. Alvarez, "Technical Report NetApp Data Compression and Deduplication Deployment and Implementation Guide: Data ONTAP 8.1 Operating in 7-Mode," [online] Available : http://www.netapp.com/us/media/tr-3958.pdf

[4] EMC Corporation, "Achieving Storage Efficiency through EMC Celerra Data Deduplication," [online] Available: http://www.emc.com/collateral/hardware/white-papers/h6065-achieve-storage-effficiency-celerra-dedup-wp.pdf

[5] T. Matsumoto, T. Onoyama, and N. Komoda, "File Size Distribution Model in Enterprise File Server toward Efficient Operational Management," International Conference on Systems Engineering and Engineering Management (ICSEEM'12), 2012.

[6] D.T. Meyer and W.J. Bolosky, "A Study of Practical Deduplication," in Proc. USENIX Conference on File and Storage Technologies (FAST'11), pp.1-13, 2011.

[7] Bolosky, W. J., Corbin S., Goebel D., and Douceur, J. R. :Single Instance Storage in Windows 2000, Proc 4th USENIX Windows Systems Symposium, pp.13-24, 2000.

[8] M.A. Olson, K. Bostic, and M.I. Seltzer, "Berkeley DB," in Proc. USENIX Annual Technical Conference, FREENIX Track, pp.183-191, 1999.

[9] " fio," [online] Available: http://freecode.com/projects/fio.

[10] " drop_caches," [online] Available: http://www.kernel.org/doc/Documentation/sysctl/vm.txt.

[11] G. Lu, Y.J. Nam, and D.H.C. Du, "BloomStore: Bloom-Filter based Memory-efficient Key-Value Store for Indexing of Data Deduplication on Flash," The 28th IEEE Conference on Massive Data Storage, 2012.

[12] B.H. Bloom, "Space/Time Trade-offs in Hash Coding with Allowable Errors," Communications of The ACM, pp.422-426, 1970.

[13] B. Debnath, S. Sengupta, and J. Li, "ChunkStash: Speeding up Inline Storage Deduplication using Flash Memory," in Proc. of USENIX annual technical conference, 2010.

Iterative Synthesis Techniques for Multiple-Valued Logic Functions – A Review and Comparison

Mostafa Abd-El-Barr
Department of Information Science, Kuwait University, Kuwait.

Abstract *- A number of heuristics for near optimal functional synthesis of Multi-Valued Logic (MVL) have been reported in the literature. Among the well-known heuristics is the Direct Cover algorithm (DCA). We have introduced a number of improved versions of the DCA. These include the Weighted Direct Cover (WDC), the Ordered Direct Cover (ODC), and the Fuzzy Direct Cover (FDC). In this paper, we review and compare the performance of those heuristic iterative techniques using two set of benchmarks. The first consists of 50000 randomly generated 2-variable 4-valued functions and the second consists of 50000 2-variable 5-valued functions. The average number of product terms required to synthesize a given MVL function is used as the criterion for comparison. The results obtained show that the modified iterative synthesis heuristics outperformed the DCA and that among the modified techniques the FDC produces the best results.*

Keywords: Direct-Cover algorithms (DCA), Weighted DC (WDC), Ordered DC (ODC), Fuzzified DC (FDC), non-binary digital signal processing (DSP)

1 Introduction

Digital information processing using Multiple-Valued Logic (MVL) is carried out using more than discrete logic levels. Due to technological reasons and for easy interfacing with the predominantly existing binary digital systems, 4-valued logic has been the most widely used. Recent advances in Very Large Scale Integration (VLSI) technology made it possible to fabricate more efficient 4-valued circuits using binary CMOS (Complementary Metal Oxide Semiconductor) technology [1], [5], and [7]. These circuits have shown considerable reduction both in processing time and chip area compared to their binary counterparts [1-8].

The MVL functional synthesis problem is however more complex when compared to its binary counterpart. This is because of the massive size of the MVL functional search space. Consider, for example, the case of two-variable functions. While there are only 16 2-variable binary functions there are $4^{16} = 4294967296$ 2-variable 4-valued functions. Exact minimization of MVL functions is prohibitively expensive [9]. A number of iterative heuristics for near minimal synthesis of MVL functions have been introduced see, for example, [9]-[16]. Fuzzy-based synthesis of MVL functions has also been reported in the literature [17].

An n-variable r-valued function $f(X)$ is a mapping $f : R^n \rightarrow R$, where $R = \{0,1,\cdots,r-1\}$ is a set of r logic values with $r \geq 2$ and $X = \{x_1, x_2, \cdots, x_n\}$ is a set of r-valued n variables. The followings are sample MVL logic operators.

(1) The window literal

$$ {}^a x^b = \begin{cases} (r-1) & \text{if } (a \leq x \leq b) \\ 0 & \text{otherwise} \end{cases} $$

where $a, b \in R$ and $a \leq b$

(2) *The tsum (truncated sum)*

$$ tsum(a_1, a_2, ..., a_n) = a_1 \oplus a_2 \oplus ... \oplus a_n = \begin{cases} a_1 + a_2 + ... + a_n & \text{if } a_1 + a_2 + ... + a_n < r-1 \\ r-1 & \text{otherwise} \end{cases} $$

Where $a_i \in R$ and $\oplus$ represents the truncated sum operation.

(3) The maximum (MAX) of two MVL variables

$$ MAX(x_1, x_2) = \begin{cases} x_1 & \text{if } x_1 \geq x_2 \\ x_2 & \text{otherwise} \end{cases} $$

(4) The minimum (MIN) of two MVL variables

$$ MIN(x_1, x_2) = \begin{cases} x_1 & \text{if } x_1 \leq x_2 \\ x_2 & \text{otherwise} \end{cases} $$

Fig. 1 shows an example of a 2-varaible 4-valued function. In this figure $1\bullet{}^0X_1{}^0\bullet{}^3X_2{}^3$, $2\bullet{}^0X_1{}^0\bullet{}^1X_2{}^1$ and $3\bullet{}^0X_1{}^0\bullet{}^2X_2{}^2$ are examples for minterms while $2\bullet{}^0X_1{}^1\bullet{}^1X_2{}^1$and $2\bullet{}^0X_1{}^1\bullet{}^1X_2{}^2$ are examples for *implicants*.

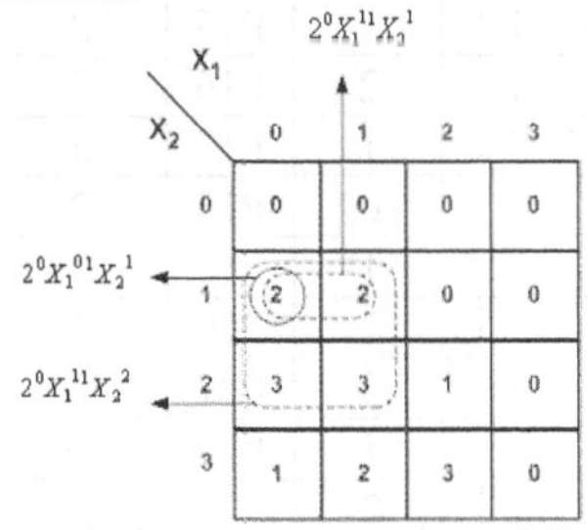

Fig. 1: A Tabular Representation of $f(X_1, X_2)$.

2 The Direct Cover Algorithm

The Direct Cover Algorithm (DCA) for synthesis of MVL functions [10]-[13] consist of the following main steps:

1. Choose a minterm (see Definition 3),
2. Identify a suitable implicant (see Definition 4) that covers the chosen minterm,

3. Obtain a reduced function by removing the identified implicant, and
4. Repeat steps 1 to 3 until no more minterms remain uncovered.

The selection of appropriate minterms and the implicants covering them play an important role in obtaining less number of product terms to cover a given function. The DCAs reported in the literature differ in the way appropriate minterms are chosen. They also differ in the way appropriate implicants are identified. Different metrics to select minterms have been proposed in the literature. We have presented a comprehensive analysis of the DCAs in [15]. The outcome of this analysis has indicated that improvements to the DCA are still possible. We have introduced three iterative-based heuristics as improvements to the DCA. These are explained below.

3 Weighted Direct Cover (WDC)

It is observed in [15] that all criteria used for selection of minterms and/or implicants have linear and monotonic function. All criteria, except for RBC and NRC, assume values greater than or equal to 0. We use the term *weight pattern* to specify the weight for each selection criterion for both minterm and implicant and that the weight should be in the set {0, 1, 2, 3}. A minterm weight pattern 112 means that $w_{CF}=1$, $w_{CFN}=1$, and $w_{IW}=2$. Combining the weight patterns for minterms with the weight patterns for implicants, we will have 4096 different patterns (P-1, P-2, ...). Representatives of different weight scenarios are examined (see Table 1). These weight patterns will be used for both minterm and implicant. In total, the number of different algorithms (because of different patterns) tested in this paper is $(24)^2 = 576$.

Table 1 : Different Weighting Scenarios.

	WM-1	WM-2	WM-3		WM-1	WM-2	WM-3
P1	0	0	1	P13	1	2	2
P2	0	1	0	P14	1	2	3
P3	0	1	1	P15	2	0	1
P4	0	1	2	P16	2	1	0
P5	0	2	1	P17	2	1	1
P6	1	0	0	P18	2	1	2
P7	1	0	1	P19	2	1	3
P8	1	0	2	P20	2	2	1
P9	1	1	0	P21	2	3	1
P10	1	1	1	P22	3	1	2
P11	1	1	2	P23	3	2	1
P12	1	2	1	P24	3	3	1

All of the 576 patterns will be tested using our benchmark. Since presenting all results from the 576 different algorithms is not practical, we only present the best 10 results (in terms of average PTs) for both 2-variable 4-valued and 2-variable 5-valued functions among the benchmarks used. Tables 2 and Table 3 show these results, respectively. The results presented in these tables show that the best result is obtained using the following pattern: for minterm, CF = 0, CFN = 1 and IW = 2 and for implicant, RBC = 1, NRC = 0 and LRZ = 0. Using this pattern (written shortly as 012-100), the average number of product terms (PTs) required to cover a given 2-variable 4-valed function is 7.24914 while it is 12.1658 in the case of a 2-variable 5-valed function.

Table 2 : The best 10 weight patterns for 2-variable 4-valued

	Minterms			Implecant			#PTs
	CF	CFN	IW	RBC	NRC	LRZ	
P1	0	1	2	1	0	0	7.2491
P2	1	2	3	1	0	0	7.2502
P3	0	0	1	2	1	3	7.2623
P4	0	1	1	1	0	0	7.2625
P5	1	2	2	1	0	0	7.2629
P6	0	0	1	2	1	2	7.2636
P7	0	0	1	3	1	2	7.2636
P8	1	1	2	1	0	0	7.2636
P9	0	0	1	2	1	1	7.2650
P10	1	2	3	2	1	0	7.2707

Table 3 : The best 10 weight patterns for 2-variable 5-valued

	Minterms			Implecant			#PTs
	CF	CFN	IW	RBC	NRC	LRZ	
P1	0	1	2	1	0	0	12.166
P2	1	2	3	1	0	0	12.175
P3	1	1	2	1	0	0	12.189
P4	1	2	2	1	0	0	12.196
P5	0	1	1	1	0	0	12.197
P6	1	1	1	1	0	0	12.208
P7	0	2	1	1	0	0	12.213
P8	1	2	1	1	0	0	12.222
P9	2	2	1	1	0	0	12.224
P10	2	3	1	1	0	0	12.229

4 Ordered Direct Cover (ODC)

According to this approach selection criteria are ordered based on a given priority [16]. There are three criteria for minterm selection. These are Smallest CF, Smallest CFN, and Smallest IW. There are three criteria for implicant selection. These are Smallest RBC, Smallest NRC, and Largest LRZ. Assume that for minterm selection we set Criterion 1 as 'Samllest CF", Criterion 2 as "Smallest CFN" and Criterion 3 as "Smallest IW" and for implicant selection we set Criterion 1 as "Samllest RBC", Criterion 2 as "Smallest NRC, and Criterion 3 as "Largest LRZ" (See Table 4). In Table 5, we summarize the different scenarios for ordering (O-1, O-2, ...) the above mentioned criteria.

The performance of the WDC algorithm is assessed through the results obtained using a benchmark consisting of 50000 randomly generated 2-variable 4-valued functions and a benchmark consisting of 50000 randomly generated 2-varaiable 5-valued functions. This assessment is presented in Section 6.

Table 4: Criteria used for ODC Algorithm.

	Criterion 1	Criterion 2	Criterion 3
Minterm	Smallest CF	Smallest CFN	Smallest IW
Implicant	Smallest RBC	Smallest NRC	Largest LRZ

Table 5: Different Order Scenario.

	Order-1	Order-2	Order-3
P1	CR1	~	~
P2	CR1	CR2	~
P3	CR1	CR3	~
P4	CR1	CR2	CR3
P5	CR1	CR2	CR3
P6	CR2	~	~
P7	CR2	CR1	~
P8	CR2	CR3	~
P9	CR2	CR1	CR3
P10	CR2	CR3	CR1
P11	CR3	~	~
P12	CR3	CR1	~
P13	CR3	CR2	~
P14	CR3	CR1	CR2
P15	CR3	CR2	CR1

We assess the performance of the ODC through the results obtained using the same benchmark used in the case of the WDC. Table 6 and Table 7 show ten orderings that give the best results for 2-variable 4-valued and 2-variable 5-valued functions, respectively.

Table 6: The best 10 results of ODC for 2-variable 4 valued

Order Pattern						#PTs
Minterm			Implicant			
Order 1	Order 2	Order 3	Order 1	Order 2	Order 3	
Smallest IW			Smallest RBC	Largest LRZ		7.20234
Smallest IW			Smallest RBC	Largest LRZ	Smallest NRC	7.20234
Smallest IW	Smallest CF		Smallest RBC	Largest LRZ		7.20248
Smallest IW	Smallest CF		Smallest RBC	Largest LRZ	Smallest NRC	7.20248
Smallest IW	Smallest CFN		Smallest RBC	Largest LRZ		7.20248
Smallest IW	Smallest CFN		Smallest RBC	Largest LRZ	Smallest NRC	7.20248
Smallest IW	Smallest CF	Smallest CFN	Smallest RBC	Largest LRZ		7.20248
Smallest IW	Smallest CF	Smallest CFN	Smallest RBC	Largest LRZ	Smallest NRC	7.20248
Smallest IW	Smallest CFN	Smallest CF	Smallest RBC	Largest LRZ		7.20248
Smallest IW	Smallest CFN	Smallest CF	Smallest RBC	Largest LRZ	Smallest NRC	7.20248

The performance of the ODC algorithm is assessed through the results obtained using a benchmark consisting of 50000 randomly generated 2-variable 4-valued functions and a benchmark consisting of 50000 randomly generated 2-varaiable 5-valued functions. This assessment is presented in Section 6.

Table 7: The best 10 results of ODC for 2-variable 5 valued

Order Pattern						#PTs
Minterm			Implicant			
Order 1	Order 2	Order 3	Order 1	Order 2	Order 3	
Smallest IW	Smallest CF		Smallest RBC	Largest LRZ		12.0682
Smallest IW	Smallest CF		Smallest RBC	Largest LRZ	Smallest NRC	12.0682
Smallest IW	Smallest CFN		Smallest RBC	Largest LRZ		12.0682
Smallest IW	Smallest CFN		Smallest RBC	Largest LRZ	Smallest NRC	12.0682
Smallest IW	Smallest CF	Smallest CFN	Smallest RBC	Largest LRZ		12.0682
Smallest IW	Smallest CF	Smallest CFN	Smallest RBC	Largest LRZ	Smallest NRC	12.0682
Smallest IW	Smallest CFN	Smallest CF	Smallest RBC	Largest LRZ		12.0682
Smallest IW	Smallest CFN	Smallest CF	Smallest RBC	Largest LRZ	Smallest NRC	12.0682
Smallest IW	Smallest CF		Smallest RBC	Largest LRZ		12.0685
Smallest IW	Smallest CF		Smallest RBC	Largest LRZ	Smallest NRC	12.0685

5 Fuzzy-based Direct Cover (FDC)

The Fuzzy Direct Cover (FDC) algorithm employs fuzzy rules to select the best minterm and the best implicant covering it [17]. A fuzzy logic rule expresses the way in which linguistic variables (objectives) are interrelated, the relationship between these objectives, and the overall function value [18]. The goal is to find a high quality solution, represented by a linguistic variable. See the next two illustrative examples.

1. ***IF*** a minterm has a good CF ***OR*** good CFN ***OR*** good IW, ***THEN*** it is a good minterm for selection.
2. ***IF*** an implicant has a good RBC ***OR*** a good LRZ ***OR*** a good NRC, ***THEN*** it is a good implicant for selection.

Our proposed Fuzzy-based Direct Cover (FZDC) algorithm employs fuzzy rules (along with preferences) to select the best set of minterm and the most appropriate implicant covering each such that the whole function is covered. The goodness of a minterm (implicant) is examined using the abovementioned fuzzy rules and preferences. Looking at these rules, it is easy to deduce that we can use the 'OR-'like operator to aggregate all decision criteria. Table 8 shows the mathematical formulae we introduced for each membership function in the minterm selection. Table 9 shows the same for implicant selection.

Efficiency of the proposed fuzzy selection process is influenced by the parameter used in fuzzy operators, i.e. the value of β in OWA operator. In addition to that, fuzzy preference rules will also impact the performance of the proposed algorithm. Since there are three criteria for each of the minterm and implicant selection, there will be additional 6 parameters to fine tuned in order to get the best performance of the algorithm. In order to obtain the best result using the proposed fuzzy-based selection criteria, the following set of experiments are conducted:

1. Experiments with different fuzzy operators
2. Experiments with parameters in fuzzy operators

Table 8: Membership functions in Min terms selection.

Minterm Selection		
Technique	Criterion	Formulated Membership Function
DM [10]	CF	$\mu_{CF} = \begin{cases} 1 & \text{if } CF=0 \\ \frac{Max_{CF} - CF}{Max_{CF}} & \text{if } 0<CF<Max_{CF} \\ 0 & \text{if otherwise} \end{cases}$
ND [8]	CFN	$\mu_{CFN} = \begin{cases} 1 & \text{if } CFN = 0 \\ \frac{Max_{CFN} - CFN}{Max_{CFN}} & \text{if } 0 < CFN < Max_{CFN} \\ 0 & \text{otherwise} \end{cases}$
BS [3]	IW	$\mu_{IW} = \begin{cases} 1 & \text{if } IW = Min_{IW} \\ \frac{Max_{IW} - IW}{Max_{IW} - Min_{IW}} & \text{if } Min_{IW} < IW < Max_{IW} \\ 0 & \text{otherwise} \end{cases}$

Table 9: Membership functions in implicant selection.

Implicant Selection		
Technique	Criterion	Formulated Membership Function
DM [10]	RBC	$\mu_{RBC} = \begin{cases} 1 & \text{if } RBC = Min_{RBC} \\ \frac{MAX_{RBC} - RBC}{Max_{RBC} - Min_{RBC}} & \text{if } MIN_{RBC} < RBC < Max_{RBC} \\ 0 & \text{otherwise} \end{cases}$
ND [8]	NRC	$\mu_{NRC} = \begin{cases} 1 & \text{if } NRC = Min_{NRC} \\ \frac{MAX_{NRC} - NRC}{Max_{NRC} - Min_{NRC}} & \text{if } MIN_{NRC} < NRC < Max_{NRC} \\ 0 & \text{otherwise} \end{cases}$
BS [3]	LRZ	$\mu_{LRZ} = \begin{cases} 1 & \text{if } LRZ = Max_{LRZ} \\ \frac{LRZ}{Max_{LRZ}} & \text{if } 0 < LRZ < Max_{LRZ} \\ 0 & \text{otherwise} \end{cases}$

Table 10 shows the fuzzy preference used for the first experiment.

Table 10: Fuzzy preference for minterm and implicant.

Minterm		Implicant	
Criteria	Fuzzy Preference	Criteria	Fuzzy Preference
IW	0.9	RBC	0.9
CF	0.2	LRZ	0.2
CFN	0.1	NRC	0.1

Using the above mentioned fuzzy preferences, we tested the proposed fuzzy selection criteria against the 50000 randomly generated 2-variables 4-valued MVL functions. Five different fuzzy operators are used for this purpose. Table 11 shows the results of the experiment. It should be noted that we list the results obtained in two cases: not considering minterm values in any order (No CMV) and taking minterm values in ascending orders; lower to higher values (With CMV). We set $\beta = 0.5$ while collecting the results reported in Table 11.

Table 11: Performance of different fuzzy operator in FDC.

Operator	# PT No CMV	# PT With CMV
Max	8.5513	8.0301
Max with pref.	7.30344	7.21964
OWA	7.38226	7.28898
OWA with pref.	7.27186	7.19450
Weighted Average	7.30646	7.19784

6 Comparison

In this section we provide a comparison among the iterative heuristics presented above. The results shown in Table 12 reveal that the three heuristic algorithms outperform other existing DC-based techniques, regardless of the number of minterms in the given MVL function. Among the three introduced algorithms, it is clear that in the worst case, the FDC produces results that are as good as those produced by the other two algorithms. However, in vast majority of the cases, the FDC produces results that are better than those produced by the other two algorithms in terms of the average number of product terms needed to synthesize a given function.

Table 12: Average #PT with Respect to Different Number of Minterms of MVL Functions used.

# minterm	# functions	Promper	Besslich	Dueck	ODC	WDC	FDC
16	500	7.594	7.562	7.002	7.086	7.01	6.946
15	2679	8.295	8.307	7.51	7.481	7.501	7.423
14	6589	8.355	8.405	7.569	7.516	7.559	7.500
13	10585	8.275	8.352	7.541	7.491	7.545	7.484
12	11230	8.049	8.098	7.382	7.33	7.383	7.320
11	9003	7.707	7.757	7.129	7.086	7.134	7.087
10	5434	7.323	7.366	6.831	6.787	6.837	6.794
9	2575	6.871	6.879	6.473	6.436	6.479	6.444
8	1038	6.309	6.322	6.023	5.978	6.022	5.981
7	277	5.726	5.751	5.527	5.484	5.523	5.505
6	75	5.133	5.147	4.973	4.96	4.987	4.960
5	13	4	4	4	3.923	4	4
4	1	4	4	4	4	4	4
3	1	3	3	3	3	3	3
Total	50000						

The following tables 13 to 15 provides tabular forms of the obtained percentage improvements achieved using the three iterative heuristics as compared to the results obtained using the conventional DC heuristics.

Table 13: The percentage of improvement achieved by FDC.

Type of functions	Number of functions	% functions
≥ 12% improvement Functions	6589	≅ 13.2%
10% ≤ improvement <12%	(2679+10585+11230) = 24494	≅ 49%
< 10% improvement ≤ 5%	(500+9003+5434+2575+1038) = 18550	≅ 37.1%
< 5% improvement	(277+75)= 352	≅ 0.7%
No improvement	15	≅ 0.03%

Table 14: The percentage of improvement achieved by WDC

Type of functions	Number of functions	% functions
Functions with improvement ≥ 10%	(2679+6589+10585)=19853	≅ 39.7%
Functions with 5% ≤ improvement <10%	(500+11230+9003+5434+2575) = 28742	≅ 57.48%
Functions with improvement < %5	(1038+277+75) = 1390	≅ 2.78%
Functions with no improvement	15	≅ 0.03%

Table 15: The percentage of improvement achieved by ODC.

Type of functions	Number of functions	% functions
≥ 10% improvement	(2679+6589+10585+11230) = 31083	≅ 62.1%
5% ≤ improvement <10%	(500+9003+5434+2575 +1038) = 18550	≅ 37.1%
< %5 improvement	(277+75+13) = 365	≅ 0.73%
No improvement	2	≅ 0.004%

From Table 13, we can see that the maximum percentage of improvement achieved using the FDC heuristic over all DC-based techniques is 12.067% and this is achieved in 6589 functions out of the 50000 (about 13.2% of the benchmark functions). From Table 14, we can see that the maximum percentage of improvement achieved using the WDC heuristic over all DC-based techniques is 11.192%. This has been achieved in 6589 functions (about 13.2% of the 50000 benchmark functions). From Table 15, we can see that the maximum percentage of improvement achieved using the ODC heuristic over all DC-based techniques is 11.828%. This has been achieved in 6589 functions (about 13.2% of the 50000 benchmark functions).

A summary of the results obtained using the three heuristic algorithms is provided in Table 16 in the form of an overall comparison among the heuristic algorithms and the existing DC-based algorithms in terms of the average number of PTs used using the randomly generated 50000 2-variable 4-valued and the 50000 2-variable 5-valued benchmarks.

Table 16: Comparison among three different heuristic algorithms

	#PT (2-variable 5-valued)	#PT (2-variable 4-valued)
Promper	13.4404	7.89012
Besslich	13.6507	7.93882
Dueck	12.1525	7.24786
WDC	12.1525	7.24914
ODC	12.0682	7.20234
FDC	12.0694	7.19422

7 Concluding Remarks

In this paper, we have presented three iterative heuristics for synthesis of MVL functions: the WDC, ODC, and FDC. We have also compared the results obtained using these algorithms through simulating the three algorithms using two benchmarks: 50000 2-variable 4-valued and 2-variable 5-valued functions. The results obtained showed that the three heuristics outperform the conventional DCs. Among the three heuristics the FDC achieved the best improvements.

Acknowledgement

The author would like to acknowledge the support of Kuwait University provided in the form of the funded research project WI 04/10.

References

[1] Dubrova, E., "Multiple-Valued Logic in VLSI", International Journal on Multiple-Valued Logic and Soft Computing, 2002, pp. 1-17.

[2] Naiff, K., Rich, D., and Smalley, K., "A Four-State ROM using Multi-level Process Technology", IEEE Journal of Solid-State Circuits, vol. 19, no. 2, April 1984, pp. 174-179.

[3] Razavi, H. And Bou-Ghazale, S., "Design of a Fast CMOS Ternary Adder", Proceedings IEEE International Symposium on Multiple-Valued Logic (ISMVL), May 1987, pp. 20-23.

[4] Hanyu, T. And Kameyama, M., "A 200 MHz Pipelined Multiplier using 1.5 V-Supply Multiple-Valued MOS Current-Mode Circuits with Dual-Rail Source-Coupled Logic", IEEE Journal of Solid-State Circuits, vol. 30, no. 11, November 1995, pp. 1239-1245.

[5] Patel, V. And Gurmurthy, K., "Arithmetic Operations in Multi-Valued Logic", International Journal of VLSI & Communication Systems (VLSICS), vol. 1, no. 1, March 2010, pp. 21-32.

[6] Manikas, T. And Teeters, D., "Multiple-Valued Logic Memory System Design using Nano-Scale Electro-Chemical Cells", Proceedings ISMVL-2008, May 2008, pp. 197-201.

[7] Hosseinzadeh, M., Jassbi, S., and Navi, K., "A Novel Multiple-Valued Logic OHRNS Modulo Adder Circuit", Proceedings World Academy of Science, Engineering, and Technology, vol. 25, November 2007, ISSN 1307-6884, pp. 128-133.

[8] Kouretus, I. And Puliourus, V., "High-Radix Redundant Circuits for RNS Modulo $r^n - 1, r^n, OR\ r^n + 1$", Proceedings IEEE International Symposium on Circuits and Systems (ISCAS-2003), vol. 5, 2003, pp. V-229-V-232.

[9] Dubrova, E., Jiang Y., and Brayton, R., "Minimization of multi-valued functions in Post algebra", Proceedings International Workshop on Logic and Synthesis, 2001, pp. 132-137.

[10] Promper, G., Armstrong A., "Representation of multiple valued functions using the direct cover method", IEEE Transactions on Computers (TC), September 1981, pp. 674-679.

[11] Besslich, W., "Heuristic Minimization of MVL Functions: A Direct Cover Approach", IEEE Transactions on Computers (TC), vol. C-35, no. 2, February 1986, pp. 134-144.

[12] Dueck, G., Miller, M., "A Direct Cover MVL Minimization Using the Truncated Sum", Proceedings ISMVL-87, May 1987, pp. 221-227.

[13] Yang, C., and Wang, Y., "A neighbourhood decoupling algorithm for truncated sum minimization", Proceedings ISMVL-90, pp. 153-160.

[14] Lee, K., El-Sharkawi, M., "Modern Heuristic Optimization Techniques", Institute of Electrical and Electronics Engineers (IEEE), ISBN 9780470225868, 2008.

[15] Abd-El-Barr, M., and Al-Awami, L., "Analysis of Direct Cover Algorithms for Minimization of MVL Functions", International Conference on Microelectronics (ICM 03), 2003, pp. 308- 312.

[16] Abd-El-Barr, M., Sarif, B., "Weighted and Ordered Direct Cover Algorithms for Minimization of MVL Functions", Proceedings ISMVL-2007, May 2007, pp. 48-53.

[17] Sarif, B., and Abd-El-Barr, M, "Fuzzy-based Direct Cover Algorithm for Synthesis of Multiple-Valued Logic Functions", Proceedings IASTED Circuits and Systems, Hawaii 2008, pp. 625-630.

[18] Zadeh, L., "Fuzzy Sets", Information and Control, vol. 8, 1965, pp. 338-353.

FPGA-based Hexapod Robot Spider

Yuhua Li
Dept. of Computer Science and Technology
Xi'an Jiaotong University, City College
Xi'an, China
yhli@mail.xjtu.edu.cn

Huimin Ma
Dept. of Computer Science and Technology
Xi'an Jiaotong University, City College
Xi'an, China
mlhfm@yahoo.com.cn

***Abstract*—This paper describes a FPGA-based hexapod robot spider, which is used for student education purposes. In the paper mechanical design, kinematic analysis, electro-mechanical device and FPGA system are introduced. Some key points about gait mode, non-stop PWM signal, filter of reflex ultrasonic wave and Bluetooth control are given in detail. At the end of the paper a discussion section gives some technical opinions about FPGA-based system, gait mode, filter of sonar echo and remote control.**

***Index Terms*—FPGA, robot spider, mini-sever, PWM , Bluetooth Control**

I. INTRODUCTION

Robot spiders are widely built and researched for a variety of purposes, including space exploration, mine cleaning in battle fields and rescue work in disasters. Robot spiders can be used in such application situations because of their special leg-walking mode. Compared with wheel mode robot, the efficiency of robot spider is not higher, but a robot spider can easily cross over obstacles.

The hexapod robot spider CC-Balck5 described in the paper is used for educational purposes for college students. They can take it as an experiment platform, and write their own VHDL program to realize varieties of movements.

II. MECHANICAL DESIGN

The robot spider CC-Black5 consists of 6 legs, which are located on both sides of the body, as shown in Fig.1. Each leg has 2 joints, i.e. each leg includes 2 freedoms. One freedom is rotating around lengthways axis. This is defined as the small-leg joint. Another freedom is rotating around the crosswise axis and it is defined as the big-leg joint. The whole structure includes 12 freedoms. Some mechanical data are listed in TABLE I.

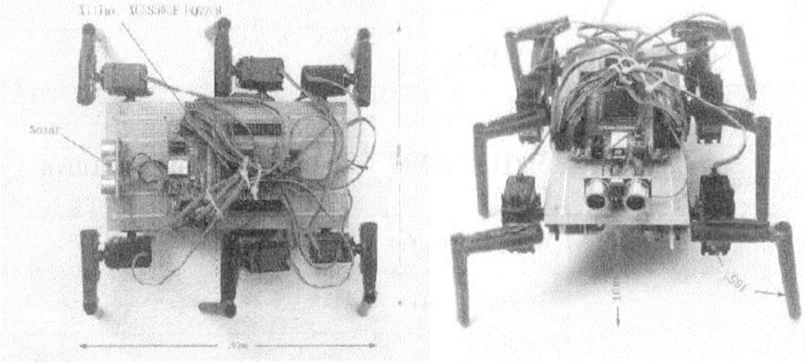

Fig.1 Top view and front view of CC-Black5

TABLE I. MECHANICAL CHARACTERISTICS

length	250(mm)
width	230(mm)
height	130(mm)
Height of bottom space	100(mm)
Total mass	615(g)
mass of each leg including 2 joints	82(g)
stride	50(mm)
speed	50(mm/s)

III. KINEMATICS ANALYSIS

A. Gait Mode

A robot spider with six legs could have a lot of gait modes. The gait mode of CC-Black5 is similar to the mode of coxswainles-six-oar rowboat. With the rowboat mode the movement of all six paddles are same at the same time, but for CC-Black5 there are some differences. All six legs of CC-Black5 are divided into two groups: Group A and Group B, as shown in Fig.2. Group A includes two left legs, L1,L3 and one right leg, R2. Group B includes two right legs, R1,R3 and one left leg, L2.Each group forms a triangle. All three legs which are in one group will make the same movement at the same time. The main consideration is that, when the legs of one group leave from the ground, then the other three legs of the other group keep standing on the ground. This can keep CC-Black5's movement stable.

In term of kinematics design, the movement of each leg includes four beats: leg rising→return stroke→leg descending →paddling. The movement is like as human arm in free style swim, or like as paddle in a rowboat. The positions of one right leg of CC-Black5 during 4 beats is shown in Fig.3, where in states 3 and 4, the leg contacts the ground, in states 1 and 2, the leg leaves the ground. In state 4, the leg carries CC-Black5 forwards. At this moment, the three joints of the three big legs in one group output the maximum power. The CC-Black5 takes 250ms for one beat. Four beasts form a loop, which takes one second. A stride length of a loop is 50mm.

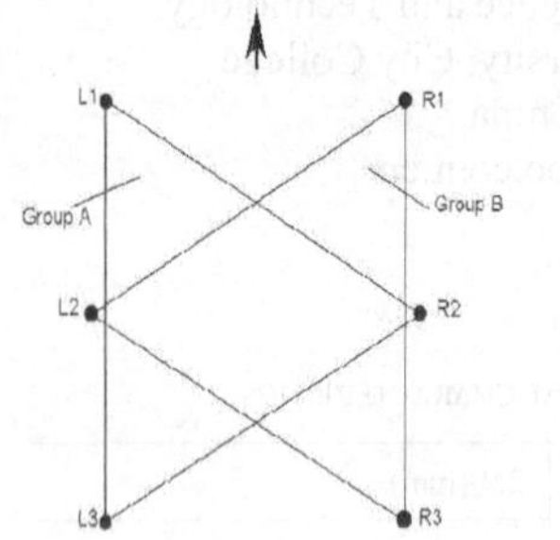

Fig.2 Two groups of legs

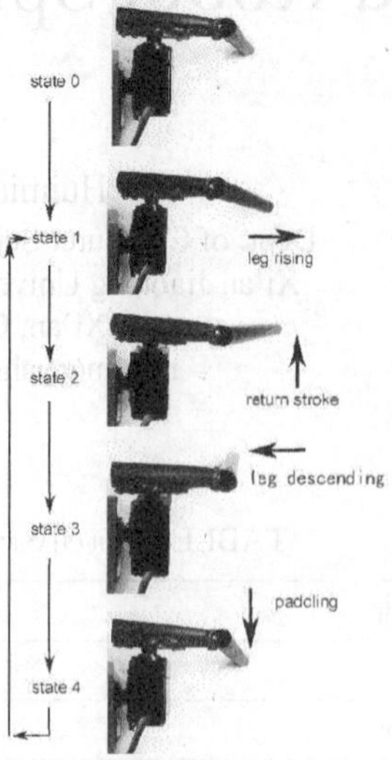

Fig.3 Four-beat movement mode

B. Eight-beat gait or four-beat gait mode

The experimental program has been tested for two ways of gait: 8-beat gait and 4-beat gait.

In the 8-beat gait program, Group B is standing on the ground until 4-beat movement of Group A is completed, and vice versa. The 8-beat sequence is: Group A leg rising→return stroke→leg descending→paddling→Group B leg rising→return stroke→leg descending→paddling. In this way CC-Black5 moves very stably. But the efficiency is lower. One loop of walking costs 2 seconds, and because there are always 3 legs standing on the ground, a bigger friction occurs.

In the 4-beat gait program, Group A and Group B move simultaneously following 4-beat mode, but two groups have 2-beat phase difference. The 4-beat sequence is: Group A leg rising and Group B leg descending→Group A return stroke and Group B paddling→Group A leg decending and Group B leg rising→Group A paddling and Group B return stroke. In this way the movement of CC-Black5 is faster and more lively. One loop of walking takes 1 second.

However it is very important to notice that, in 4-beat gait program beat 1 and beat 3 demand 3 legs rising and 3 legs descending simultaneously. In fact it leads to a strongly harmful push-up movement. A fine adjustment of time sequence during beat 1 and beat 3 must be made. With adjustment every time leg-rising allways occurs a little bit later than leg-descending. This adjustment makes the walking of CC-Black5 more stable and stronger.

C. Basic Status

The basic statuses of CC-Black5 are: standing, going forward, going backward, turning left and turning right. The standing status is the most important one, and all joints of CC-Black5 are located in their middle position. Because of mechanical deviation, the duty values of each PWM signal for each jiont is not in the same. These initialization values must be carefully adjusted. All other statuses need only off-set parameters based on standing status. All off-set parameters are nearly the same. Other additional statuses, such as hand-waving, body up-down, swing dance are also possible to configurate.

IV. ELECTRO-MECHANICAL DEVICE

The electro-mechanical device used as a joint of legs is a mini-server, as shown in Fig.4. Its electrical and mechnical characteristics are listed in the TABLE II.

A mini-server consists of an IC for control-drive, a DC motor, a gear set and a proportional potentiometer, as shown in Fig.4 and Fig.5. Control-drive module can detect a specific PWM signal and drive the DC motor. The gear set reduces the rotating speed of the motor. According to the duty time of a signal the control module fixes the axis of the mini-server to a certain position. The proportional potentiometer outputs an electrical level to the control module to correct this position. So the mini-server then rotates to a fixed position between 0 and 180 degree according to the duty of PWM signal(see Fig.7). Because the gear set has no self-lock characterristics, the mini-server can not keep this position if the signal disappears, or is broken. Fig.6 shows the control conception of a mini-server.

Fig.4 Mini-server

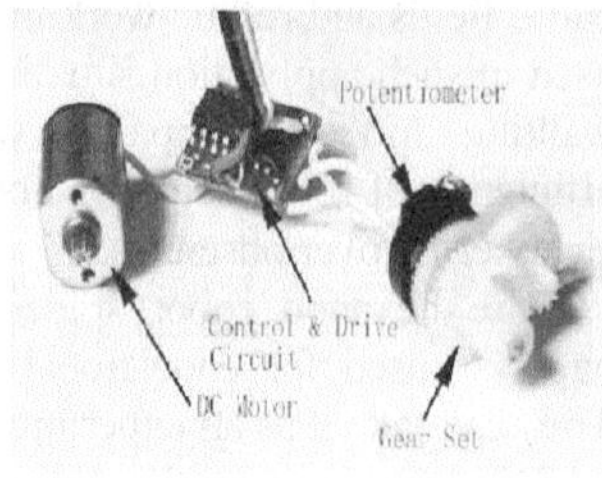

Fig.5 Structure of mini-server

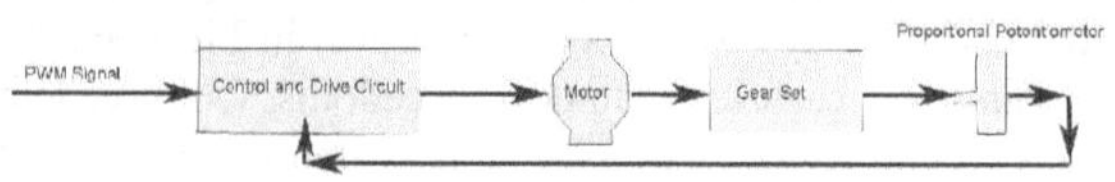

Fig.6 Control conception of a mini-server

TABLE II. ELECTRICAL AND MECHANICAL CHARACTERISTICS OF MINI-SERVER

power	5(V DC)
Max. current	100(mA)
Control signal	50(Hz), PWM with duty 0.5(ms) – 2.5(ms), LVTTL
Rotating angle	0 – 180(degree)
torque	≥20(N-cm)
weight	35(g)

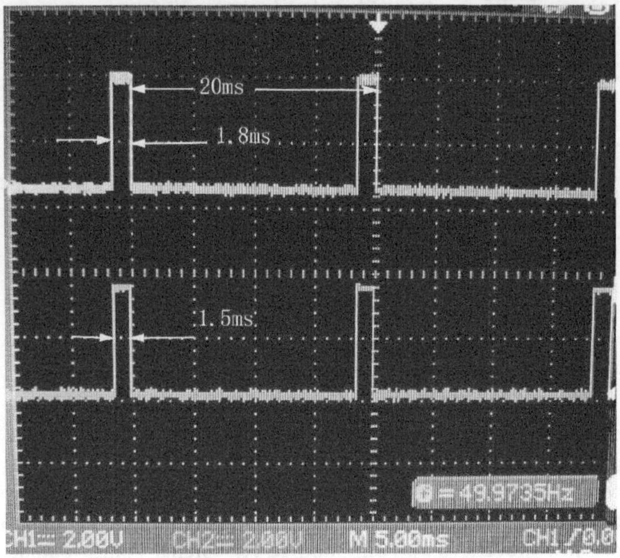

Fig.7 PWM signals of 2 mini-servers

V. FPGA SYSTEM

A. Minimum System of FPGA

The movement of CC-Black5 is all under the control of a FPGA(Field-Programmable Gate Array) system. A standard minimum system of FPGA is used in CC-Black5, according to the system recommended by Xilinx Inc. Other than this minimum system no other additional components and devices are used. The hardware design is based on the Master Serial Mode as shown in Fig.8. It is a low cost, high-performance solution for a robot spider.

The system consists of two ICs only. The main one is FPGA, which type is XC3S500E-PQ208. It belongs to Spartan-3E FPGA family of Xilinx Inc. Inside of the chip 500K system gates, 158 I/O pins are integrated. The run speed of FPGA is high up to 300MHz. Another chip in Fig.8 is a flash memory, which type is XCF04S of Platform PROM family of Xilinx Inc. The size of XCF04S is 4 Mb. It is used to keep the configuration data of FPGA. The configuration data is programmed with VHDL(Very high speed Hardware Description Language), and is down loaded into the flash memory through JTAG interface.

B. Sonar device

A sonar device as shown in Fig.9 is used to measure the distance between CC-Black5 and a wall. If the distance is smaller than 10cm, CC-Black5 will turn back and change forward direction. A speaker of the device sends 40kHz ultrasonic wave. The receiver has the same size as the speaker. Both of them are resonated under 40kHz ultrasonic wave. The transmission speed of ultrasonic wave in the air is 340m/s. A counter in FPGA measure the response time of the echo, and gives a signal to change the the walking direction when the response time is shorter than 0.59ms.

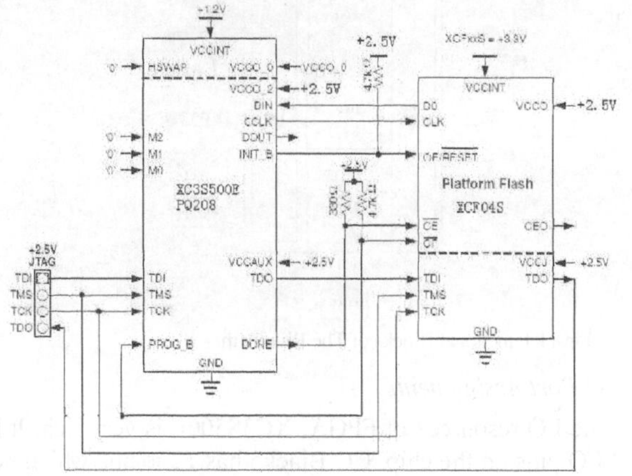

Fig.8 FPGA system based on Master Serial Mode

Fig.9 Sonar device

C. Bluetooth Module

A Bluetooth module as shown in Fig.10 is used to control CC-Black5.Through it man can use a mobile phone or a laptop to remote control movements of CC-Black5. The control distance is more than 50m. The frequency of the Bluetooth module is 2.4GHz. The control commands include "stop", "forward", "backward", "turn right", "turn left", and "hand waving". The communication between the host and the Bluetooth module is on the basis of protocol V2.1+ EDR. The interface between Bluetooth module and FPGA is LVTTL-UART with 115,200 Baud rate. The Bluetooth module consists of the chip BlueCore4-Ext (CSR Ltd.) and a MCU. The functional block diagram is shown in Fig.11.

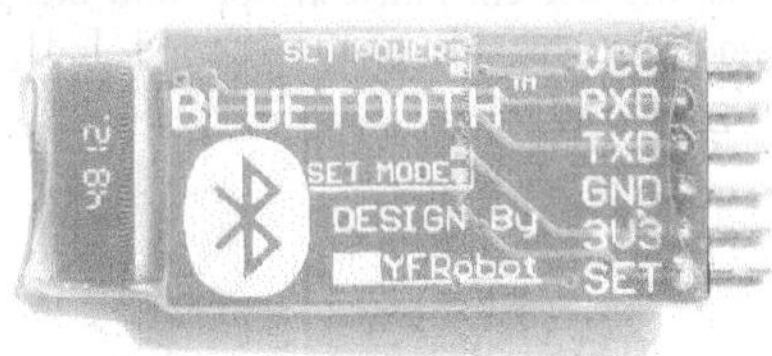

Fig.10 Bluetooth Module

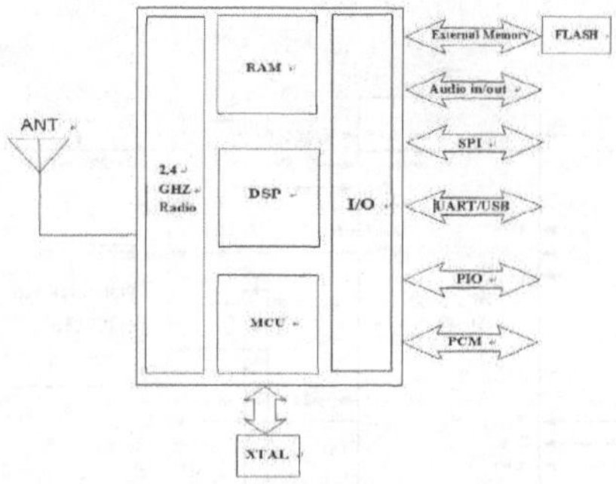

Fig.11 Functional Blocks of The Bluetooth

D. I/O Port Assignments

The I/O resourece of FPGA, XC3S500E is very rich. It has 158 I/O pins on the chip. CC-Black5 has 12 joints, which need 12 I/O ports. The sonar device needs one input to get the response of the echo and one output to trigger ultrasonic wave. The Bluetooth module needs one output pin to connect its RXD, and one input pin to connect its TXD. Additional 2 outputs are used for LEDs as indicators. All 18 I/O ports occupy only a small part of the I/O resource of FPGA. Fig.12 shows the I/O assignment of FPGA.

E. Synchronous and Non-Stop PWM Signal

The all 12 PWM signals are synchronous. Fig.7 shows only 2 signals of the 12 signals, and they are exactly synchronous. The FPGA is clocked with an external 50MHz crystal oscillator. Through frequency divides it results in some basic clocks: 50Hz for PWM signal, 4Hz for beats of walking, and other clocks for the Sonar and for UART of the Bluetooth module. Because of concurrent characteristics of FPGA it is easy to keep all 12 PWM signals non-stop and synchronous. It means that during the whole running cycle of CC-Black5 all 12 PWM signals will never be broken, but can be changed. It is important for mini-server. If the PWM signal stops, the rotate position of mini-server will be easily changed under a load. It will make a robot spider weaker and instable.

Using Xilinx hardware design tool ISE it is easy to create the schematic of the FPGA system of CC-Black5, as shown in Fig.13 and Fig.14. Fig.13 shows that the FPGA system becomes an ASIC(Application Specific IC), having three input pins on the left side of the IC: clk pin, echo pin and txd pin, and 16 output pins on the right side of the IC: led, led1, 12 mini-server signals, trig and rxd pins.

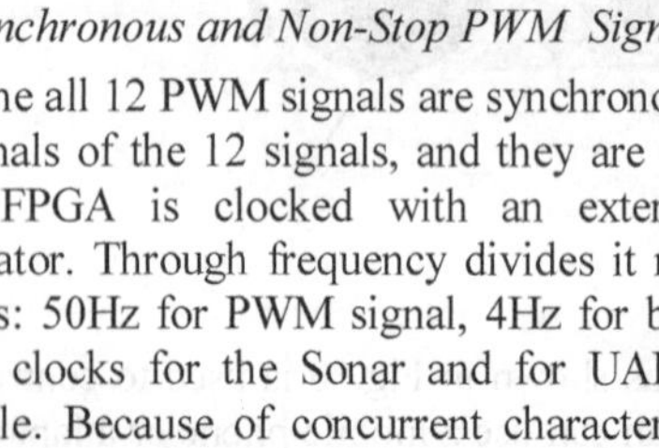

Fig.12. Assignment of I/O pins

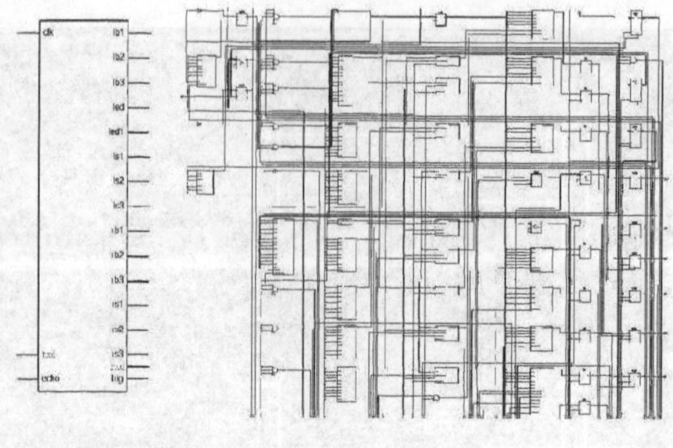

Fig.13 Schematic of FPGA Fig.14 Fine schematic

The input clk pin gets external 50MHz clock, the input echo pin gets a reflex ultrasonic wave signal, and the input txd pin gets signals from Bluetooth module, which form a 8-bit command. The signal type of the three input pins is rising-edge of externals. Both led pin and led1 pin output high level (3.3V) or low level (0V). 12 mini-server signal pins output synchronous non-stop PWM signals, which control movements of spider legs. The trig pin outputs a rising-edge signal to start the sonar device. The rxd pin outputs an acknowledge to the Bluetooth module after the command is implemented. Fig.14 shows a detail of schematic, which includes a lot of counters to divide frequency and FFs(flip-flop) to capture rising-edge of signals and output synchronous signals.

In the field of robot spider, some of them have been built based on the 32-bit embedded system. For these kind of robot spider to keep all PWM signals synchronous and non-stop is not so easy. Compared with control by the embedded system, the FPGA-base robot spider CC-Black5 walks more stably.

F. Communication of the Bluetooth Module

Between the host and Bluetooth module the communication is 2.4GHz RF according to the protocol V2.1+ EDR. The host can be an android mobile phone, or a windows laptop. The App for Bluetooth on the mobile phone must support UART format. The communication between the Bluetooth module and FPGA is LVTTL-UART. The Baudrate for both of them are set as 115,200.

For example, if the host sends a character "r", the Bluetooth module gets it, then transmits it to FPGA through its TXD pin. According to "r" FPGA changes its moving status into "turning right", and gives a response character back to RXD pin of the Bluetooth module. The Bluetooth module sends the response back to the host. It is a complete transaction.

VI. DISCUSSION

By the concurrent feature of FPGA and its rich resources of I/O, the demand for more synchronous and non-stop PWM signals can be easily met. In the authors' point of view, FPGA system is more suitable to such loading case than the 32-bit embedded system.

CC-Black5 uses 12 mini-servers, which can be drived by FPGA XC3S500E directly. If more powerful big servers are used, then additional drive modules are needed to insert between output pins of FPGA and servers.

Because the gait mode is not as stable as the wheel mode, it causes instable reflex ultrasonic waves. A filter design for sonar device in FPGA is then necessary. In CC-Black5 , when a reflex echo continues more than 2 seconds, it can be confirmed that there is a real obstacle wall in front. Sometimes when a reflex ultrasonic wave from the floor reaches to the receiver of the device, the filter will ignore it.

The UART interface as a process in FPGA has been programmed. The remote control can be easily realized with various devices. Except of the Bluetooth module, the GSM base-band module SIM300S, or SIM900A(Siemens) are successfully constructed in CC-Black5. A Man-Spider communication through a mobile phone can be set up.

The battery is always a problem just like in other kind of robots. Here, CC-Black5 needs 5V and maximum 1.5A power supply.

ACKNOWLEDGMENT

We would like to express our deep gratitude to Professor Lina Lu, whose encouragement and support to CC-Black5 project are greatly appreciated. We also thank the other team members, Mr. Zhe Zhang, Mr. Chao Sun and Mrs. Roumei Jiang, for their hard working and full co-operation. The CC-Black5 project has been supported by Xilinx University Program. For this valuable supporting we give our special thanks to Dr. Kevin Xie, Great China Manager of Xilinx University Program.

REFERENCES

[1] Wang Jintong, Wang Zhouyi and Li Hongkai, "Movement of a Spider on a Horizonal Surface", Chinese Science Bulletin. Beijing, October 2011.

[2] Din Xilun, Wang Zhiying and Alberto Rovetta, "Typical Gaits and Motion Analysis of Hexagonal Symmetrical Hexapod Robot", Robot, Vol.32, November 2011.

[3] LiuuJianhui and Ye Jing, "Gait Study of a Bionic Spider", Journal of Liaoning Technical University, June 2008.

[4] www.xilinx.com, "Spartan-3E FPGA Family", Data Sheet. August 2009.

[5] www.xilinx.com, "Platform Flash PROM User Guide", October 2009.

[6] Peter Wilson, "Deign Recipes for FPGAs", Elsevier(Singapore) Pte Ltd., 2009.

3D Lattice Monte Carlo Simulations on FPGAs

A. Gilman[1], A. Leist[2] and K.A. Hawick[1]
[1] Institute of Natural and Mathematical Sciences,
[2] School of Engineering and Advanced Technology,
Massey University, North Shore 102-904, Auckland, New Zealand
email: { a.gilman, a.leist, k.a.hawick }@massey.ac.nz
Tel: +64 9 414 0800 Fax: +64 9 441 8181

Abstract— *Field Programmable Gate Arrays (FPGAs) offer significant performance advantages over general purpose compute architectures for certain scientific problems, including lattice-based Monte Carlo simulations of complex systems models. We report on a custom logic design for the 3D-lattice Ising model that keeps the entire system state in on-chip memory to achieve very high throughput rates. The pipelined architecture, which is implemented in Verilog, is able to process an entire row of cells per clock cycle. When processing a system of 256^3 spins on a Xilinx Virtex-7 device, about 3000 full system sweeps can be performed per second. We discuss implementation issues and solutions that apply in similar ways to a variety of nearest neighbour, lattice-based Monte Carlo simulations, as well as the performance of the Ising model implementation on two FPGA architectures.*

Keywords: FPGA-based design; simulation; complex systems; parallel computing; performance evaluation.

1. Introduction

While Field Programmable Gate Arrays (FPGAs) were at first predominantly used by engineers to implement time-critical applications, recent advances in FPGA technology [1]–[3] have led to an increasing interest from the scientific high-performance computing community.

FPGAs are now more and more frequently utilised to accelerate complex systems simulations that were previously the domain of general purpose compute clusters, supercomputers or data-parallel accelerators such as graphics processing units [4], [5]. They have been successfully employed to accelerate physics calculations [6], bio-informatics data processing [7], image processing [8]–[10], and agent-based models [11] to name but a few.

We are interested in three-dimensional (3D) Monte Carlo simulations [12] and explore the FPGA platform for these types of problems using the Ising model [13], one of the most widely studied systems of interacting particles, which remains an important tool for theoretical and numerical analysis of phase transitions in critical systems. Real magnets exhibit phase transitions at the Curie temperature – above which iron for example ceases to exhibit spontaneous ferromagnetism – and this macroscopic phenomena can be reproduced and scrutinised with the Ising model.

While the Ising model has been solved analytically [14] on both one and two-dimensional lattices, the three-dimensional Ising model remains intractable and its properties have only been investigated using numerical simulations. The critical temperature and critical exponents have been determined to some degree of precision using computer simulations [15], but to compare the 3D Ising model with other models and systems, greater accuracy is needed. This can only be obtained using very large system sizes, which in turn require parallel computing solutions to be practically feasible. While specialist processor and accelerator units and computer clusters have been brought to bear on the 3D Ising model and associated problems [16], there is still scope for considerably improved computational performance.

FPGAs have already been applied to the 2D Ising model [17], which is useful as numerical properties can be compared to the known analytic solutions. It is however the 3D Ising system that represents the great unknown and it is hoped that modern FPGA accelerators may provide a more feasible route towards a greater precision answer.

This paper presents an investigation into using FPGA processing elements to address the problem of using Monte Carlo methods to simulate large systems like the 3D Ising model. We give an overview of the Ising model in section 2 and explain our approach to implementing the model on FPGAs in section 3. Section 4 describes the results of the chosen approach and sections 5 and 6 discuss our findings and offer some conclusions respectively.

2. Ising Model Simulation

The Ising model is used to investigate the properties of the phase transition from unordered (non-ferromagnetic) to ordered (ferromagnetic) domains, and vice versa, of a computational ferromagnet as the system temperature is adjusted. This transition occurs at the Curie temperature T_c for models with more than one dimension. In general, the Ising model can be used to study macroscopic phenomena caused by pairwise correlations between neighbouring sites on the microscopic scale. For instance, it can be applied to the propagation of opinions in a network of social interactions [18].

The widespread interest in the Ising model can be attributed to its simplicity, which makes it a good test case for new approximate methods for the investigation of systems of interacting particles. As Newell and Montroll put it: "If a proposed method cannot deal with the Ising model, it can hardly be expected to be powerful enough to give reliable results in more complicated cases" [19].

The common approach to dealing with the lack of an analytic solution for the 3D Ising model is to use Monte Carlo simulations to approximate the critical temperature and exponents through random sampling.

Each spin in the Ising model takes on one of only two possible values, "up" and "down" or $+1$ and -1, but an extension to Q spin values can be found in the Q-state Potts model [20]. The spins are arranged in a graph, most commonly a lattice, but irregular graph structures are also of interest, as these structures more accurately represent some natural systems. Examples of the latter include Ising model studies on small-world networks [21], [22] and scale-free graphs [23].

The simulation typically starts with a random "hot" spin configuration, which is then quenched to a temperature T. If this temperature is at or below the Curie temperature T_c, then clusters of like-spins begin to form, creating order in the initially random system. Neighbouring spins interact according to an energy function or Hamiltonian of the form [24]:

$$\mathcal{H} = -\sum_{\langle i,j \rangle} J_{ij}\sigma_i\sigma_j, \tag{1}$$

where $\sigma_i = \pm 1$, $i = 1, 2, ...N$ sites. $J_{ij} = 1/k_B T$ is the ferromagnetic coupling over neighbouring sites i and j, T is the temperature and k_B is the Boltzmann constant. The total energy E of a particular system configuration is obtained from the Hamiltonian. The magnetisation M is defined as [24]:

$$M = \frac{1}{N}\left|\sum_i \sigma_i\right| \tag{2}$$

Different Monte Carlo algorithms have been proposed to investigate the Ising model [25]–[29], with the the Markov-chain method of Metropolis *et al.* [25] being the scheme most commonly used. It was later generalised by Hastings [30] and is now commonly referred to as the Metropolis-Hastings algorithm. Subject to certain procedural limitations on the way the update is conducted, this method is known to produce an appropriate sampling of the Ising model configuration space.

In practice great care is needed so that the probabilities of updating a spin site are chosen with the correct weights. The Boltzmann factors described below must be computed on the basis of the states of the nearest neighbouring spins and neighbouring spins cannot therefore be updated simultaneously. However, as will be described later in this present paper, choosing the order of update is crucial to being able to exploit the parallelism inherent from having many FPGA processing elements working together.

For the latter half of the 20th century it was believed that a very strict ordering of the spins to update was necessary to obtain the strong detailed balance condition [31] and that a systematic sweep order of the update violated this. More recent work [32] using a transition matrix formulation has shown that providing the updates of neighbours that are energetically linked to one another is avoided, then the order in which the updates are performed is not important. This is an important consideration and it allows us to arrange our parallel updates to be performed in an order that best exploits the data locality available in the processing pipeline, providing we do not update immediate neighbours at once.

Table 1: This lookup table specifies the probability to flip a spin and thus transition to a new state for every possible ΔE, which is directly related to the number of unlike neighbouring spins x_μ in the current state. The factor of two in the exponent adjusts for the bidirectional nature of the spin neighbourhood.

x_μ	ΔE	$e^{-2\beta\Delta E}$
0	6	$p_0 = e^{-12\beta}$
1	4	$p_1 = e^{-8\beta}$
2	2	$p_2 = e^{-4\beta}$
3	0	always flip
4	-2	
5	-4	
6	-6	

At each discrete time step, the Metropolis algorithm chooses a random spin and flips its value if:

- the system energy E of the proposed configuration is lower than or equal to the current configuration, i.e. $\Delta E \leq 0$, or
- the proposed configuration is accepted with random probability $e^{-\beta\Delta E}$, where $\beta = \frac{1}{k_B T}$.

If neither of these conditions is fulfilled, then the change is rejected and the system remains in its previous state. Table 1 expresses this as a lookup table for all possible values of the number of unlike neighbouring spins in the current configuration x_μ.

Due to the local nature of the system updates in the Metropolis algorithm, it is well suited for parallel implementations of the Ising model. Parallel implementations can exploit the knowledge that, assuming the spins are arranged on a regular lattice, the checkerboard pattern can be used to update half of the sites concurrently without the risk of race conditions, as neighbouring spins will never be updated at the same time. We have previously demonstrated [33], [34] that this approach can be used to efficiently implement the Metropolis algorithm on graphics processing units.

3. FPGA Implementation

To achieve any significant advantage over the software implementations, computation of updates must be highly paralellized. We were able to successfully achieve this in our previous work [35] – implementing the Game of Life cellular automata – resulting in some significant computational throughputs. The implementation of the Ising model, however, carries a number of additional complications:

- the lattice is 3-dimensional and must be linearized to be stored in memory
- the on-chip block RAM (BRAM) is used, which has large bandwidth, but limited capacity
- 7 memory reads and 1 write are required for each spin computation (current state + six neighbouring states + writing the result)
- periodic boundary conditions on 6 sides
- a (pseudo-) random number is required for each spin computation

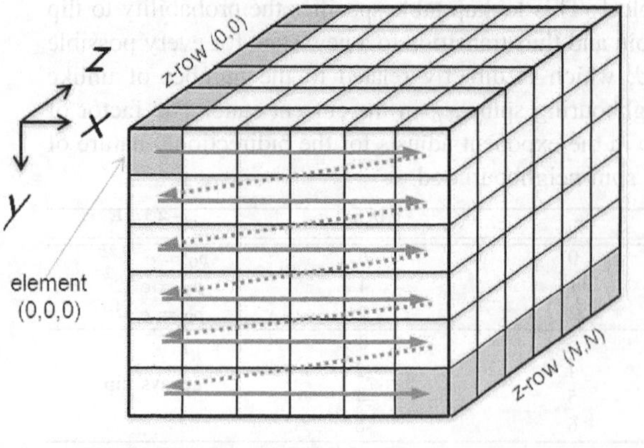

Fig. 1: The 3D lattice arrangement for the spins of the Ising system. The neighbourhood of a spin (x, y, z) consists of the spins $\{x^-, x^+, y^-, y^+, z^-, z^+\}$, which refer to the cells to the left, right, above, below, in front and behind respectively. Periodic boundary conditions apply.

- cannot compute updates for neighbouring spins simultaneously

We opted for a similar strategy to our previous work – designing a N wide by N^2 deep dual port memory to store the N^3 lattice, with the whole row of spin states along the z-dimension bit-packed into a single memory word. By pipelining memory access and processing, one complete z-row can be read from memory, another complete z-row processed to update the spin states and another one written back to memory in a single clock cycle. z-rows are read and processed in ascending order along the x-dimension (see Figure 1), which has the effect that z-row $(x + 1, y)$ trails row (x, y) in the pipeline.

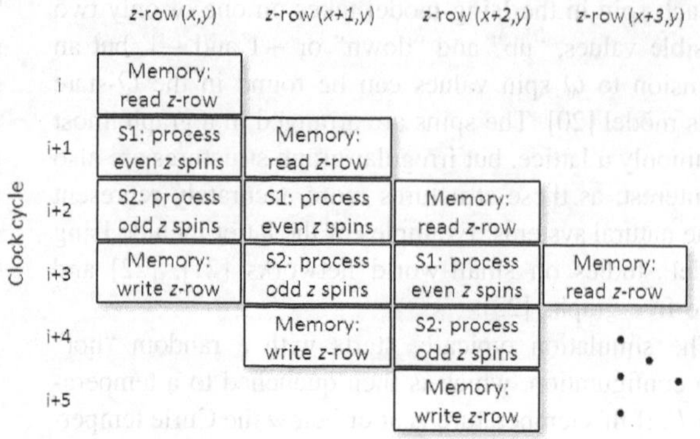

Fig. 2: The movement of z-rows from memory, through the processing stages of the pipeline and back into memory.

However, due to the constraint that neighbouring cells cannot be updated at the same time, our architecture only processes half of the elements in the z-row at a time, by separating the processing into two pipelined stages. This means that when the z-row at (x, y) is in processing stage 1 of the pipeline, which processes all cells with an even index in the vector, the z-row at $(x - 1, y)$ is in stage 2, which processes all cells with an odd index. Figure 2 illustrates this process. The pipeline is in full use at clock cycle $i + 3$ in the diagram, where

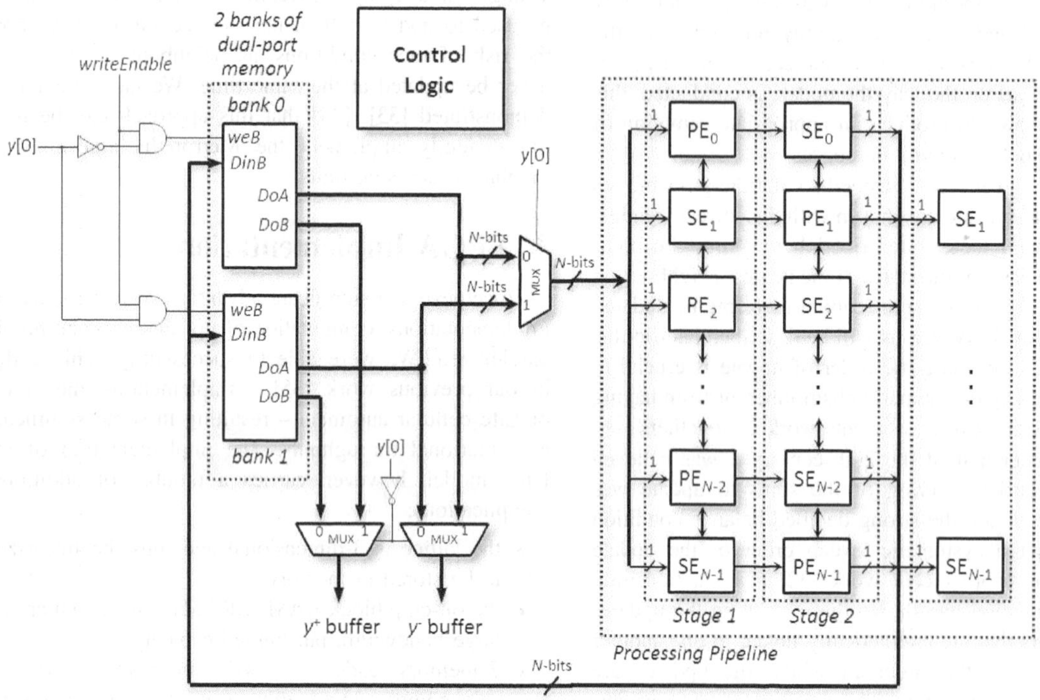

Fig. 3: Architecture of the 3D Ising model compute module: 2 banks of dual-port memory to store the spin states, 2-stage processing pipeline to update odd and even spins separately and the control logic. See text for a detailed explanation.

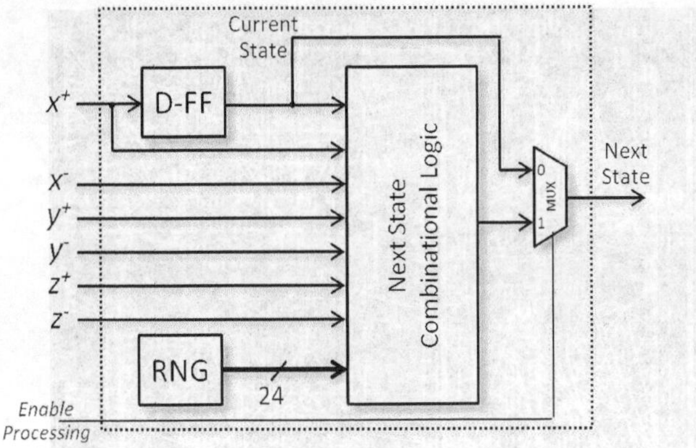

Fig. 4: Each processing element consists of a D-type flip-flop to store the current spin state, a 24-bit random number generator and combinational logic to compute the next state.

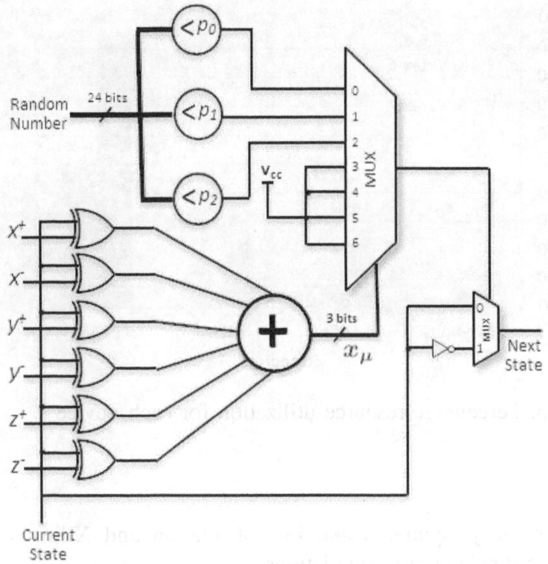

Fig. 5: Combinational logic implementing the Metropolis update algorithm. The number of unlike states x_μ drives a multiplexor that either unconditionally flips the current state ($x_\mu = \{3, 4, 5, 6\}$) or flips the current state with probabilities p_0, p_1 or p_2 (for x_μ = 0, 1 or 2 respectively).

z-row (x, y) has been processed and is being written to memory, $(x + 1, y)$ is in processing stage 2, $(x + 2, y)$ is in processing stage 1 and $(x + 3, y)$ is being read from memory. It remains fully utilised until the end of the x-row is reached, at which point three flush cycles are needed to move the remaining z-rows through the pipeline and write the results to memory. Similarly, when processing begins at the start of the new x-row, three prime cycles are necessary to place the required data into the correct stages of the pipeline for z-row $(0, y)$ to begin processing. This differs from traditional parallel implementations that utilize the checkerboard pattern, as some neighbouring elements for each cell have already been updated for this generation and some have not been updated.

One advantage of processing an entire z-row of data within the pipeline is that neighbours z^+ and z^- have also been read from memory and can be made available to the appropriate processing elements from the same stage with simple buffering. The right hand side of Figure 3 depicts the architecture of the processing pipeline, showing processing elements (PE) being interleaved with storage elements (SE) that buffer these values. Spins x^+ and x^- can be accessed from the earlier and later stages of the pipeline respectively. To access neighbouring spins y^+ and y^-, the respective z-rows $(x, y + 1)$ and $(x, y - 1)$ are loaded into and moved through collections of storage elements (running in parallel to the processing pipeline) as (x, y) moves through the pipeline. In order to be able to read these two extra z-rows into the y^+ and y^- buffers, as well as read a new z-row into the processing pipeline and write a processed z-row into the memory in a single clock cycle (4 separate memory accesses) we split the memory into 2 banks with $bank0$ storing only elements with even y value and $bank1$ storing elements with odd y value. Now each bank either reads a new z-row into the processing pipeline using port A and writes a processed z-row using port B or alternatively reads $(x, y + 1)$ and $(x, y - 1)$ z-rows into the y^+ and y^- buffers. This is controlled by the least significant bit of the y coordinate, as can be seen in Figure 3.

The design of the processing elements is illustrated in Figure 4 consisting of a single D-type flip-flop to store the current state, a 24-bit pseudo-random number generator and the combinational logic that implements the Metropolis update algorithm. This logic is shown in Figure 5 and represents the direct implementation of the look-up table detailed in Table 1.

A 63-bit linear-feedback shift register (with XNOR feedback from last and next to last taps) has been employed for the generation of pseudo-random numbers. This was selected because of its efficient FPGA implementation using the shift register primitives (see [36] for detail) - it can be implemented using a single CLB. Each PE contains 24 of these LFSRs connected in parallel to produce a new 24 bit random number every clock cycle.

To take care of the periodic boundary conditions, z-row $(l - 1, y)$ has to be fed into the pipeline before $(0, y)$ without being processed and this is accomplished during the pipeline priming with the use of the 'Enable Processing' signal (seen in Figure 4), which can turn off the state update logic as necessary. The 'writeEnable' signal (seen in Figure 3) is also used during priming to stop garbage outputs from being written to the memory.

4. Results

The design was described using Verilog HDL and implemented on two Xilinx FPGA development boards. One hosting a Virtex-6 family device (xc6vlx240t) and one hosting a Virtex-7 family device (xc7vx485t). The advantage of using these development boards is the presence of an on-board PCIe interface that can be used for exchanging the data between the host PC and the FPGA. We have used Xilinx ISE Design Suite 14.3 for HDL

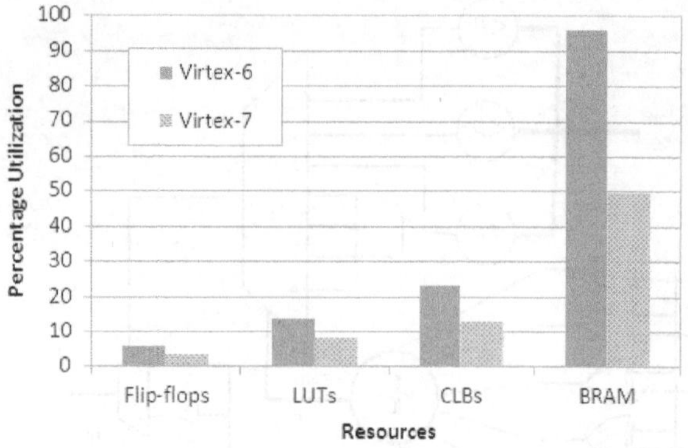

Fig. 6: Percentage resource utilization for each device

design entry, synthesis and implementation and Xilinx ISIM for behavioural simulations.

The available resources on the two FPGAs are summarized in Table 2. It was our original intention to implement a 256^3 Ising model, but unfortunately the Virtex-6 device did not have enough on-chip memory for this and we opted for a 200^3 model on Virtex-6 and a 256^3 model on Virtex-7.

The implementation results are summarized in Table 3, showing the resource utilization (the number of utilized flip-flops and look-up tables and also the total number of used CLBs), the maximum clock frequency in megahertz and the compilation time in minutes for the two model sizes. As expected, the resource utilization ratio between the two devices is 30% (Virtex-6 has 200 PEs in the pipeline vs 256 on Virtex-7). A large difference in the maximum frequency can be partly attributed to the manufacturing process: 40 nm for Virtex-6 and 28 nm for Virtex-7. The resulting throughput is 24 and 51.2 billion individual spin updates per second for Virtex-6 and Virtex-7 respectively, equivalent to around 3,000 full 3D field generation updates per second. Figure 6 shows that logic and register utilization is very small, whereas the BRAM utilization is at 96% for Virtex-6 and 50% for Virtex-7.

Our first implementation attempt on Virtex-6 resulted in fairly poor timing because of large routing delays. To improve this, each bank of memory was implemented using BRAMs configured as 1 bit wide by 32768 deep and 200 of these were used in parallel to store a single z-row at each address. This configuration was selected to associate each bit of the pipeline output with a single BRAM (all of the spins with the same z-coordinate are stored in the same BRAM). This allowed for placement of the storage and processing elements associated with the computation of each bit relatively close to the BRAM where those bits are stored (as Figure 7 demonstrates). This has improved the timing somewhat, however, there were still large delays associated with memory address and write-enable signals that are shared by all BRAMs in one bank. Compare the relatively short nets connecting processing pipeline outputs to BRAMs with the very large net connecting one bit of the memory address register to all of the BRAMs in Figure 8. Pipelining these signals,

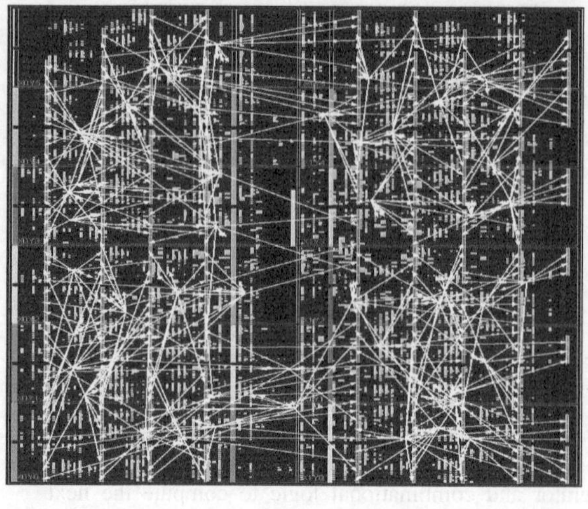

Fig. 7: White arrows indicate the relative location of each of the 200 bits of pipeline output and their associated BRAM on the Virtex-6 device.

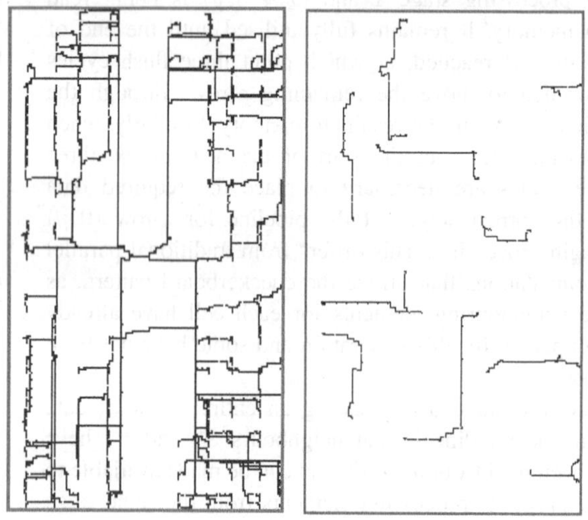

Fig. 8: Left image shows a very large net connecting memory address register (bit 3) to BRAM blocks. Right image shows relatively short nets connecting every 20th bit of the pipeline output to corresponding BRAM blocks.

	xc6vlx240t	xc7vx485t
Flip-flops	301,440	607,200
LUTs	150,720	303,600
CLBs	37,680	75,900
36Kb bRAM	416	1,030

Table 2: FPGA resource summary.

as well as register replication has helped to achieve the frequency of 120 MHz. Further low-level optimisations are possible, but they come at a big cost of time and not being able to modify the design at higher level, as it would undo all of the low-level optimisations.

	200^3	256^3
Flip-flops	17,563	22,314
LUTs	20,781	25,548
CLBs	8,673	9,842
BRAMs	400	512
Max clock (MHz)	120	200
Compilation Time (min)	30	98

Table 3: Resource utilization for different size simulations. **Note:** 200^3 implemented on xc6vlx240t and 256^3 implemented on xc7vx485t.

5. Discussion

We have shown how a 3D Ising model can be implemented on an FPGA system with encouraging performance results.

There are a number of strategies that could be employed to obtain useful statistical results to attempt better estimates of the critical properties of the model. One is to deploy FPGA accelerators on a large scale cluster with independent statistical jobs farmed out to processors and their slave FPGA units. This can be analysed using conventional techniques based upon the Binder cumulant and other moments [37]. Another is to attempt a renormalisation group calculation using a still larger Ising system size that can be block-averaged and analysed using techniques such as [15], [38].

In both cases it will be desirable to have model systems be as large as possible which is constrained by available memory on the FPGA units at present. It may be required to deploy external memory units to support the FPGA processing elements, but this would significantly reduce the available bandwidth from the current 200 Gb/s to around 7.5 Gb/s for quad-bank DDR3 SDRAM and dramatically increase the hardware costs.

Beyond applying these techniques to the simple Ising model there is also scope to address variants of the model for which less is known and for which smaller simulation systems are necessary as lower numerical precision of critical temperature and exponents are needed. Such system include the dilute or damaged Ising model where some bond links are removed to mimic crystal defects, or the frustrated Ising model where some links have a reverse in the sign of the coupling J to mimic impurities or mixtures at the atomic level.

6. Conclusions

We have shown that it is possible to implement a 256^3 lattice of Ising model spins on a modern FPGA device using on-chip memory. Using a pipelined implementation of the Metropolis Monte Carlo algorithm, our design is capable of 3000 full system updates per second.

We found the system size to be limited by the amount of available on-chip memory and the maximum frequency to be mostly limited by routing propagation delays, which can be optimised using standard digital design techniques; however, at a high manual labour cost. Alternatively, the computational throughput may be increased through further parallelisation. Additional processing elements can be easily added as the current logic resource utilization is low.

Another use for the available logic resources could be the implementation of a true-random number generator to seed the pseudo-random number generators initially and at regular intervals to increase average entropy per bit.

This approach has great scope for investigations to obtain greater precision on the critical properties of the Ising model itself but also variations of it such as dilute and frustrated magnetic systems.

References

[1] Oldfield, J.V., Dorf, R.C.: Field programmable gate arrays - Reconfigurable logic for rapid prototyping and implementation of digital systems. Number ISBN 0-471-55665-3. Wiley (1995)

[2] Chu, P.P.: FPGA Prototyping by VERILOG Examples. Number ISBN 978-0-470-18532-2. Wiley (2008)

[3] Herbordt, M.C., Gu, Y., VanCourt, T., Model, J., Sukhwani, B., Chiu, M.: Computing Models for FPGA-Based Accelerators. Computing in Science & Engineering **10**(6) (November/December 2008) 35–45

[4] Leist, A., Playne, D.P., Hawick, K.A.: Exploiting Graphical Processing Units for Data-Parallel Scientific Applications. Concurrency and Computation: Practice and Experience **21**(18) (25 December 2009) 2400–2437 CSTN-065.

[5] Preis, T., Virnau, P., Paul, W., Schneider, J.J.: GPU accelerated Monte Carlo simulation of the 2D and 3D Ising model. Journal of Computational Physics **228**(12) (2009) 4468–4477

[6] Danese, G., Leporati, F., Bera, M., Giachero, M., Nazzicari, N., Spelgatti, A.: An accelerator for physics simulations. Computing in Science and Engineering **9**(5) (September 2007) 16–25

[7] Anan'ko, A.G., Lysakov, K., Shadrin, M.Y., Lavrentiev, M.M.: Development and application of an fpga based special processor for solving bioinformatics problems. Pattern Recognition and Image Analysis **21**(3) (2011) 370–372

[8] Gribbon, K.T., Bailey, D.G., Bainbridge-Smith, A.: Development issues in using fpgas for image processing. In: Development Issues in Using FPGAs for Image Processing?, Proceedings of Image and Vision Computing New Zealand 2007, Hamilton, New Zealand (2007) 217–222

[9] Bailey, D.: Design for Embedded Image Processing on FPGAs. Wiley (2011) ISBN 9780470828496.

[10] Huang, Q., Wang, Y., Chang, S.: High-performance fpga implementation of discrete wavelet transform for image processing. In: Proc. 2011 Symposium on Photonics and Optoelectronics (SOPO), Wuhan (16-18 May 2011 2011) 1–4

[11] Chen, E., Lesau, V.G., Sabaz, D., Shannon, L., Gruver, W.A.: Fpga framework for agent systems using dynamic partial reconfiguration. In: Proc. 5th Int. Conf on Industrial Applications of Holonic and Multi-Agent Systems (HoloMAS). Number 6867 in LNAI, Toulouse, rance (29-31 August 2011) 94–102

[12] Metropolis, N., Ulam, S.: The monte carlo method. J. American Statistical Association **44**(247) (September 1949) 335–341

[13] Ising, E.: Beitrag zur Theorie des Ferromagnetismus. Zeitschrift fuer Physik A Hadrons and Nuclei **31**(1) (1925) 253–258

[14] Onsager, L.: Crystal Statistics. I. A Two-Dimensional Model with an Order-Disorder Transition. Physical Review **65**(3-4) (1944) 117–149

[15] Baillie, C., Gupta, R., Hawick, K., Pawley, G.: Monte-Carlo Renormalisation Group Study of the Three-Dimensional Ising Model. Phys.Rev.B **45** (1992) 10438–10453

[16] Hawick, K., Poon, W.C.K., Ackland, G.: Relaxation in the Dilute Ising Model. Journal of Magnetism and Magnetic Materials **104-107** (1992) 423–424 International Conference on Magnetism,Edinburgh 1991.

[17] Lin, Y., Wang, F., Zheng, X., Gao, H., Zhang, L.: Monte carlo simulation of the ising model on fpga. Journal of Computational Physics **237** (2013) 224–234

[18] Svenson, P.: Damage spreading in small world Ising models. Physical Review E **65**(3) (2002) 036105

[19] Newell, G.F., Montroll, E.W.: On The Theory Of The Ising Model Of Ferromagnetism. Reviews of Modern Physics **25**(2) (1953) 353–389

[20] Potts, R.B.: Some Generalized Order-Disorder Transformations. In: Proceedings of the Cambridge Philosophical Society. Volume 48. (1952)

[21] Barrat, A., Weigt, M.: On the properties of small-world network models. The European Physical Journal B **13**(3) (2000) 547–560

[22] Herrero, C.P.: Ising model in small-world networks. Physical Review E **65**(6) (2002) 066110

[23] Herrero, C.P.: Ising model in scale-free networks: A Monte Carlo simulation. Physical Review E **69**(6) (2004) 067109

[24] Binney, J.J., Dowrick, N.J., Fisher, A.J., Newman, M.E.J.: 2 Statistical mechanics. In: The Theory of Critical Phenomena - An Introduction to the Renormalization Group. Oxford University Press (1992) 33–53

[25] Metropolis, N., Rosenbluth, A.W., Rosenbluth, M.N., Teller, A.H., Teller, E.: Equation of State Calculations by Fast Computing Machines. Journal of Chemical Physics **21**(6) (1953) 1087–1092

[26] Glauber, R.J.: Time-Dependent Statistics of the Ising Model. Journal of Mathematical Physics **4**(2) (1963) 294–307

[27] Swendsen, R.H., Wang, J.S.: Nonuniversal Critical Dynamics in Monte Carlo Simulations. Physical Review Letters **58**(2) (1987) 86–88

[28] Wolff, U.: Comparison Between Cluster Monte Carlo Algorithms in the Ising Model. Physics Letters B **228**(3) (1989) 379–382

[29] Marinari, E., Parisi, G.: Simulated Tempering - a New Monte-Carlo Scheme. Europhysics Letters **19**(6) (July 1992) 451–458

[30] Hastings, W.K.: Monte-Carlo Sampling Methods Using Markov Chains And Their Applications. Biometrika **57**(1) (1970) 97–107

[31] Parisi, G.: Statistical Field Theory. Paperback edn. Westview Press (1998) ISBN 978-0738200514.

[32] Manousiouthakis, V.I., Deem, M.W.: Strict Detailed Balance is Unneccessary in Monte Carlo Simulation. J. Chem. Phys. **110**(2753) (1999)

[33] Hawick, K.A., Leist, A., Playne, D.P.: Regular Lattice and Small-World Spin Model Simulations using CUDA and GPUs. Int. J. Parallel Prog. **39**(CSTN-093) (2011) 183–201

[34] Leist, A., Hawick, K.A., Playne, D.P.: Hybrid update algorithms for regular lattice and small-world ising models on graphical processing units. In: Proc. Int. Conf. on Scientific Computing (CSC'12), Las Vegas, USA, CSREA (16-19 July 2012) 228–234

[35] Gilman, A., Hawick, K.A.: Field Programmable Gate Arrays for Computational Acceleration of Lattice-Oriented Simulation Models. In: Proc. International Conference on Computer Design (CDES'12), Las Vegas, USA (16-19 July 2012)

[36] George, M., Alfke, P.: Linear Feedback Shift Registers in Virtex Devices. Technical report, Xilinx (2001)

[37] Binder, K., ed.: Monte Carlo Methods in Statistical Physics. 2 edn. Topics in Current Physics. Springer-Verlag (1986) Number 7.

[38] Pawley, G.S., Swendsen, R.H., Wallace, D.J., Wilson, K.G.: Monte-Carlo renormalization group calculations of critical behaviour in the simple cubic Ising model. Phys. Rev. B **29**(7) (Apr 1984) 4030–4040

Redundancy + Reconfigurability = Recoverability

Simon Monkman[1], **and Igor Schagaev**[2]
[1] ITACS Ltd, 157 Shephall View, Stevenage, SG1 1RR, England
[2]Faculty of Computing, London Metropolitan University, 166-220 Holloway Road, London, N7 8DB, England

Abstract - *An approach to consider computers and connected computer systems using structural, time and information redundancies is proposed. An application of redundancy for reconfigurability and recoverability of computer and connected computer systems is discussed, gaining performance, reliability and power-saving in operation. A paradigm of recoverability is introduced and, if followed, shifts connected computer systems toward real-time applications. Use of redundancy for connected computers is analysed in terms of recoverability, where two supportive algorithms of forward and backward tracing are proposed and explained. As an example, growth of mission reliability is formulated.*

Keywords: redundancy; reconfigurability; recoverability; performance-reliability-energy-wise systems

1 Why Recoverability: Instead of Introduction

The human world evolves and progresses by applying knowledge derived from observations of and familiarity with repeatable aspects of nature. Our perceptions, understanding, and ability to model reality enables us to develop the policies, processes, and products required, in order to attempt to control the behaviour of natural phenomena, or human-made objects.

Nature tends to achieve stable and reliable progress (sustainable growth) and avoid regression and degradation. Sustainable growth can be considered as a fundamental descriptor of living matter, while regression and degradation are descriptors of dead matter. A clear differentiation between live and dead is required, but, so far, there has been no substantial research, or projects, on it.

The authors of this paper believe that the fundamental distinction and difference between living processes and dead matter is *recoverability*.

Essentially, recoverability in the system is based on the ability to use available redundancy to recover from environmental, or internal impacts and shocks. Two things are worth mentioning here: first—redundancy is necessary for recoverability, and second—redundancy must be deliberately introduced into systems, policies, and processes to make them resilient and efficient.

The recoverability approach and its analysis, application, and conceptual development in the domain of computers is one of the aims of this paper. The second aim is the analysis of the phases required for the implementation of recoverability for stand-alone and connected computers.

Usually, connected computer systems display fluctuations due to changes in the underlying systems. Reasons for this may include, for instance, workload, software completeness, consistency, and size of applications, or changes and shocks emanating from their environment. So far, networks sporadically and inconsistently exploit recoverability phenomena to tolerate these various fluctuations.

Connected computer (further CC) systems can be considered in terms of time, i.e., as a process of operation. Recoverability can then be applied to keep this process within a restricted set of properties, "smoothing" the process. We can apply and investigate various recovery algorithms implicit in such systems and tune the underlying parameters, reducing the extent of fluctuations and hence, reducing the cost they impose in structure, information, or performance.

Natural recoverability phenomena exist in almost any natural system, but we do not understand them. Hence, we cannot specify how the algorithm works and therefore, use it properly. This is exactly the purpose of the methodology proposed in this paper. In a practical sense, an understanding of recoverability enables us to advocate for the re-design of the whole world of CC systems, making them resilient to internal and external fluctuations.

1.1 Why Reconfigurability: An Example

Let us consider a case: an element is deformed by environmental impact. Destructive deformation of the element could cause the loss of its properties.

Let's assume an element has internal structural resources (redundancy). Redundancy of the element structure might enable the element to return to its previous state, or condition, after impact. The external impact does not change the element, if redundancy is applied and sufficient. A second impact might occur and be tolerated in exactly the same way. Let us now consider a situation where the element has properties of being alive, such as amoeba.

If an amoeba has sufficient resources available to it to use and to protect itself from the destructive energy of the environment or an impact, it will recover and continue to live—the amoeba exhibits redundancy in order to survive.

If the external event is repeated, the amoeba can self-tune and be able to react to the impact faster, tolerate the event for longer, and as a consequence, suffer less long-term damage. The external event itself might be periodic heat from the sun, cold water, fire or gas, electric discharge, etc.

Having sufficient internal redundancy to tolerate repeated external impacts caused by various events makes recovery possible. Live matter differs from man-made systems in terms of the time required for recovery and the use of available redundancy. The speed of recovery increases when the impact is the same. Here, "recovery training" takes place and either the level of redundancy, or speed of recovery, or both increase. A sequence of impacts and element recovery is presented in Figure 1.

Figure 1. Periodic impacts, element's time to recover

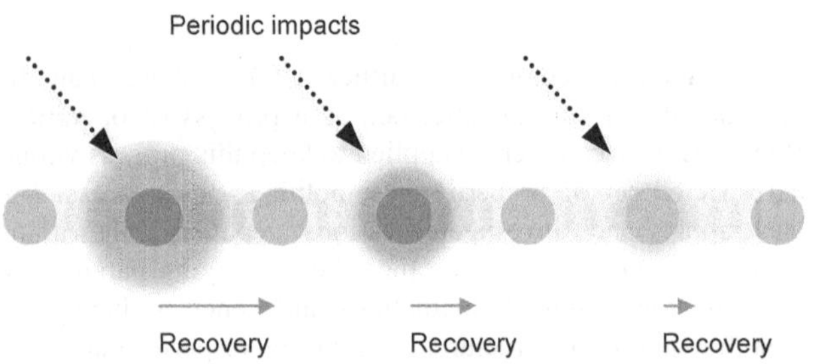

The circles show the state of an element over time, where green indicates an element in a good, or acceptable steady state and red indicates an element under recovery. Figure 1 indicates an element that adapts to the periodic external stimulus, can decrease the time for its recovery.

Where the element may be considered alive, such as in the case of the amoeba, using redundancy for recovery can reduce the time it takes to react to the same event, provided the event is periodic. Thus, life might be defined as the following:

An element is called alive, if in repeatable conditions, it is able to recover progressively, using internal redundancy actively.

The adaptability of the live element has its limits. Figure 2 shows, for example, an element approaching the limit of its adaptability and the role of its ability to recover. Whilst wildlife evolution may be seen as similar to the lower curve, the evolution of "smart" species should be smoother and faster to reach the same, or higher, limit of adaptability—the shortened curve in the diagram.

Thus, our design of information processing systems, computers, especially complex systems such as connected computers, can be measured in terms of efficiency of recovery/resilience in comparison with wildlife phenomena, where available redundancy is used and adaptability grows. In other words, how good we are at designing our systems to be adaptable can be checked against living objects.

What is the point of this? Without external repeatability of events, evolution is hardly possible; having internal redundancy to recover is not enough. Evolution depends on the repetition of the same external events—*i.e., no repetition, no evolution.*

Figure 2. The adaptability of a live element to a repeated external stimulus has its own limits

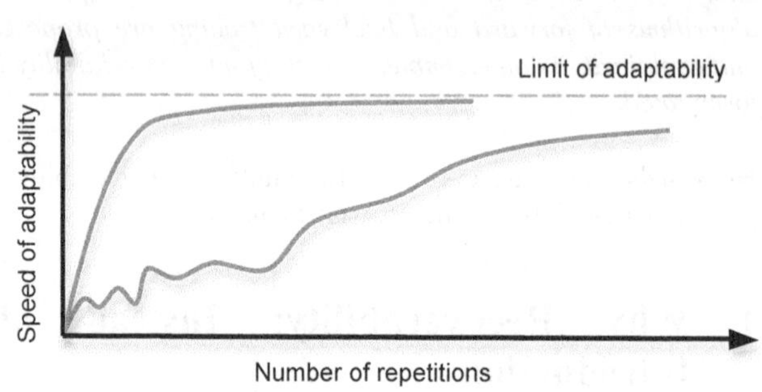

It means, for example, that the merit of sending a NASA probe searching for advanced forms of life on asteroids is worth questioning. An asteroid does not have the repeatability of environmental events during its flight. Even if life forms were there initially, their redundancy was spent for nothing in attempting to tolerate sporadic impacts.

1.2 Organization of the paper

How is this two-part introduction about recoverability and reconfigurability related to CC systems? At first, nature-made living systems are much more reliable and resilient than human-made ones. Therefore, some of the key principles of "mother nature designs" are good to adapt for CCs. Secondly, an analysis of existing technologies and applications, even if it is brief one, might highlight what is required to make our designs smarter.

Further, commercially and technologically speaking, we will address recoverability and other properties that might be required for connected computer systems. Why do we need to make this clear? Market segmentation in computer and CC systems might be reduced, or eliminated, enabling unified and modernized technologies to be applied.

We will discuss properties such as reliability and some ways to achieve it, using deliberate redundancy and recoverability when required. We extend redundancy from fault tolerance to PRE-smart system design. PRE here stands for Performance-, Reliability-, and Energy-smart systems. Later, we will be able to estimate the efficiency of redundancy use for reconfigurability and recoverability for CC systems, balancing the trade-off between PRE properties.

2 Connected computers: technologies and applications

CC technologies in general are divided into two almost independent clusters: Communication and Computer, as Figure 3 shows.

Figure 3. Connected computers - technologies and applications

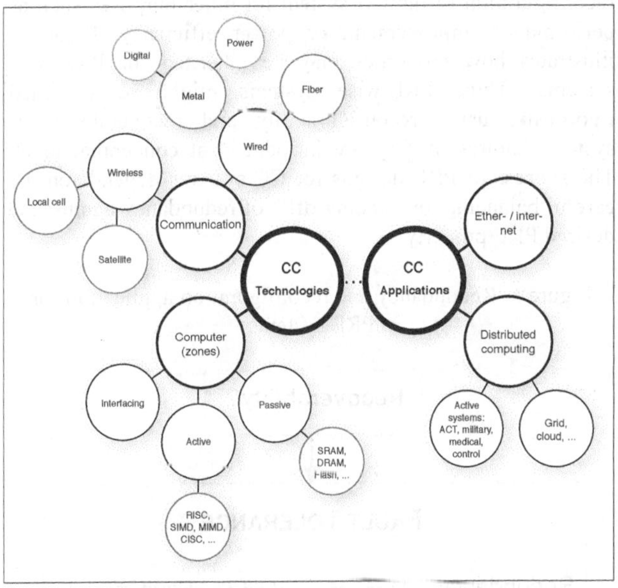

The Communication cluster deals with various media (wired, wireless) using different signal carriers (copper, fibre, air). The cluster faces problems of complexity and the volume of data that needs to be transferred, together with requirements of timely data delivery over complex interconnected networks.

The Computer cluster addresses all three zones of information processing to make them faster and technologically feasible. The zones differ semantically. The Active zone is the one where information is transformed and is currently known: in the form of complex instruction set computers (CISC), reduced instruction set computers (RISC), single instruction multiple data (SIMD) architecture and multiple instructions multiple data (MIMD) architectures. Flynn's [1] classification was used to reference these architectures. The Passive zone is known in the form of static and dynamic memories, flash memory, disks, etc. The Interfacing zone deals with data transfer between zones and getting them in and out from environment.

Historically, computer systems were not really fit for purpose for working within CC systems, which reduces our expectations when addressing the aspect of distributed computing by design. Attempts, such as a transputer, also prove that introducing distributiveness into CC is challenging and not an easy task. CC systems such as the Internet and Ethernet are expanding enormously in terms of data transfer, video, audio and e-mails and are moving in a strange direction, allowing home-makers, young people, financial sector operatives and bureaucrats communicate and "deliver their messages and instructions".

All of the aforementioned applications are not critical in terms of real-time operation; VOIP requires some traffic shaping to deliver packages with time and other constraints, known as Quality of Service. This is what the vast majority of CC systems are using. At the moment, according to various sources, around two billion IP addresses are allocated permanently. This prodigious amount of data requires handling procedures that need to be much more effective, as everyday life becomes dependent on the "health" of CC systems. There is a visible shift in the distributed computing paradigm (using distributed, connected computers to solve large-scale tasks), toward distributed databases, financial services such as ATM, and so-called "cloud computing". Putting scepticism aside and leaving other papers and researchers to discuss what is the real technological progress of cloud computing, we note here only that the efficiency of large-scale applications, including cloud computing, depends on the algorithmic skeleton—graphs of data, control and address dependencies [4] and their use, in order to prepare flexible, reconfigurable and resource-efficient algorithms for distributed computing.

To be effective, distributed computing requires a periodic "tuning" of the CC topology and computers as the elements in that topology. These tunings of application software, system software, topology, and internal structure of the computers should be handled statically, before execution and supported dynamically, during execution.

So far, there has been no visible progress in this direction, in spite of substantial investment under the flag of cloud computing. At the same time, there is a segment of human life that really requires attention and the involvement of CC: safety-critical, real-time active control systems, military applications, health monitoring, etc. All these applications should benefit from CC, but they require the integrity of a CC system, in terms of hardware, system and application software, user and system data, and the billions of connected computers to be applied much more efficiently, following the maxima:

Remark 1. Technology must help people to become better, not to be more comfortable.

Therefore, safety critical applications (military, health monitoring, emergency management, air-traffic control, traffic control at large) should emerge and exploit existing connected computers. Two approaches to making CC useful are becoming obvious: the application of existing CC to wider and more challenging areas and the use of specially-built, safety-critical systems for "common" applications, as a part of the family of CC.

Ignoring any of theses approaches will lead to bigger market clustering and industry segmentation, resulting in the communication between entities becoming less efficient and which contributes to increased energy and ecological overheads - an unforgivable waste of resources for human race.

2.1 Problems and properties

To avoid this segmentation in technology and market clustering a CC system should be redesigned to have new properties. In addition to the requirement for trustworthy CCs (security of hardware, system and application software and user data), widening CC adoption in terms of application use requires the development of *recoverability*. *Recoverability* requires an implementation of a generalized algorithm of fault tolerance (GAFT). Note also that recoverability is practical, if it is invisible for the application software. GAFT assumes the execution of several sequential steps related to hardware (HW) and software (SW), in terms of proving the integrity of the system, (step A), detection of a fault and determination of its type (step B), defining the "level of damages" Permanent of malfunction (step C), location of faulty element (step D) and reconfiguration of the hardware (step E) and proof of correctness of integrity of software (step F) and determination of correct state (step G) and software to correct in order to continue operation. GAFT has two main phases - one for hardware (steps A-E), another for software (steps F and G). GAFT is initiated if a fault of CC, or any other deviation, has been detected. During the first step, it recognizes fault type in order to gauge location and tolerance.

Figure 4. Redundancy application for GAFT

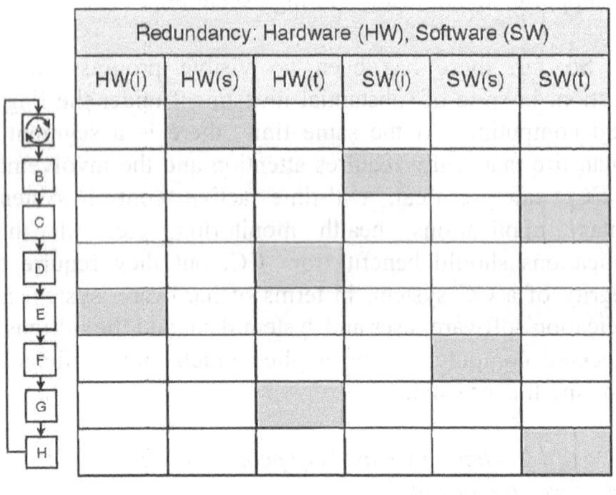

As Figure 4 shows the redundancy types application for fault tolerance are based on the categories of *structure* "*s*", *information* "*i*" and *time* "*t*". The white boxes show a possible application of fault tolerance, using the described redundancies.

While we are capable of using redundancy for checking, reconfiguration and recovery within a CC system, we should ask ourselves:

Could we use this redundancy for other purposes?

Introducing system redundancy might allow us to achieve recoverability. We need all the ingredients - redundancy, reconfigurability and fault modelling - in order to understand and analyse existing mutual dependencies at every stage of the design and development process.

At the same time, redundancy can be used for reconfiguration of the CC system for other purposes such as performance improvement, or power efficiency. Figure 5 illustrates how properties may be inherited for PRE-wise systems. Thus, PRE-wise systems might be designed rigorously, using reconfigurability and recoverability as system features, if they are introduced at conceptual level. The success of PRE designs for CC systems depends on the careful balancing, or "trading-off", of redundancy against the desired PRE property.

Figure 5. Redundancy and reconfiguration application for PRE systems

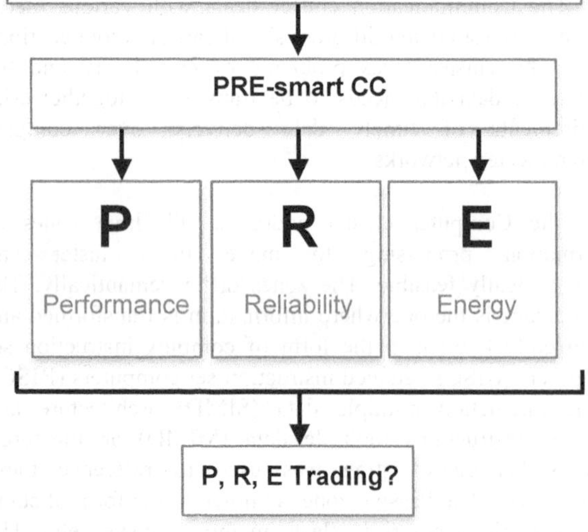

2.2 Trading P, R, E

Structure, *Information* and *Time*, as the various types of redundancy, might be weighted, say, in units or values, with or without reference to the steps of GAFT, or any other algorithm where redundancy has been applied to achieve performance-, reliability- or energy-wise features. The relative importance (and cost) of the redundancy type chosen for the steps in the algorithms shown might be introduced as a coefficient α_i, related to the cell i (Figure 4). Similar "valuations" of redundancy types might be applied for any other algorithms designed for the implementation of PRE properties.

While time and information is understandable in units - seconds and bits, the structure, especially structural redundancy requires some extra effort. Note also that time, information and structure are considered as independent variables. Structural redundancy for our purposes might be measured using the graph-related notation:

$$dS: \ < dV, dE >$$

where dS denotes introduced structural redundancy, while dV and dE denote extra vertices and edges added into the structure in order to implement the steps of GAFT, or any other algorithm.

Then, our efforts toward the goal of PRE can be measured quantitatively, as a vector of redundancy use:

$$dR \ = \ < dT, dS, dI >$$

In determining the cost of each type of redundancy used and describing the steps of an algorithm to achieve performance-, reliability- or energy-wise improvement, we can quantify each solution, according to the redundancy types applied.

This approach explains and quantifies, for example, the limitations of system software-based developments using Java - it will always consume more time, hardware, software and energy to store and process. In other words, we always will waste much more energy than really required.

Furthermore, the over-use of flash-based memory will also add to the energy wastage, as the activation of one memory cell in flash requires the application of power to the bulk of a 64K, or 64M memory segment.

The principles of PRE- design should be applied to the CC system as a whole, using the redundancy- and reconfigurability-wise approach for each of the goals. That being the case, tables similar to those proposed above have to be crafted individually for various purposes.

A PRE-wise system design paradigm is the future. When a computer, or CC system is designed with redundancy and reconfigurability in mind, with possible smart configurations and reconfigurations for PRE purposes, the market segmentation of information computer technologies (ICT) will be reduced dramatically. The combination of steps in the sequence described above implementing the declared properties is a simplification, as design of a system is not, in fact, sequential. It most likely follows a pattern as illustrated by Figure 6, where the various steps are dependent on and have feedback loops with other steps.

One approach to cope with these forms of dependencies in the algorithm (or project) phases assumes the application of a semi-Markov model to analyse the impact of these feedbacks on design efficiency [2,5].

Figure 6. Dependencies of project phases

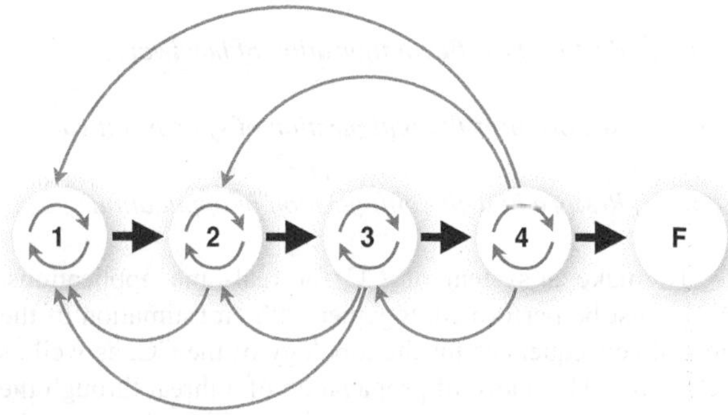

2.3 Recoverability in connected computer systems

Applying the same approach to CC systems to suit real-time and safety-critical applications highlight differences between stand-alone and CC structures:

- Redundancy in CC systems already exists (each computer "deals" with neighbour);
- Latency of threat impact for CC systems is unavoidable;
- Propagation of threat impact for CC systems is similar to flooding.

Let us look at a notional segment of a CC topology with incoming and internal connections as Figure 7 presents. Incoming and out-going edges are shown with arrows. Threats here mean physical faults (permanent, or as a malfunction) of hardware, incomplete or deliberately damaged software, viruses, worms, etc. Thus, the recoverability of a CC system might require more effort and extend GAFT actions, namely:

- *Find where threat propagates;*
- *Estimate damages;*
- *Stop propagation;*
- *Find source of the threat (internal, or external);*
- *Exclude, or block the source;*
- *Restore best-fit configuration of hardware;*
- *Restore best-fit configuration of system software;*
- *Restore best-fit configuration of applications.*

To make a system of CC for real-time applications, GAFT must be performed, together with an estimation of the potential consequences for the topology of the CC, as well as its elements. The speed of propagation of a threat through the topology has to be addressed as a factor of performance for recovery.

The potential damages caused as a result of the threat may differ in severity - sometimes substantial and exponentially dangerous (gateway routers), if we do not react accordingly.

Figure 7. Connected computers topology (fragment)

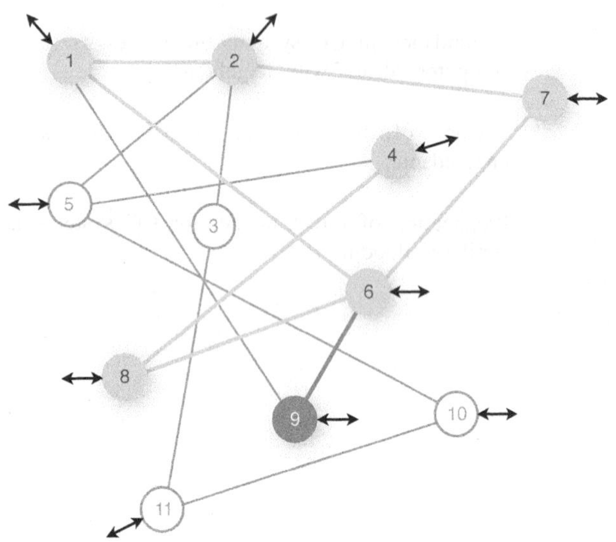

Existing solutions with local restarts and segmental switching do not comply with the requirements of real-time, or safety-critical applications. A CC system can be presented in the form of probabilities of the propagation of a threat (or symptom of a fault) through the topology, where thickness of the edges defines the strength of dependency between vertices. The dependencies between vertices are not symmetrical: vertex 9 might have, say, a much higher impact on vertex 6, than vertex 6 might have on vertex 9.

A propagation of a threat along the CC system might be described as a vector P of predicates {pi} that define the condition for each vertex:

$$P = \left\{p_1\left(m_1\left(v_1\left(d_1(t)\right)\right)\right),\ p_2\left(m_2\left(v_2\left(d_2(t)\right)\right)\right),\ \ldots,\ p_k\left(m_k\left(v_k\left(d_k(t)\right)\right)\right)\right\} \quad (1)$$

where *m1,...,mk* stand for models of vertices in terms of vulnerability to threat; *v1,...,vk* are vertices, *d1, ...,dk* are data available about each vertex condition.

Data about each vertex might be accumulated using checking (testing, or online checking, including historic knowledge and their combination), as well as processed in real time.

Note that for a CC system, we assume flood-like threat propagation; i.e. all adjacent vertices to the initial point, namely for vertex 1, one has to consider adjacency with the 2nd, 6th and 9th vertices, vertex 11's adjacency to vertex 3 and 10, etc. The role of the initial point that starts off the process of recovery requires further discussion.

2.4 How this works

The recoverability of CC systems assumes the involvement of two algorithms: Forward Tracing and Backward Tracing. When the symptoms of a threat are manifested through the detection of a change in behaviour at an element, the Tracing algorithm searches through a Dependency Matrix for the subsequent propagation of that threat along the system. The potential consequences to the system can be hereby identified, starting from the vertex from where the threat presence was first detected.

Performing the Forward Tracing algorithm, a cumulative probability is calculated along each possible path (of edges) until a termination threshold ε is reached. Threshold ε is defined empirically using engineering expertise and considered as constant for a particular configuration of a CC.

Another termination condition for searching the path of threat propagation is obvious - checking all dependent vertices. When all elements have been traced, one can fully guarantee 100% threat checking coverage. Unfortunately, this termination condition becomes scale-dependent on CC system size.

Note here that the probabilistic matrix for a system from Figure 7 is not Markovian, because the sum of probabilities on the edges at each node may not be equal to 1; in contrast, several edges of a single node may have significant probabilities.

Figure 8. Forward tracing of possible consequences

```
Algorithm Tracing (s, D(N),Ds, {Π(ps,x), x Ds } )
// Input: Dependency matrix D(N) with N elements of a weighted graph G=<V, E>
// Input: The start node s and the reaching node j
// Output:  The set of nodes Ds where x  Ds and Π(ps,x)> ε
// Output:  The highest probability Π(ps,j) of node j reached by node s
Q  // a priority queue based on the higher probability of nodes reached by s
L  // the set of nodes already visited, used to avoid tracing loops
Initialize(Q)  // initialize nodes priority queue to empty
For each node v in V do
  ps,v ←ε; // set default probability to ε
  Insert (Q,v,ps,v) //initialize the priority queue
  ps,s ←1; Increase(Q,s,ps,s)  //update priority of s with ps,s
  Ds←Empty // presume all elements are safe
  L←Empty
for i←0 to N-1 do
   a*←DeleteMax(Q)  //delete the maximum priority element
   while pi,a*>ε
     do
     Ds←Ds { a*};L←L { a*}; Π(ps,a*)=pi,a*
     for every node a in V- Ds- L that is adjacent to a* do
        if ps,a* * Da*,a> ps,a then
        ps,a = ps,a* * Da*,a;
        Increase(Q,a,ps,a)
      end for
    end while
end for
Terminate
```

2.5 Probability along the path

In the tracing algorithm, the cumulative probability of threat propagation from one element (vertex) to another along the edges from the suspected node *i* to node *j* (possibly via a series of other nodes), is defined as Π(pi,j).

When several paths lead from node *di* to node *dj*, all possible Π(pi,j) are ranked and nodes along the paths are included into the set of suspected nodes. Starting from the vertex, *i*, that manifests the threat, its impact is evaluated by searching from *d1* to all directly, or indirectly connected nodes (elements). The result of this search is a ranked list of the nodes most likely to be affected - the "consequence" of threat propagation. As the threat paths from each node are evaluated, only the edge with the highest probability is followed at each node. At most, each node is only ever included once in any path to ensure termination in a graph which contains loops.

The proposed Forward Tracing algorithm does not solve the problem of threat elimination from CC systems and, at its best, can only be part of the solution. The reason is explained in Figure 9. The time gap between the appearance of a threat at one vertex and the detection of it impact at another has arbitrary duration. Above all, while the consequences are being detected, threat propagation continues. Thus, the Forward Tracing algorithm helps to localize damages, and assist when possible, in order to block propagation, but does not solve the whole problem.

To locate the first damaged node and discover the real reason for its changed behaviour, we need another algorithm called Backward Tracing, Figure 10. This algorithm discovers the source(s), or reason(s) from the sequences of exhibited threat symptoms and defines areas where each element (vertex) was involved. Thus, we search for the reason, not just the symptoms.

When the elements that are likely to be the cause of the manifest discrepancies are detected, the recovery is initiated from the vertex where the threat first appeared dealing with the damaged area only, reducing the need for the brute force of a restart, saving real-time mode for the whole CC system. The results of the recovery process also need to be saved for security improvement, monitoring of reliability and maintenance efficiency.

Figure 9. Threat propagation timing along a CC system

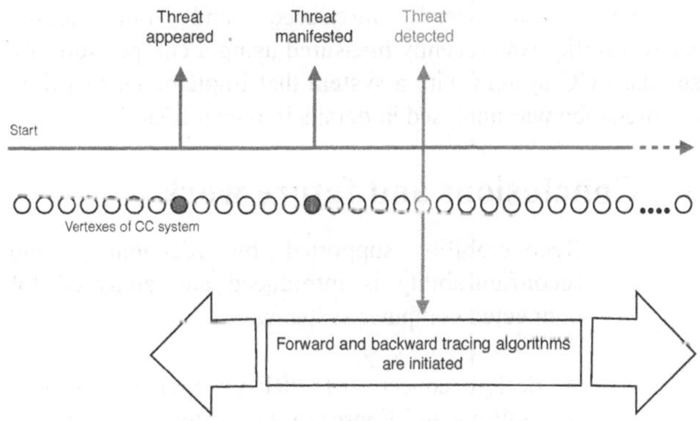

The threat checking procedure over a CC system might be activated, either by a signal indicating that there is a discrepancy in behaviour of one or more elements (vertices), or by a predefined sequence of maintenance, if necessary. For the purpose of maintaining CC system integrity, the procedures for condition checking might be initiated by choosing any vertex of the CC system at random, or even in a loop, covering all vertices, when it is convenient.

Figure 10. Backward threat tracing for a CC system

```
Algorithm Backward Tracing (s, R^(N), S_s, {Π(p_{s,x}), x∈R_s})

// Input:  The Recovery matrix R^(N) with N elements of a weighted connected graph G=<V, E>
// Input:  The suspected node s
// Output:  The set of nodes S_s in which x ∈S_s and Π(p_{x,s}) > ε
// Output:  The highest probability Π(p_{j,s}) of node j reaching node s

Q // a priority queue based on the higher probability of nodes reaching s
L // a set of node have been visited. It is to avoid loop tracing
Initialize(Q)  //initialize nodes priority queue to empty
For every node v in V do
p_{v,s} ←ε;
Insert(Q,v,p_{v,s}) //initialize the priority queue
p_{s,s} ←1; Increase(Q,s,p_{s,s}) //update priority of s with p_{s,s}
S_s←Empty //initialize the set of originating node to empty
L←Empty //nodes have been visited is set to empty
for i←0 to N-1 do
   a*←DeleteMax(Q) //delete the maximum priority element
   if p_{a*,i}>ε
    Then
    S_s←S_s∪{ a*};L←L∪{ a*}; Π(p_{a*,s})=p_{a*,i};
      for every node a in V- S_s- L that is adjacent to a* do
        if p_{a*,s} * R_{a,a*} > p_{a,s}
          p_{a,s} = p_{a*,s} * R_{a,a*};
         Increase(Q,a,p_{a,s});
   else //correspond to p_{a*,i}<ε
     Terminate
```

2.6 How much recoverability costs

As shown above, recoverability requires the introduction of several new processes into CC system management, including online checking of CC conditions and the implementation of two mentioned above algorithms. The gradient of this change is a function of the quality of checking (coverage), success of recovery (algorithms of tracing) and quality of maintenance shifting it to the "light" mode with preventive actions against threats.

The gain from introduced and implemented recoverability was recently measured using a comparison of a standard CC system with a system that implements real-time maintenance was analysed in details in recent book [3].

3 Conclusions and future work

- Recoverability supported by redundancy and reconfigurability is introduced and analysed for connected computer systems.
- A design concept of PRE-wise (Performance-, Reliability- and Energy-wise) systems is proposed as a unified approach.
- Shown that recoverability using Forward and Backward Tracing algorithms makes connected computer systems closer to real-time and safety-critical applications.
- As a future development, it is suggested that the development of a PRE framework, assuming mutual dependencies of phases of design, development and run time use using a semi-Markov model.

4 References

[1] Flynn M. "Some Computer Organizations and Their Effectiveness"; IEEE Trans. Comput., Vol. C-21, 948, 1972.

[2] Birolini A. "Reliability Engineering Theory and Practice." 6th ed., Springer-Verlag: Berlin, Heidelberg, Germany, 2010.

[3] Carbone J., Schagaev I. "Active Conditional Control: Analysis." Applied Cyber-Physical Systems, Springer, ISBN 978-1-4614-7335-0, 2013.

[4] Gutkneht J., Kaegi T., Schagaev I. "ERA: Evolving Reconfigurable Architecture"; SNPD, 11th ACIS International Conference on Software Engineering, Artificial Intelligences, Networking and Parallel/Distributed Computing, London, UK, 9–11 June 2010.

[5] Plyaskota S., Schagaev I. "Economic Effectiveness Of Fault Tolerance"; Automatic and Remote Control, No. 7, 131-143, 1995.

[6] Schagaev, I.; Kirk, B.; Schagaev, A. "Method and Apparatus for Active Safety Systems"; UK Patent GB 2448351, INT CL: G05 9/02 (2006.01), Granted 21.09.2011.